# Multicultural Families, Home Literacies, and Mainstream Schooling

*a volume in*
Literacy, Language, and Learning

*Series Editor:*
Patricia Ruggiano Schmidt,
*Le Moyne College*

# Literacy, Language, and Learning

Patricia Ruggiano Schmidt, Series Editor

*African-American Middle-Income Parents:*
*How Are They Involved in Their Children's Literacy Development?* (2007)
by Ethel Swindell Robinson

*Closing the Gap: English Educators Address the Tensions Between Teacher*
*Preparation and Teaching Writing in Secondary Schools* (2007)
edited by Karen Keaton Jackson and Sandra Vavra

*Research and Reflection:*
*Teachers Take Action for Literacy Development* (2006)
edited by Andrea Izzo

*ABC's of Cultural Understanding and Communication:*
*National and International Adaptations* (2006)
edited by Patricia Ruggiano Schmidt and Claudia Finkbeiner

*Preparing Educators to Communicate and Connect with*
*Families and Communities* (2006)
edited by Patricia Ruggiano Schmidt

*Reading and Writing Ourselves Into Being:*
*The Literacy of Certain Nineteenth-Century Young Women* (2004)
by Claire White Putala

*Reconceptualizing Literacy in the New Age of*
*Multiculturalism and Pluralism* (2001)
edited by Patricia Ruggiano Schmidt and Peter B. Mosenthal

# Multicultural Families, Home Literacies, and Mainstream Schooling

*edited by*

**Guofang Li**
*Michigan State University*

**Information Age Publishing, Inc.**
Charlotte, North Carolina • www.infoagepub.com

**Library of Congress Cataloging-in-Publication Data**

Multicultural families, home literacies, and mainstream schooling / edited by Guofang Li.

p. cm.—(Language, literacy, and learning)

Includes bibliographical references.

ISBN 978-1-60752-035-1 (pbk.)—ISBN 978-1-60752-036-8 (hardcover)

1. Children of minorities—Education—United States—Case studies. 2. Children of immigrants—Education—United States—Case studies. 3. English language—Study and teaching—Foreign speakers—Case studies. 4. Home and school—United States—Case studies. 5. Multiculturalism—United States—Case studies. I. Li, Guofang, 1972-

LC3731.M82 2009

371.82900973—dc22

2008051152

Printed in the United States of America

# CONTENTS

## PART IV: HOME LITERACIES AND
## MAINSTREAM SCHOOLING—A CONCLUSION

# FOREWORD

## Patricia Ruggiano Schmidt

*Multicultural Families, Home Literacies, and Mainstream Schooling*, edited by Guofang Li, integrates family literacy and linguistic, cultural, and economic diversity via powerful educational stories. As a result of these compelling narratives, we are forced to examine our nation's educational system and search for answers to the following significant question, "How should teachers and administrators be prepared to work successfully with multicultural families?"

Recent and past research repeatedly sends the message that well-prepared teachers and administrators are key factors in the successful education of children from underrepresented groups in our nation (Chenoweth, 2007; Ladson-Billings, 1995; Schmidt, 1998a). The collection of ethnographic studies in this volume reminded me of a story that occurred 17 years ago when a teacher, Mrs. Starr, described by the principal as a "superb building leader," invited me to observe two language minority children in her kindergarten classroom who were demonstrating problem behaviors that she could not remedy. The children, Peley and Raji, were born in the United States and were the only two children of color in the kindergarten classroom.

Peley and Raji had learned English and their home languages simultaneously, but were struggling socially and academically. Raji, whose family

*Multicultural Families, Home Literacies, and Mainstream Schooling*
pp. ix–xiii
Copyright © 2009 by Information Age Publishing
All rights of reproduction in any form reserved.

came from India, rarely talked with other children whether in class or on the playground. He enjoyed creating detailed drawings of designs, seldom chose books to read, and avoided writing/drawing stories. Peley, whose family came from Cambodia and Vietnam, was loud and belligerent; she was avoided. Peley selected Dr. Seuss books and enjoyed writing, drawing, and reading silly stories, hoping to garner giggles from classmates. She was desperate for friends, but did not seem to know how to attract them. She attempted to critique classmates' work, but they quickly rebelled against her bossy attitudes.

Mrs. Starr had not been prepared to work with children and families from diverse cultural, linguistic, or lower socioeconomic backgrounds. Raised in a middle income, European American environment, she remembered seeing one student from China in her high school and one student of African American descent at college. During the first months of school, she surmised that Raji's and Peley's behaviors were preventing academic and social achievement and concluded that their families contributed to their problems. She guessed that Peley's family did not care about school, since they appeared a day late for their first parent conference and Raji's family was putting too much pressure on their child, since they requested homework for him. In both cases, Mrs. Starr was wrong. Peley's mother worked the day shift and her father worked the night shift at a local factory. They knew very little English and were confused by the information sent home. Raji's family was college educated and wanted to help their son with English, so he could better communicate with neighborhood children. At the end of the school year, when ethnographic data were revealed to Mrs. Starr, she was shocked into action. She asked me to work with her during that summer. And so we studied research related to the sociocultural perspective and began to create and develop new literacy practices that could be described as culturally responsive.

Though Mrs. Starr eventually became a superb building leader who embraced diversity in her teaching, many of our current teachers still share Mrs. Starr's early struggles in working with families from linguistic and cultural backgrounds different from their own. There is much research concerning the cultural conflicts and struggles of children and families who do not fit the image of mainstream suburban United States, but few teacher preparation programs have successfully incorporated the teaching of children from diverse backgrounds and experiences. As a result, it is important for teachers and teacher educators to understand the urgency and importance of their roles in making life palatable and meaningful for families and children of underrepresented groups. It is apparent to me that our schools and teacher education programs should do better. And this book, *Multicultural Families, Home Literacies, and Mainstream Schooling*, artfully edited by Guofang Li, explicitly tells us this through poignant stories. *So how do we make a difference? How should teachers and administrators be prepared to work successfully with multicultural families?*

The necessary first steps for change are well-prepared educators who possess the understanding and compassion to successfully educate children from linguistically, culturally, and economically diverse backgrounds. Previous research and practice demonstrate that strong home, school, and community connections not only help students make sense of the school curriculum, but also promote literacy development (Au, 1993; Moll, 1992; Schmidt, 2000), yet, in recent years, home, school, and community connections have become a significant challenge. As school populations have become increasingly diverse, both culturally and ethnically, teaching populations have remained homogeneous. Teachers are usually from European American, suburban, cultural backgrounds who typically describe themselves as "an American, [who] don't have a culture" (Schmidt & Finkbeiner, 2006). Most present and future teachers have not had sustained relationships with people from different ethnic, cultural, and lower socioeconomic backgrounds. As a result, much of their knowledge about diversity has been influenced by media stereotypes (Pattnaik, 1997; Payne, 1999). Also, school curriculum, methods, and materials usually reflect only European American or white culture and ignore the backgrounds and experiences of students and families from lower socioeconomic levels and differing ethnic and cultural backgrounds (Nieto, 1996). Furthermore, many teacher education programs do not adequately prepare educators for "culturally relevant pedagogy" (Ladson-Billings & Tate, 1995). Consequently, this disconnect has become a national problem whose influence has been linked to poor literacy development and extremely high dropout rates among students from different linguistic, cultural and economic backgrounds.

Therefore, in teacher educational programs, teacher self-knowledge should be the first and foremost consideration when attempting to help teachers understand diverse groups of students (Schmidt, 1998b, 2005a). Additionally, teacher education programs that combine in depth self-analyses, culturally responsive teaching, and prolonged authentic encounters with people from different backgrounds and experiences are more capable of changing lifelong emotions and attitudes that promote stereotyping, low expectations, and negative attitudes (Finkbeiner, 2006; Tatum, 1992). When teacher education programs deal first with these issues, the next step is to promote the implementation of culturally responsive teaching.

Teachers who reach out to families and create connections to the curriculum are actually implementing culturally relevant pedagogy or culturally responsive teaching. This pedagogy connects the curriculum to the knowledge and experiences of the diverse cultures in the classrooms by validating student family backgrounds and experiences, and using the literacies found in the students' cultures. And when families from diverse linguistic and cultural backgrounds and lower socioeconomic levels become connected with the school, as resources for learning, there is often a narrowing of the academic gap and an increase in positive attitudes toward school. For instance, Moll's (1992) "funds of knowledge" demonstrates that many Latino students have mechanical abilities involving literacy skills related to their community's needs that usually go unrecognized in schools. Similarly, African American community literacies, such as oral storytelling, recitation, song, and poetry may also be ignored (e.g., Edwards, Dandridge, McMillon, & Pleasant, 2001). Additionally, ethnographic research (Trueba, Jacobs & Kirton, 1990) has demonstrated that when Asian family knowledge and traditions are recognized in the classroom, the positive social results help students erase the anger and frustration that comes from being ignored and disempowered.

So, there is hope. The research studies presented in this important volume inform us concerning the literacies in culturally, linguistically, and economically diverse families and prepare teachers to work with students from diverse backgrounds. This collection of literacies as they occur in these different families as they navigate mainstream schooling serves as a foundation to stimulate teacher educators to make changes in programs. So teacher educators must pursue new ways to help our in-serve and pre-service teachers to understand the relationship between culturally relevant literacy learning and academic and social achievement.

This is a moral imperative in our time. In the families' localized narratives told for *Multicultural Families, Home Literacies, and Mainstream Schooling*, tragic global economic, political, and social events and our nation's flawed discriminatory policies *are evident*. We are given unforgettable pictures of the long and arduous journeys families make in the attempt to gain respect and equal opportunity. All of the groups have hoped for a better life for themselves and their children, but are often confronted with academic and social traumas in the very educational environments that were seen as the means to success. As a result, this timely book should encourage teacher educators and teachers to stop, reflect, and act upon what needs to happen NOW in our programs at colleges and universities.

## REFERENCES

Au, K. (1993). *Literacy instruction in multicultural settings*. New York: Harcourt, Brace Javanovich.

Chenoweth, K. (2007). *"It's being done": Academic success in unexpected schools*. Cambridge, MA: Harvard Education Press.

Edwards, P. A., Dandridge, J., McMillon, G. T., & Pleasants, H. M. (2001). Taking ownership of literacy: Who has the power?. In P. R. Schmidt & P. B. Mosenthal (Eds.), *Reconceptualizing literacy in the new age of multiculturalism and pluralism* (pp. 111-134). Greenwich, CT: Information Age.

Finkbeiner, C. (2006). Constructing third space: The principles of reciprocity and cooperation. In P. R. Schmidt & C. Finkbeiner (Eds.), *ABC's of cultural understanding and communication: National and international adaptations* (pp. 19-42). Greenwich, CT: Information Age.

Ladson-Billings, G. (1995). Toward a theory of culturally relevant pedagogy. *American Educational Research Journal, 32*, 465-491.

Moll, L. C. (1992). Bilingual classroom studies and community analysis: Recent Trends. *Educational Researcher, 21*(2), 20-24.

Nieto, S. (1996). *Affirming diversity: The sociopolitical context of multicultural education*. New York: Longman.

Pattnaik, J. (1997). Cultural stereotypes and preservice education: Moving beyond our biases. *Equity and Excellence in Education, 30*(3), 40-50.

Payne, R. K. (1999). *Framework for understanding poverty*. Highlands, TX: Aha Process.

Schmidt, P. R. (1998a). *Cultural conflict and struggle: Literacy learning in a kindergarten program*. New York: Peter Lang

Schmidt, P. R. (1998b). The ABC's of cultural understanding and communication. *Equity and Excellence in Education, 31*(2), 28-38.

Schmidt, P. R. (2000). Teachers connecting and communicating with families for literacy development. In T. Shanahan & F. Rodriguez-Brown (Eds.), *National Reading Conference yearbook, 49th* (pp. 194-208). Chicago: National Reading Conference.

Schmidt, P. R. (2005). *Preparing educators to communicate and connect with families and communities*. Greenwich, CT: Information Age.

Schmidt, P. R. & Finkbeiner, C. (2006). *ABC's of cultural understanding and communication: National and international adaptations*. Greenwich, CT: Information Age.

Tatum, B. (1992). Talking about race, learning about racism: The application of racial identity theory in the classroom. *Harvard Educational Review, 62*(1), 1-24.

Trueba, H. T., Jacobs, L. & Kirton, E. (1990). *Cultural conflict and adaptation: The case of the Hmong students in American society*. New York: The Falmer Press.

# INTRODUCTION

## Toward a Situated Perspective on Multicultural Families and Their Home Literacy Practices

### Guofang Li

*All literacy users are members of a defined culture with a cultural identity, and the degree to which they engage in learning or using literacy is a function of this cultural identity.*

Betha Pérez (2004, p. 5)

Much research on immigrant and/or minority language and literacy acquisition has focused mainly on linguistic and cognitive aspects of English learning in traditional school sites. Although it has yielded significant knowledge to the field, such a narrow focus often ignores the funds of knowledge students may acquire outside school in their homes and communities and the important complexities associated with their learning in these unofficial settings (Dyson, 2003; Hull & Shultz, 2001; Li, 2002, 2007; Moll & González, 1994). Lack of knowledge about students' learning outside school has also contributed to the difficulties edu-

*Multicultural Families, Home Literacies, and Mainstream Schooling*
pp. xv–xxvii
Copyright © 2009 by Information Age Publishing

cators encounter when trying to embrace cultural diversity as many do not have the knowledge base about immigrant and minority children's culturally specific ways of learning in non-school settings. Given the changing cultural landscapes in today's schools, we have an imperative to develop more situated understandings of children's literacy learning experiences embedded in the social and cultural fabrics of their everyday lives outside school.

Efforts to bridge the literacy gaps and differences inside and outside school have been carried out through a variety of family literacy programs. Many of these programs, however, have been heavily criticized. One common critique is that these programs often focus on familiarizing minority parents or caretakers with mainstream, Eurocentric literacy practices that are detached from the cultural practices of the families who are often from non-White middle class backgrounds and are therefore built upon a deficit model that devalues minority families as sources of information and literacy leaning (Auerbach, 1995; De Carvalho, 2001; Handel, 1999). One of the main reasons for this critique is that the literacy activities of the home and the cultural context of home practices are often not readily accessible to school personnel, program developers, policy makers or even researchers and educators (Handel, 1999). Therefore, there is a need for a better understanding of literacy practices from the inside of the culturally diverse homes to ensure culturally responsive program development that will empower, not impede, all children's learning.

This volume of research will meet these important needs in the field. It features research on home literacy practices that are lived, negotiated, and transmitted in families of various ethnic and cultural backgrounds. It not only focuses on the complexity of literacy learning in diverse home contexts, but also examines how literacy is practiced and lived in multiple ways within families of various cultures including those of Asian, African American, Hispanic, White European, and mixed race backgrounds. In addition, it explores how these various culturally embedded home practices will inform school education and policy making in a larger socio-political context. The goals of this book are therefore to provide: (1) understandings of home literacy practices including immigrant and/or minority and mainstream parents and students' everyday experiences and cultural beliefs on their children's language and literacy learning to determine the needs and barriers for successful adaptation to schooling; and (2) understandings of how the knowledge of home practices can help building school and home links to suggest recommendations regarding better policies and strategies for effective school-home-community collaborations and teacher education.

## TOWARD A SITUATED PERSPECTIVE
## ON HOME LITERACY PRACTICES

The research studies included in this book are based on a situated perspective to literacy that seeks to understand literacy practices within the social and cultural contexts in which they occur (Vygotsky, 1978). Viewed from this perspective, language and literacy are treated as social practices rather than a narrow set of reading and writing skills to be learned through formal education (Gee, 1989; Street, 2003). It is a contextually based, broad concept that is grounded in cultural practices. Literacy learning, therefore, is much more than acquiring rudimentary skills but involves developing knowledges, attitudes and understandings about the forms, functions and purposes of literacy in particular sociocultural contexts (Li, 2002; Street, 2003). As Li (2006) writes,

> Literacy is no longer thought of as a technical ability to read and write, nor the ability of individuals to function within social contexts associated with daily living. Rather, beyond these capacities, it is an ability to think and reason, a way of living, a means of looking at the world we know and how we behave in the world. (p. 18)

Literacy as a way of living is part of a culture (Li, 2002, 2006). Literacy itself is an individual cognitive as well as a cultural phenomenon—it permeates in the life of an individual through ongoing exchanges of meanings with significant others (Halliday, 1978, p. 1). The uses of language and literacy (e.g., ways of speaking and writing, choices of words) are culturally encoded as language and literacy reflect and reinforce "the values and beliefs of a given culture and at the same time are shaped by that culture" (Halliday, 1978, p. 14). Therefore, the learning of language(s) and literacies is also "a key part of cultural apprenticeship (i.e., essential to how one learns to be a member of culture)" (Zentella, 2005, p. 6). During this cultural apprenticeship, children not only acquire the conventions of reading and writing, but also the sociocultural values that are attached to their particular literacy practices (Heath, 1983; Li, 2006; Rogoff, 1990).

Since different cultural groups have different social and cultural norms, literacy practices—their functions, meanings, and methods of transmission—vary from one cultural group to another and from family to family (Langer, 1987; Li, 2002; Wagner, 1991). In this volume, we include studies of families from five different racial and/or ethnic backgrounds. We hope to capture a snap shot of how the culturally different families socialize their children as cultural members of their communities by documenting both the visible element of learning (e.g., reading and writing practices) and the less visible but equally poignant element of literacy learning at home—"the familial and cultural histories, experiences, and expectations that help learners frame and revise their goals, plans, and approaches to learning literacy" (Gadsden, 2004, p. 402). We hope that the nuances of their everyday living and learning (which may or may not be unique to the family or its culture) will serve as "cultural data sets" or cultural texts which teachers and educators can tap when they design learning environments and manage learning interactions in school (Lee, 2007).

While we try to reflect the cultural pluralism of social contexts in which literacy is used, we do not, however, intend to essentialize the cultural differences across or within the ethnic groups. Rather, through uncovering the processes of literacy learning as a social practice in culturally different home milieus, we hope to draw attention to both *cultural variability* and *universality* of home literacy practices across the groups and families. Though families as basic social institutions share many characteristics, in different societies, families have different family lives and worldviews; and even within one society or one culture, "patterns of family life differ in terms of values, education, occupation, income, religion, and ethnicity" (Li, 2002, p. 17). Therefore, we do not assume that all parents from a particular group will socialize their children the same way or there are no similarities in socialization patterns among different cultures. Rather, we take the universality and variability in family literacy practices into consideration, and attempt to reflect the individual family or group's cultural practices shaped by family or group characteristics as well as the collective experiences that are common to all families and/or groups. We try to neither essentialize nor fragment various social categories or ethnic cultures by presenting a sample picture of the varying diversity in ways that different racial groups in America might encounter (Li, 2008). The attention to both the universality and cultural variability of the home literacy practices, as González, Moll, and Amanti (2005) theorized, is "a strategic way of reducing theoretically (but with plenty of respect) the complexity of people's everyday experiences without losing the rich and dynamic totality of their lives" (p. 21). It is our hope that through displaying these different "household analyses" or "funds of knowledge" side by side (González et al., 2005), we can generate a deeper inter- and intracultural sensitivity and more cross-cultural dialogues and contacts.

In this volume, we emphasize the important role of social context and interaction in language and literacy acquisition, that is, the homes of the multicultural families, where literacy is an inherent part of the cultural fabric in which the children and their families live their lives. The chapters included pay attention to not only the physical environment (e.g., level of economic and educational resources, availability of print materials in the setting) and individual differences such as child and parent characteristics, but also the interpersonal interaction between parents and children and among siblings and others in the home in relation to literacy events), as well as socioemotional and motivational climates within the home milieu (Leichter, 1984; Wasik & Herrmann, 2004). We examine different domains of literacy activities ranging from daily living, entertainment, religion, to school- and work-related activities (Anderson & Stokes, 1984; Cairney & Ruge, 1998; Farr, 1994). The distinctive world of literacy that exists in people's home surroundings and, in particular, their different ways of passing on literacy values and skills through these different domains of literacy activities, reflect the cultural experiences that are essential to their lives (Li, 2002, 2006).

In addition to the contexts of literacy practices, we also pay attention to the processes of cultural apprenticeship. From a situated perspective toward literacy, literacy learning in the home context is seen as an *interactive* process. Building on the work of Lave and Wenger (1991), Rogoff (1990), and Vygotsky (1978), we examine the mutual roles of the individual (both adults and children) and the sociocultural context and the social processes by which the individual appropriates and extends skill and understanding from their involvement through participation in culturally laden literacy activities. As the chapters demonstrate, we examine different levels of interaction within the home milieu including interactions between individuals or groups (such as between parents and children around literacy, among siblings, and between the researcher and the researched), interactions among the individual, the family, and the external environment such as the socioeconomic system and the racial climate, and interactions among the individual, the family, and other major social institutions such as the schools, the government, and the church. The relationships between the individual, the family as a whole unit, the social environments and institutions are seen as mutually interactive and reciprocal (Webb, 2001). We believe it is these reciprocal influences between the individual, the family, and their socio-cultural environments and institutions that shape the families and children's home literacy practices and their experiences with schools.

Within these different levels of interaction, we emphasize the agency and independency of the family members in the processes of cultural apprenticeship. We do not assume that all family members are the same. Rather, we see literacy learning and socialization in the family is context dependent and learner-specific. As Gadsden (1994) notes, not all components of the same family environment are shared or affect the individual's literacy learning the same way; therefore, there are both *similarities* and *differences* in literacy learning among family members in the same family. Further, we do not assume that cultural transmission is unidirectional from adults to children. Rather, we believe that children are active meaning makers who coconstruct knowledge in the social practices at home.

Therefore, we emphasize *reciprocal influences* between parents and children and between siblings, and in some cases, between the researcher and the researched (e.g., Lynch chapter, this volume). As Germain and Gitterman (1987) argue, "neither the people served, nor their environments, can be fully understood except in relationship to each other" (p. 493).

## MULTICULTURAL FAMILIES, HOME LITERACY PRACTICES, AND IMPLICATIONS FOR EDUCATION: OUTLINE OF CHAPTERS

This book brings together a number of researchers and educators who will make important contributions to understanding students' out-of-school literacy and learning, culturally different patterns of parental involvement in the home milieu, their interactions with the mainstream schools, and policy implications of such knowledge for minority and teacher education. The book is divided into four parts: (1) Theorizing Research on Home Literacy Practices and Mainstream Schooling; (2) Multicultural Families and Home Literacy Practices; (3) School-Home Literacy Connections and the Directions of Minority Literacy Education; and (4) Home Literacies and Mainstream Schooling—A Conclusion.

In part I, Theorizing Research on Home Literacy Practices and Mainstream Schooling, Trevor Cairney provides a review of key theoretical insights that have shaped policy and school-based practices in literacy and an overview of key developments in our understanding of the relationship between the cultural practices of families and the way literacy is taught in schools. Cairney attempts to problematize the existing research literature in this area and discuss possible future directions by drawing on the broader international research literature. This chapter provides a theoretical foundation and framework for the following chapters.

Part II, Multicultural Families and Home Literacy Practices consists of nine chapters that examine the diverse home literacy practices among families from five different cultural and ethnic backgrounds. Though all chapters focus on literacy practices, each chapter addresses different facets of literacy practices that are specific to the home contexts under study. Thus, each chapter makes a special contribution and together they present a complex and multidimensional nature of home literacies in multicultural families.

Chapters 2 and 3 are dedicated to families of African and African American backgrounds. In chapter 2, Catherine Compton-Lilly presents the stories of three African American children. She explores the ways their literacy practices are situated within home contexts that feature not only activities related to reading and writing but rich relationships that accompany those practices and expansive social and historical roots that led to these literacy practices. In particular, she focuses on two types of literacy practices that children and parents shared over the course of the 8-year research project: literacy practices that parents use to teach children to read and those children share with their siblings and peers. In chapter 3, Patricia Lynch explores the experiences of one Somali Bantu refugee family as they learned to negotiate the language and culture of the United States, and describes her evolving role as she assisted in literacy learning while attempting to learn the family's language and culture herself. Through these reciprocal influences, Lynch discovers that each family member took different kinds of risks in their engagement with language and are culturally situated to learn from a variety of mediators and resources, and that she was the best teacher when she became the most vulnerable learner.

Chapters 4 and 5 are about families of Asian heritage. In chapter 4, Hye-Young Park describes the specific difficulties and differences that she encountered during the interactions with her 12 year-old son in his writing development in Korean and English. She discovers that their interactions around Korean writing often involved considerable communication breakdowns while English writing often proceeded smoothly, which resulted from differences in linguistic/cultural understanding between her and her son who have varied degrees of acculturation to the American culture. In chapter 5, Guofang Li documents a Chinese immigrant family—the Li family's home literacy practices as they make their cultural and literacy transitions to North American society. She unveils what home literacy is like and the ways the Li parents facilitate their son's adaptation to the new learning environments. Specifically, she focuses on four aspects of the Li family's home literacy practices: literacy opportunities inside and outside home, the parents' culturally specific instructional strategies, cooperation and interaction between parents and child, and the socio-emotional quality in the home milieu.

The next two chapters are studies of families of Hispanic backgrounds. In chapter 6, Maria Coady presents a case study of two migrant farmworking families' home literacy practices and the ways in which the families negotiated literacy ideologies in rural, northern Florida. Data from this study reveal that home literacy practices were informed socioculturally and historically by patents' experiences with literacy in the country of origin and shaped further by the religious ideologies of the families upon relocation to the United States. Coady also discovers that the parents' (principally the mothers') home country experiences with literacy and books contrasted with schools' (mainstream) literacy ideologies and expectations, and that the use of religious materials and texts was also an important literacy tool. However, despite parental efforts and practices to support the education of their children, parents were essentially unaware of mainstream assumptions of literacy and how those assumptions interact with the educational experiences of their children. In chapter 7, Leslie Reese documents purposes of literacy uses among immigrant Latino families including school, church, and work. Similar to the findings in Coady's study, Reese finds that the values and beliefs guiding and shaping these literacy practices, derived in part from the home country experiences of the families as well as from their interactions in U.S. social contexts, shape the ways in which family members carry out literacy practices. A key concept explored is that of complementarities between mainstream practices and school expectations and the literacy practices of Latino families that may not be identical to mainstream practices but which nonetheless serve to promote children's literacy development and support their academic success.

Following these two chapters are two studies on White American families from different socioeconomic backgrounds. In chapter 8, Billie Enz and Dawn Foley describe the 5-year journey of Anne, a child from an upper-middle class White background, to becoming an accomplished communicator and sophisticated interpreter and consumer of print. They examine the wide range of language and print that is pouring into Annie's environment through multiple sources—radio, videos/DVDs, television programming, books, environmental print, games, and especially family talk. Enz and Foley also conclude that adults in Annie's life such as parents and grandparents play heavily into her development as a competent communicator, reader, and writer and will also impact her future success in school as she was socialized into different literacy practices from infancy. In contrast to the upper-middle class White family, in chapter 9, Guofang Li introduces two low-socioeconomic status (SES) White families in an inner-city environment where they were a racial minority. She explores not only their literacy experiences at home and in school but also how their particular race and class locations (e.g., being White but poor and a racial minority) shape their daily literacy practices as they cross borders between home and school. Data analysis reveals that reading and writing for school-related purposes is one of the major domains of literacy used in the homes of the two families. The parents tried their best to respond to school demands and cultivate cultural capital to support their children's school learning. These efforts, however, were constantly thwarted by family socio-economic status and constrained by hostile racial relationships, increasingly unsafe community environments, and declining school cultures.

The last chapter in this section, chapter 10, is concerned with a family of mixed heritages. Mariana Souto-Manning and Dice present a "kidwatching" study highlighting literacy practices within a bicultural and bilingual context in a Latin American household. They examine how a young child negotiates a third space between the official and unofficial literacy practices, and how Latino and American models of literacy practices inform each other syncretically in his biliteracy and bicultural development. They also discover that different conceptualizations of literacy practices that surround each parent's cultural belief systems beyond language differences also play a role in shaping the child's syncretic literacy practices.

Part III: School-Home Literacy Connections and the Directions of Minority Literacy Education contains three chapters. In chapter 11, Sarah J. McCarthey illustrates the influence of both home and school on students' emerging identities from three different theoretical perspectives: the dialogic theory, the theory of communities of practice, and the narrative theory. In chapter 12, Jennifer Turner and Patricia Edwards explore critical issues about home literacies in relation to three educational contexts: teacher education programs, K-12 schools and classrooms, and family literacy programs. Through the discussion concerning the impact of home literacies research on preparing teachers to teach literacy to children from diverse cultural and linguistic backgrounds, they highlight how diversity has been a "hot topic" in teacher education for several years, yet preservice teacher education programs still have not adequately prepared literacy teachers to build on their students' home literacy backgrounds. Next, they theorize about how research on home literacies has shaped our current understanding of culturally responsive literacy instruction in K-12 classrooms. Finally, they describe the tensions and disconnections between the "theory" of family literacy and the "practices" of family literacy education programs. They conclude the chapter by raising new questions, proposing next steps, and offering possible directions for future research on home and school literacies.

Finally, in part IV, Home Literacies and Mainstream Schooling: A Conclusion, Diane Lapp concludes the book by discussing the implications of home literacy research for schools. She highlights three major areas of focus for the preparation of future teachers namely, teachers' knowledge and attitudes about the home literacies of their students, teachers' knowledge and skills in coconstructing with their students a classroom culture of inclusion, and teachers' knowledge and ability to support their students in understanding the learning process.

## WHERE DO WE GO FROM HERE?

The studies in this volume demonstrate that home literacies are complex and multidimensional. While all chapters point to the role of culture plays in shaping home literacy practices, culture plays out differently in different families depending on the individual family's sociohistorical and sociocultural backgrounds, their beliefs and attitudes about and experiences with literacy, as well as their race and class locations. For example, while religious texts play an important role in some of Hispanic and African American families, they do not hold such a place in other families such as the Asian or the White families. While all parents play an active role in shaping the children as well as the families' literacy practices, what and how parents socialize their children into home literacy practices differ widely depending on parent characteristics such as their own proficiency in the mainstream language, their educational background, and their SES status. As the chapters demonstrate, parents who have higher education (e.g., those in Li, chapter 4, Enz & Foley, this volume) are more familiar with mainstream literacy and are thus able to provide school-like literacy supports at home while other low-SES parents are not. In fact, Li (chapter 9, this volume), Coady, and Compton-Lilly (this volume) illustrate, many minority parents are not familiar with mainstream literacy practices endorsed by school and how their different assumptions about literacy might influence their children's educational experiences. Although we see cases of complementary practices between school and home (Reese, this volume), more often we see evidence of disconnect between mainstream schooled literacy practices and social and cultural practices in the minority home contexts. Unless all children learn to successfully negotiate a third space where both literacy traditions and practices are valued (like Diego in Souto-Manning and Dice, this volume), they are likely to experience disconnections between school and home learning that further place them at an academic disadvantage.

The knowledge accumulated through this volume speaks to the need for schools to revisit issues concerning minority literacy education. Though a large body of research has pointed to the need for schools to build on students' cultural backgrounds, little research has been conducted to examine the strategies and approaches that help teachers use students' "cultural data sets" in their design of lessons and management of classroom learning. Many current approaches such as Gonzalez, Moll, and Amanti's (2005) "funds of knowledge" approach and Lee's (2007) "cultural modeling" are examples of good practices but mostly with a specific minority population (e.g., Latinos or African Americans). More research is needed to expand this type of work by developing strategies and pedagogical models that can help teachers translate this knowledge into their lesson planning that addresses students from diverse/multiple cultural traditions and backgrounds.

To do so, further work is needed to make these "cultural data sets" more accessible to teachers, policy makers, as well as parents themselves. In fact, much research to date has adopted a unidirectional approach in examining how home practices might inform school practices. Little research is conducted to examine the reciprocal relationship between school practices and home practices. Given the need to better involve parents in children's literacy learning in school and home, future research can help teachers as well as parents become aware of the family as a system—how some developmental and contextual structures within the family can serve as either incentives or barriers to learning (Gadsden, 1994) and become familiar with how schools as a system works and how it can interact with the home system to impede or facilitate learning.

Future research must also focus on children's learning processes—not just what they learn, but also how they learn and how learning is transferred in multiple contexts. For example, how and in what conditions can children successfully negotiate a third space for multiple languages and literacies? What are the barriers and incentives to achieve such success? What are the other pathways to success for children who are border crossers? What and how do teachers and parents help to facilitate such conditions and developments?

Finally, given the complex and multidimensional nature of the home literacies, we need more interdisciplinary, collaborative work that explores the various variables that affect the families and their learning. As Gadsden (1994) argues:

> A convergence of families and literacy as a research domain stresses the cross-disciplinary nature of literacy research and practice (e.g., the interrelationships among contributing disciplines—reading, sociology, psychology, and social work) … this view would expand the field to focus on the conditions and circumstances that affect families and seek to understand the most effective ways to meet the multiple and varied educational needs and social demands within different home settings. (pp. 73-74)

With this note, I invite you to meet the children, parents, teachers, and researchers in this volume as their literacies learning and teaching and their realities in and out of school unfold in the chapters that follow.

## REFERENCES

Anderson, A. B., & Stokes, S. J. (1984). Social and institutional influences on the development and practice on literacy. In H. Goelman, A. A. Oberg, & F. Smith (Eds.), *Awakening to literacy* (pp. 24-37). Exeter, NH: Heinemann.

Auerbach, E. (1995). Deconstructing the discourse of strengths in family literacy. *Journal of Reading Behavior, 27*, 643-659.

Cairney, T. H., & Ruge, J. (1998). *Community literacy practices and schooling: Towards effective support for students.* Canberra, Australia: Department of Employment, Education & Training.

De Carvalho, M. E. P. (2001). *Rethinking family-school relations: A critique of parental involvement in schooling*. New York: Teachers College Press.

Dyson, A. H. (2003). *The brothers and sisters learn to write: Popular literacies in childhood and school cultures*. New York: Teachers College Press.

Farr, M. (1994). En los dos idiomas: Literacy practices among Chicago Mexicanos. In B. J. Moss (Ed.), *Literacy across communities* (pp. 9-47). Cresskill, NJ: Hampton Press.

Gadsden, V. L. (1994). Understanding family literacy: Conceptual issues facing the field. *Teachers College Record, 96*(1), 58-86.

Gadsden, V. L. (2004). Family literacy and culture. In B. H. Wasik (Ed.), *Handbook of family literacy* (pp. 399-400). Mahwah, NJ: Erlbaum.

Gee, J. P. (1989). Literacy, discourse, and linguistics: Introduction. *Journal of Education, 171*(1), 5-17.

Germain, C. B., & Gitterman, A. (1987). Ecological perspectives. *Encycolpedia of social work* (18th ed., pp. 488-499). Silver Springs, MD: NASW Press.

González, N., Moll, L. C., and Amanti, C. (Eds.). (2005). *Funds of knowledge: Theorizing practices in households, communities, and classrooms*. Mahwah, NJ: Erlbaum.

Halliday, M. A. K. (1978). *Language as social semiotic: The social interpretation of language and meaning*. Baltimore: University Park Press.

Handel, R. D. (1999). *Building family literacy in an urban community*. New York: Teachers College Press.

Heath, S. B. (1983). *Ways with words: Language, life, and work in communities and classrooms*. New York: Cambridge University Press.

Hull, G., & Schultz, K. (2001). Literacy and learning out of school: A review of theory and research. *Review of Educational Research, 71*(4): 575-611.

Langer, J. A. (Ed.). (1987). *Language and literacy and culture: Issues of society and schooling*. Norwood, NJ: Ablex.

Lave, J., & Wenger, E. (1991). *Situated learning: Legitimate peripheral participation*. Cambridge, United Kingdom: Cambridge University Press.

Lee, C. D. (2007). *Culture, literacy, and learning: Taking bloom in the midst of the whirlwind*. New York: Teachers College Press.

Leichter, H. J. (1984). Families as environments for literacy. In H. Goelman, A. A. Oberg, & F. Smith (Eds.), *Awakening to literacy* (pp. 38-50). Exeter, NH: Heinemann.

Li, G. (2002). *"East is east, west is west"? Home literacy, culture, and schooling*. New York: Peter Lang.

Li, G. (2006). *Culturally contested pedagogy: Battles of literacy and schooling between mainstream teachers and Asian immigrant parents*. Albany, NY: State University of New York Press.

Li, G. (2007). Home environment and second language acquisition: The importance of family capital. *British Journal of Sociology of Education, 28*(3), 285-299.

Li, G. (2008). *Culturally contested literacies: America's "rainbow underclass" and urban schools*. New York: Routledge.

Moll, L. C., & González, N. (1994). Lessons from research with language-minority children. *Journal of Reading Behavior, 26*, 439-456.

Pérez, B. (Ed.). (2004). Literacy, diversity, and programmatic responses. In *Sociocultural contexts of language and literacy* (pp. 3-24). Mahwah, NJ: Erlbaum.

Rogoff, B. (1990). *Apprenticeship in thinking: Cognitive development in social context.* Oxford, England: Oxford University Press.

Street, B. (2003). What's "new" in new literacy studies? Critical approaches to literacy in theory and practice. *Current Issues in Comparative Education, 5*(2), 77-91.

Vygotsky, L. (1978). *Mind and society: The development of higher mental processes.* Cambridge, MA: Harvard University Press.

Wagner, D. A. (1991). Literacy as culture: Emic and etic perspective. In E. M. Jennings & A. C. Purves (Eds.), *Literate systems and individual lives: Perspectives on literacy and schooling* (pp. 11-22). Albany, NY: State University of New York Press.

Wasik, B. H., & Herrmann, S. (2004). Family literacy: History, concepts, services. In B. H. Wasik (Ed.), *Handbook of family literacy* (pp. 3-22). Mahwah, NJ: Erlbaum.

Webb, N. B. (Ed.). (2001). Working with culturally diverse children and their families. In *Culturally diverse parent-child and family relationships: A guide for social workers and other practitioners* (pp. 3-28). New York: Columbia University Press.

Zentella, A. C. (Ed.). (2005). Introduction: Perspectives on language and literacy in Latino families and communities. In *Building on strength: Language and literacy in Latino families and communities* (pp. 1-12). New York: Teachers College Press.

# PART I

**THEORIZING RESEARCH ON HOME LITERACY
PRACTICES AND MAINSTREAM SCHOOLING**

CHAPTER 1

# HOME LITERACY PRACTICES AND MAINSTREAM SCHOOLING

## A Theoretical Understanding of the Field

**Trevor H. Cairney**

Research in language acquisition and early literacy development has increasingly identified the family as a critical factor in school success or failure (T. Rogers, Marshall, & Tyson, 2006). But while research has consistently shown that the family has an influence on later achievement in and out of school, explanations of the part played by families have varied greatly and often have been limited by the assumptions that underpin them. This chapter seeks to review research in this area and theorize this important topic while challenging some of these assumptions.

As part of an evaluation of Australian family literacy initiatives for the federal government detailed case studies of a range of different families were undertaken to help understand the forms of support that parents offer to their children's literacy learning (Cairney, Ruge, Buchanan, Lowe, & Munsie, 1995). We were surprised to observe just how diverse families were, not just in relation to the literacy practices we observed, but in the way literacy was defined, supported and valued. Families were different,

*Multicultural Families, Home Literacies, and Mainstream Schooling*
pp. 3–24

not just in literacy practices, but also in the relationships between members of the family where literacy and language learning was concerned, including what counted as literacy, how literacy was supported and how it was used as part of daily life. This was in stark contrast to the less varied nature of literacy in the classrooms they attended each day.

It was also obvious from this research that literacy is not a unitary skill with a limited range of communicative uses. Rather, we observed rich literacy practices. The term literacy practice is used deliberately as is the related term literacy events. These two terms are often used interchangeably. The term *literacy event* has its roots in the sociolinguistic idea of speech events dating back to the work of Dell Hymes (1962), but the concept was developed further by Heath (1982, 1983) to describe a distinct communicative situation where literacy has a key role. For Heath, a literacy event is "any occasion in which a piece of writing is integral to the nature of the participants' interactions and their interpretive processes" (1982, p. 23). "Literacy *events* are the particular activities in which literacy has a role: they may be regular repeated activities. Literacy *practices* are the general cultural ways of utilizing literacy that people draw upon in a literacy event" (Barton, 1991, p. 5). The value of the term literacy practices is that it shifts our focus from a concern with literacy as skill to that of literacy as social practices inseparable from culture. Street (1995) explains something of this relationship in exploring the distinction between literacy practices and literacy events, arguing that whenever people engage in a literacy event they have "culturally constructed models of the literacy event in [their] minds" (p. 133). This is a significant understanding that shapes the various studies conducted in this book that concern families from varied language and cultural traditions.

As a number of researchers have observed, literacy practices are situationally defined in and through the interactions and practices of students and teachers at school, and family and community members at home (Cairney, 1995; Collins & Green, 1992). When people engage in specific literacy events they act and interact in ways that socially construct, and are constructed by, the general cultural ways of using literacy. Thus, literacy events contribute to, and constitute part of the literacy practices of the particular classroom, family or community group. Literacy in varied forms is integrated with the cultural practices of the families that have been observed in the studies that are discussed in the following chapters. These forms include print-based practices of all types. In recent times some have sought to go even further and acknowledge the impact and interrelationship of new media with print literacy. Marsh (2006) for example uses the term "communicative practices" to embrace the enhanced range of multimodal meaning making events in which children engage.

Cope and Kalantzis (2000) argue that literacy and literacy teaching must include negotiating a multiplicity of discourses. First, literacy pedagogy must take account of the context of our culturally and linguistically diverse and increasingly global societies. Second, it must take account of the increasing variety of text forms associated with information and multimedia technologies. Stein and Slonimsky (2006) found that within three South African families that literacy was fundamentally multimodal, drawing on the representational resources available to them. Similarly, work by Li (2004) has demonstrated that in bilingual families this richness is even more complex with first and second language practices adding to the richness of multimodal encounters with texts of all kinds. As Souto-Manning and Dice (this volume) suggest in chapter 10 of this book, the link between parental literacy practices and children's literacy practices extends well beyond story reading and homework, to include "storytelling, rapping, shopping, cooking, participating in religious rites, dancing, acting, drawing" and so on.

Cope and Kalantzis (2000) argue that instead of talking about reading and writing we should consider the term "design" to cover the multiple forms of meaning that they see as characterizing our increasingly multimedia dominated world. They argue that the term design is free of the negative associations that plague traditional terms. The term reflects a theoretical position that semiotic activities are the creative application and combination of conventions (resources or available designs) that, in the process of design, transforms, at the same time as it reproduces, these conventions (Fairclough, 1992).

However, for many researchers the concept of design is too broad and far removed from the social practices viewed by most parents and community members as constituting literacy. Instead, researchers have used a variety of frameworks to make sense of the diverse practices that most people would call literacy. For example, in my work, I sought to move beyond simple categories of language form or descriptive labels. As a result, a system was developed to classify and make sense of literacy practices and events which could account for all of the types and uses of literacy at home and at school. A number of classification systems described in the existing research literature were considered, but none was found to be adequate for our work. Instead of focussing on function, we noted that some researchers had helpfully on purpose and decided to pursue this approach. We identified four distinct purposes for literacy in the homes and classrooms in our study: literacy for establishing and maintaining relationships; literacy for accessing or displaying information; literacy for pleasure and/or self-expression; and literacy for skills development (Cairney & Ruge, 1998).

Literacy for establishing relationships involved a rich variety of reading and writing to maintain contact with others and build common ground. Practices included letter writing, reading to and with each other, and even playing school. Literacy for accessing or displaying information and included reading store catalogs, reading maps, TV guides, games, writing shopping lists, filling in forms and reading factual texts. Literacy for pleasure and/or self-expression included reading books, magazines, cartoons, writing songs, keeping diaries, playing computer games. Literacy for skills development was typically literacy that had an instructional focus, "doing literacy," rather than using literacy. The learning of literacy for its own sake was the primary purpose and the focus of "school type" literacy which included word drills, read aloud sessions, homework activities and so on. What this framework helped us to do is move beyond a limited range of school-based written literacy practices to consider the diverse range of practices that we were observing in families.

What we found when we applied this framework to the home and school literacy practices of our 27 families was a greater richness and variation in families than in classrooms, in spite of the fact that school literacy had a significant impact on home literacy infiltrating family life for many hours and in diverse ways. This same richness is demonstrated in the various studies in this book.

Marsh (2006) in applying the Cairney and Ruge (1998) framework in more recent research found that the purposes that form the basis of the framework were still applicable. However, almost ten years on from the Cairney and Ruge research, she found that the literacy practices of 83 families were increasingly embedded within popular culture, media and new technologies. This shift continues as children encounter increasingly diverse forms of literacy in and out of school.

In the Cairney and Ruge (1998) study one, the Ahmeds, provides insight into this complexity. At home, the Ahmed children spoke Arabic to both their parents and their siblings. Mr. Ahmed read to the children in Arabic, but the children had only English books. The four children were all learning to read and write Arabic through attendance at Arabic school three times per week. They had attended Arabic lessons from a young age. Hannah, at 5 years of age, had not yet begun kindergarten but had already been attending Arabic lessons for almost a year. The two oldest children, a girl and a boy, were attending single-sex high schools. Mr. Ahmed says that, for him, provision of an Arabic language program was an important consideration in deciding where to send the children to school. The children completed most of their school homework in isolation within their rooms, and their parents played minimal part. Mr. Ahmed indicated that he was less involved in his children's school work these days and commented, "I used to help them before, but now they can do it by themselves." When his son Joe was asked what he did if he encountered difficulty with his homework, he replied, "Ask my brother or sister ... mostly it's maths; they show me how to get the answer and how to write it on the page." In this very supportive home, much of the help with school literacy comes from siblings, not from parents.

The Ahmed children were negotiating multiple literacies in two languages across varied contexts. When we visited their schools we found only limited differentiation in the forms of support given to children in each of their classes, and there appeared to be little difference in the teachers' expectations of the children as literacy learners. But in their daily lives the children assumed many roles as students and family members. At home the children also adopted varied informal roles as supporters of each other's school learning. They had different literacy needs to their parents and engaged in different literacy practices. There was also variation with age in the specific literacy and language practices of the children.

What the studies in this book demonstrate is that such complexity is demonstrated across varied cultural and language groups. This is consistent with observations of great variability across social class groups (e.g. Cairney & Ruge, 1998; Compton-Lilly, 2004; Li, 2002, 2008). Families make many and varied contributions to their children's literacy and language learning.

In contrast, while within the Cairney and Ruge (1998) study no two families were the same, the classrooms in which they were taught were remarkably similar. Our research demonstrated that schools need to be more responsive to the literacy and language complexity that children encounter outside school. We concluded that schools need to understand the rich tapestry of literacy practices that children experience and respond accordingly (Cairney et al., 1995).

What much of this research points to is a need to think carefully about the evidence relating to language and literacy variations across families and communities. As well, we need to consider the role that schools play in responding to such diversity. In the rest of this chapter I provide a theoretical framework for understanding the relationship between home and school literacy. As well as outlining some of the major research that has informed our work with multicultural families, I will provide a theoretical justification for the view that understanding the differences between the literacy practices of home and school is vital to ensuring that all students are given the best chance to succeed at school, particularly for children from families for whom English is not the first language.

## UNDERSTANDING THE DIVERSE NEEDS OF LITERACY LEARNERS

One of the great challenges for schools in today's diverse society is to understand how to cater for the needs of all students within traditional school structures. One of the imperatives for teachers in many English-speaking countries like the United States, Australia, Canada and the United Kingdom in the last 2 decades has been the need to acknowledge and build on the language and cultural diversity of the students who enter schools each day. The acquisition of English literacy has been one of the major priorities for teachers within such schools. But the achievements of schools have been mixed, with differing levels of success in meeting the diverse needs of all learners.

In commenting on inequitable outcomes in education Au (1993) has suggested that most explanations are governed by two major sets of theoretical assumptions. The first set has been called the theory of cultural discontinuity, or cultural difference, and suggests that cultural mismatches between teachers and students may result in difficulties in communication and interaction in the classroom (Erickson, 1993). These differences or mismatches, it is argued, work against the literacy learning of students whose home culture does not reflect that of the school. Studies that adopt a cultural discontinuity perspective tend to focus less on broad issues of social and economic power, and more on the day-to-day patterning of specific activities (e.g., Delgado-Gaitan, 1992; Deyhle & LeCompte, 1994; Heath, 1983; Malin, 1994; Mulhern, 1995). Au (1995) argues that a key assumption of cultural difference analyses "is that there are systematic, identifiable differences in cultural values, knowledge, and practices, and that these differences are related to students' chances for school success" (p. 90). However, this theory fails to explain the fact that children from some cultural groups have higher rates of success than others. Nor does it explain the phenomenon of children who "code switch" (Gumperz, 1982; Trudgill, 2000) regularly, indicating high proficiency with multiple languages, and yet who still struggle with English literacy at school.

The second dominant theory has been called structural inequality and looks beyond mismatches between the culture of the home and the school. It suggests that the lack of educational success of students from minority backgrounds reflects structural inequalities in the broader social, political and economic spheres (Au, 1993; Ogbu, 1993). This theory takes into account the power relationships between groups, and argues that schools function to maintain the status quo. Critical analyses of social and cultural differences and the impact of these on school success tend to adopt a "structural inequality" perspective (e.g., Fairclough, 1989; Ogbu, 1992, 1993; Luke, 1993; May, 1995; R. Rogers, 2003). This perspective attributes educational disadvantage to "oppressive social structures that create vast inequalities in power and opportunity favouring the dominant group" (Au, 1995, p. 87). Luke (1995) has argued that schools "naturalise particular interactional patterns and textual practices in ways that systematically exclude those students from economically marginal and culturally different backgrounds" (p. 16).

However, neither the cultural discontinuity theory nor the structural inequality theory appears to adequately explain the continuing educational disadvantage of students from minority backgrounds. Several, have argued instead for schools to examine pedagogy more closely before simply blaming differences in literacy practices and inequitable power relationships as the cause of school failure for some.

Ruis (1988) has argued that a better orientation is to see language as a resource. He suggests that linguistic diversity is a rich resource that needs to be nurtured. This argument is consistent with the work of Moll and his colleagues who have argued that we must recognize that all children bring with them different funds of knowledge that can have utility and importance in school. Such a perspective involves "a shift away from a view of individual learners to a view of learning as participation in a community of practice" (Moll, 1993, p. 2). The emphasis is thus, not how individual children learn, but instead, why and how people learn through their participation in the practices that define specific groups and communities, how communities organise their resources, and how participation in the culture shapes identity. This different perspective shifts the focus away from blaming families to pedagogical practices that support all learners.

Similarly, Ladson-Billings (1995a) has pointed out that much of the existing work on linking students' home and school cultures has concentrated on "improving achievement in relation to White middle-class norms" (p. 150). She argues like Au and others that this effectively treats difference as a problem to be overcome. Such studies she suggests attribute poor school achievement of minority children to differences in interaction patterns between teachers and students. She goes even further to suggest that even seemingly appropriate responses that use the terms *culturally appropriate, culturally congruent* and *culturally compatible*, are commonly based on an assumption that mainstream school culture should merely accommodate students' home culture, rather than respond to it. Ladson-Billings believes that much more is needed, arguing that schools must help students to accept and affirm their cultural identity while developing critical perspectives that challenge inequities that schools (and other institutions) perpetuate. She terms this *culturally relevant pedagogy* defining its features as an approach that develops students academically, nurtures and support cultural competence, while also supporting critical consciousness (Ladson-Billings, 1995b).

In another significant study Li (2006, p. 209) has suggested another framework for making sense of the changes that need to occur in pedagogy as well as the way that schools relate to communities. She uses the term "pedagogy of cultural reciprocity." As an outcome of detailed qualitative study of Chinese immigrant families in Vancouver, research she concludes that we need a new dialogic discourse or model for change. Such a model she suggests must encourage change in the relationship between home and school where different practices, values, traditions, understandings, and ideologies are reconfigured and acquired by both school and home agencies.

Common to views like those of Ruis, Ladson-Billings and Li is the rejection of notions that literacy is a single unitary skill, and the replacement understanding that it is a social practice with many specific manifestations (Cairney, 1995; Gee, 1990; Luke, 1993; Welch & Freebody, 1993). Furthermore, this work rests on the assumption that there are many forms of literacy, each with specific purposes and contexts in which they are used (Barton, 1994; Cairney, 1995; Cook-Gumperz, 1986; Moll, Amanti, Neff, & Gonzalez, 1992). This view of literacy as "social accomplishment of a group" (Baker & Luke, 1991; Bloome, 1986; Cairney, 1987, 2005; Cairney & Langbien, 1989; Santa Barbara Classroom Discourse Group, 1992; T. Rogers et al., 2006) suggests that all participants in schools, including teachers, students and parents construct their own models and definitions of literacy and sanction particular understandings, norms, expectations, and roles that define what it means to be literate. Hence, literacy is seen as a practice that cannot be separated from the people who use it, being learned and used in rich sociocultural contexts defined by members of a group through their actions with, through and about language. This was demonstrated above in the literacy practices of the Ahmed family as they constructed and used literacy across varied contexts.

Volk and de Acosta (2003) have argued based on ethnographic study of bilingual children that we learn to read with the support of a network of people of varying ages, language diversity and reading ability and include parents, siblings, extended family, friends and community members. Literacy is coconstructed as an extension of the many and varied relationships that characterize children's lives. They argue that literacies in homes are often syncretic[1] with participants drawing on oral and written texts from various contexts that are then reinvented.

As Souto-Manning and Dice (this volume) argue, being exposed to diverse multicultural families offer challenges and opportunities for children trying to negotiate literacy in contexts that demonstrate cultural hybridity. They experience and demonstrate diverse forms of participation in literacy and learning. These "third space" negotiations that might involve code switching also typically require constant negotiation between different family members concerning what is valued and what counts as literacy. Hence, differences across families in what constitutes literacy are to be expected (Volk & de Acosta, 2003).

I have argued elsewhere that the sociolinguistic diversity of literacy support that adults offer, makes it difficult to make simplistic statements concerning differences across literacy contexts, or even repeated occurrences of the same type of literacy event within a single context (Cairney, 2002; Cairney & Ashton, 2002). Even when families appear to use similar forms of support, there are often subtle differences in the language strategies being used that may lead to different outcomes. Hence, teachers need to understand that differences reflect sociolinguistic variations if they are to respond to the linguistic diversity present within classrooms to ensure equitable learning outcomes.

## MOVING TOWARD PARTNERSHIP, COLLABORATION AND SYNERGY BETWEEN HOME, SCHOOL AND COMMUNITY

There is obviously a big difference between acknowledging a community's diversity and knowing how as a school to deal with such diversity. As I have already argued above, the solution is not to seek simply to conform families to school expectations of what it is to be literate. One common response to the observation that specific groups experience inequitable school outcomes has been to seek greater parent involvement in schools. However, many family literacy and parent involvement programs give the impression that they are doing little more than seeking to conform families to school practices. In truth, the initiators of any home/school initiative immediately put themselves in a position of unequal power and begin to shape the agenda in ways that reflect their personal beliefs and expectations. Since schools have typically been responsible for initiating most Family and Intergenerational[2] initiatives, it is not surprising that many such initiatives have been dominated by concerns with school literacy.

For over 40 years researchers, policymakers and teacher educators have been strong advocates for greater parent involvement in children's education. Many of the early programs in the United Kingdom, the United States and Australia focussed on the need to offer parents a limited range of reading strategies to use with their children (see Cairney & Munsie, 1995a and Cairney & Ruge, 1998 for a full discussion) or were simply initiatives designed to involve parents more fully in their children's education at school (Epstein & Dauber, 1991)

However, while considerable effort and money has been put into hundreds of programs and initiatives in the United States, Nickse (1993) and Mattingly, Prislin, McKenzie, Rodriguez, and Kayzar (2002) point out that evidence concerning their effectiveness is modest. Similarly, in a review of 261 family and community literacy initiatives in Australia, Cairney et al. (1995) found that there had been little evaluation of the effectiveness of family and community literacy initiatives. As well, they found that schools initiated the majority of programs and that while they varied in terms of content (that was mainly school literacy), they offered little recognition of the richness of literacy practices within the wider community.

As a result of the inadequacies of many previous efforts to involve parents more in schooling, and the theoretical insights of the work of research like that reviewed in this chapter, there have been strident calls for collaborative initiatives that seek to develop genuine partnerships between families and schools. The call has been for partnerships that offer educational support and aim to increase awareness by each party of the other's literacy practices and needs (Delgado-Gaitan, 1992). This is very much consistent with the work of Ruis (1988), Moll (1993) and Ladson- Billings (1995b) discussed above that stresses the need to view language diversity within the home and community as a rich resource that must be used.

There is a need for a greater acknowledgement of family and community literacies. Pahl and Rowsell (2005) suggest that we need to move beyond the assumption that families lack literacy and instead bring our students' literacy practices into the classroom. Barton and Hamilton (1998) coined the term, "local literacies" to acknowledge that the participants in their Lancaster-based research engaged in a complex web of literacy practices that were related to their needs, interests and "passions" that could take many forms.

In her investigation of Asian immigrant families Li (this volume) found that many immigrant families had varied bilingual experiences of literacy and that they often faced incongruencies between the literacy practices they experienced at school and at home. This at times had an impact on the children when confronted by seemingly different definitions of literacy, views on learning and forms of support. These children were moving in and out of varied literacy milieus on a daily basis.

What research is suggesting is that literacy is learned and used in the multiple contexts of home, school and community. While the school is an important site for literacy, it is just one place where it is learned and used. Increasingly, we must acknowledge the multiliteracies of home and community and embrace multimodal forms of literacy as part of our everyday practices in school as well as outside its walls. But this will involve more than just 'adding a little, multimodal literacy to school curriculum. Such token changes to how we view literacy and build school programs misses the point that in embracing new multimodal forms of literacy we are considering a significant change not just in how we view literacy, but in how we structure schools and classrooms as well as our pedagogical practices. Indeed, as Siegel (2006) points out we will need to consider multimodal literacy as a matter of social justice. There are tricky issues here, for we know that in societies where there are literacies of power, the powerful are those who use these literacy practices well. In embracing new forms of literacy there will be resistance from teachers and parents who might well perceive that multimodal literacy is not the literacy that children need.

## DEVELOPING MORE RESPONSIVE AND RELEVANT CLASSROOM PRACTICES

Cummins' (1986) has suggested that previous attempts at education reform to increase opportunities for students from non-English speaking and minority backgrounds have been unsuccessful because of the failure to adequately consider the relationships between teachers and students, and between schools and communities, whom he argues, have remained essentially unchanged. To reverse the pattern of minority student failure, Cummins suggests that there needs to be a redefinition of the classroom interactions between teachers and students; relationships between schools and minority groups; and intergroup power relations within society as a whole. He insists that students from dominated communities will be empowered in the school context to the extent that the communities themselves are empowered through their interactions with the school. He points out that when educators involve minority parents as partners in their children's education, parents appear to develop a sense of efficacy that communicates itself to children, with positive academic consequences.

One example of seeing the problem in more relational terms has been work by Howard (1994) in the Australian context. Howard (1994) presented a model of culturally responsive pedagogy for Aboriginal children, that took advantage of the "social relationships with which they are familiar" (p. 41). He argued that there are two key processes for successful programs. The first, he suggested is the need to teach in ways that attempt to maximise Aboriginal student learning, while apprenticing them to the processes and assumptions of Western learning. In particular, he advocated the establishment of positive student-teacher relationships, application of peer learning opportunities, recognition and use of Aboriginal children's real-life skills, as well as tolerance and understanding of their autonomy. Second, he recommended a different approach to the use of time, both at the micro level (e.g., allowing longer pauses for Aboriginal children to consider their answers to questions), and at the macro level (e.g., the provision of a more flexible timetable).

The work of Luis Moll and his colleagues, mentioned earlier in this chapter, is also of great significance when considering new forms of partnership with families and communities. Working primarily with Mexican-American working-class families, Moll and his colleagues have explored the notion of the "funds of knowledge" (Moll, 1993; Moll et al., 1992; Gonzalez, Moll & Amanti, 2005) that communities and their members possess. Through their analysis of how households and families function as part of broader social and economic networks, they demonstrated that the families they worked with had important cultural and cognitive resources that sustained them through changing, and often difficult, social and economic circumstances. Through working with groups of classroom teachers, they explored ways in which these "funds of knowledge" could become pedagogically useful in linking students" home and school cultures. Teachers and researchers visited the homes of their students to develop greater knowledge and understanding of the students' home backgrounds. Teachers then developed learning modules based on information gathered from the households, with the result that students became more active in their learning and were able to draw on their own "funds of knowledge." The key to such visits is their purpose. They are not formal visits to glean information but visits in which the teachers "assume the role of learner" helping to establish a new more reciprocal relationship in which knowledge and understanding can be shared (Gonzalez et al., 2005).

What is common to the above more innovative attempts to acknowledge and build on the language and literacy diversity of home and community is that parents are viewed as equal partners, and that there is an effort to develop a reciprocal relationship between home and school. Initiatives of this type must not simply be "tokenistic" attempts to involve parents in school practices (Cairney & Munsie, 1995b). As Harry (1992) argues, parent initiatives must forge collaborative relationships that create mutual understanding between parents and teachers—a "posture of reciprocity." Such mutual understanding offers the potential for schooling to be adjusted to meet the needs of families. As well, it offers parents the opportunity to observe and understand the literacy of schooling, a literacy that ultimately empowers individuals to take their place in society. Parents voices must be heard if true partnership is to occur. As Li (2006) argues, unless the parents' voices are heard and legitimized in the classroom, true dialogue between mainstream teachers and minority immigrant families will not occur.

We need to move well beyond programs that teach skills seen as critical for parents and which assume that some families bring significant deficits in knowledge and learning that gets in the way of school literacy success. As Zentella (2005) argues, families are often blamed for the educational failures of their children. Focusing on the literacy needs of Latino children she suggests that language research must "unmask the ways in which one or more group's ways of speaking or raising children are constructed as inferior to the benefit of the continued domination of a powerful class" (Zentella, 2005, p. 16). Instead, we need to seek greater knowledge of each other that changes the relationship between families and their schools. This requires a process of reaching shared understanding, something that Vygotsky (1978) called "intersubjectivity." It involves a shared focus of attention and mutual understanding of any joint activity. To achieve this requires agreement on the selection of activities, the purpose of the program or initiatives, and strategies for achieving them. Programs that are imposed on families "for their own good" obviously fail to meet the conditions necessary for intersubjectivity to occur. Such programs frequently end with no appreciable impact on teachers and the school, and little long-term benefit for parents and their children.

It is important to stress that such approaches are not without their difficulties. Once again Volk and de Acosta's (2003, p. 37) discussion of syncretism is useful here. They argue that syncretism has the potential to transform learning, if teachers "create space for children's experiences, texts, voices, and choices," thus making learning more meaningful and giving children greater control over their learning. However, the operation of syncretism is messy due to the development of hybrid forms of text that may not be seen as acceptable to schools or even family members. One of the most dramatic examples of this has been the growth of invented spelling as a consequence of SMS messaging via cell phones. This has also led to clashes between educators, teachers, parents and literacy experts about the advisability of allowing hybrid forms of language and literacy at school.[3] In fact there has often been resistance to hybridity leading to parents arguing for standard spelling and the removal of practices like invented spelling.

Another consequence of syncretism is the potential unintended colonizing influence of school literacy practices on the home (see Cairney & Ruge, 1998). The latter reflects the desire of parents to ensure their children's school success by supporting school literacy practices at home. Related to this phenomenon is the problem of clashing school and home expectations when parents seek to have school practices limited to what are seen as basic skills. This effectively shuts out multiliteracies of the type that some minority and non-English speaking students might find more relevant and empowering. The work of the New London Group (Cope & Kalantzis, 2000) has contributed much to our discussion of multiliteracies, calling for schools to become more responsive and inclusive of the changing nature of literacy practices in the wider world. Hence, the last thing that schools should want it to see literacy practices narrowed.

Rather, the literacy of school should reflect the richness of home and community practices.

It is critical that researchers challenge existing assumptions about what counts as literacy. We need to understand the complexity of community literacies in other than school terms and in ways that transcend what Street (1984) refers to as "autonomous" models of literacy. That is, literacy is viewed as an object which people acquire as they learn decontextualized skills; it is seen as a technical and cognitive skill. Instead, Street argues that we need to see it as "ideological"; a set of practices that are embedded in communities where literacy is learned and used in relationship to other people and where it is related to the power structures within society.

Street, Baker, and Tomlin (2005) have considered how nonschool factors affect school achievement as part of the Leverhulme Programme in the United Kingdom. This 5-year longitudinal project sought to examine the meanings and uses of numeracy in school and community settings. It also looked at the language practices associated with numeracy, namely reading, writing, speaking and listening. A particular consideration was the influence of home contexts on school achievement. The project has attempted to develop ways of measuring pupil progression across a five-year period. The researchers' observations on numeracy and language practices are of great relevance. The researchers found that when questions were asked of parents about numeracy that discussions often turned to school practices. The researchers were left with the key question "how are the borders between numeracy practices and other social practices constructed by researchers, schools and families?" This led the researchers to ask a related question, "How damaging are any omissions?" Such observations and questions have relevance to the observation that school literacy practices dominate home practices. Could our observations of school literacy practices that apparently dominating home literacy reflect (at least in part) a masking of other practices that researchers as participants simply don't count or define as literacy.

This theme is picked up by Pahl and Rowsell (2006) as they argue that increasingly children are growing up in post-industrial economies in environments saturated by multimodal information and literacy. They argue that outside school children are immersed in varied literacy practices experienced as part of television viewing, video games, popular music, print media, the internet and the varied images and messages of popular culture. Understanding the changing face of literacy is obviously an important part of any changes that we might make to pedagogy and school practices that seek to acknowledge and build on the increasing diversity of the children and families that schools serve.

## IMPLICATIONS

The review that has been provided in this chapter suggests a number of implications for researchers, schools and teachers. In other publications (Cairney, 2003, 2005) I have discussed such implications in detail but a summary will suffice for the purposes of this chapter. The studies that are outlined in this book are consistent with the implications that were drawn.

First, researchers need to increasingly problematize the work in this area. We need more studies that consider factors such as gender, social class and culture while examining literacy across diverse contexts. There is also a need to examine in more detail the synergistic relationship between the literacy of home and school. We need further research that examines the impact of school literacy on the shaping of family literacy practices as well as an increased understanding of how family literacy intersects with community literacy. Added to this is the impact of hybridity and the challenges it brings for schools as they seek to acknowledge community literacies and languages.

The impact of multimedia and digital literacy demands on families and schools is also of critical importance. What impact do changing literacy practices have on families and how should schools respond to the growth of new literacy practices? While we know that literacy practices in our world are changing (see, for example, Cairney, 1995; Cope & Kalantzis, 2000; Lankshear, 1997; Makin & Jones-Diaz, 2002; Pahl & Rowsell, 2005), far less is known about the impact this has had on the literacy practices of the average family. As well, we need to give deep consideration to the impact of changes that we embrace. In considering families and their needs we cannot ignore their values and desires. As pointed out earlier in this chapter, moves to embrace new multimodal forms of literacy might meet resistance from parents and community leaders as they argue for the critical importance of autonomous forms of literacy. As well, teachers and researchers need to examine the ideologies that drive us, and critique our own quest to see schools transformed. There is a danger that old ideologies might be replaced by new ideologies and lead to practices that disadvantage new groups or perhaps simply entrench even more deeply existing power relationships.

Second, a great deal also needs to be done in relation to the use of our increasing knowledge of key pedagogical practices (see, for example, Louden et al., 2005) in reshaping how we structure classroom literacy learning contexts and teaching practices. There is a need for teachers to understand literacy discourse practices within their classrooms and to appreciate the differences that may exist between these and home literacy practices. Teachers need to apply our emerging research knowledge to the development of more responsive curriculum practices. This might include consideration of the way they question students, the way they permit interaction and its impact on learning, the forms of cooperation permitted or not permitted, the language of instruction that is used, the knowledge that is privileged in classrooms, the diversity of communication and literacy forms and even the text types and instructional practices we use. Au (1993) for example, suggests that redefining school literacy may be achieved through expanding the types of texts students read and write, as well as changing the nature of instructional activities and implementing culturally responsive instruction.

Third, we need to reconsider the discourses that shape how we relate to families and the pedagogies that we employ in schools. This is one of the major and unique contributions of this book that presents studies that cut across many cultural and language groups. This is hard, but armed with the research evidence already outlined in this chapter the various researchers have pursued this priority. When schools often seek to engage with families it is frequently motivated by a desire to change home literacy practices, to conform family practices to school practices, and to have parents support school literacy at home (Cairney & Munsie, 1995). What is now required is a radical (and bold) shift. If we embrace models for change such as Li's (2006) pedagogy of cultural reciprocity then we will accept that some home practices will (and probably should) change just as school practices change. However, to this point in our history there has been little reciprocity, families have needed to change to reflect schools. What the rapidly changing face of literacy in our world has done has to create an opportunity (indeed and imperative) for schools to understand and respond to their communities. As Li (2006, p. 209) points out, different practices, values, traditions, understandings and ideologies will be shared as "new cultural patterns are reconfigured and acquired by both school and home agencies."

Finally, the type of adjustments that are being suggested above will lead to raised expectations in relation to professional practice. This in turn will probably require changes in the way we train and equip teachers at the preservice level and also in relation to ongoing professional development. One possible response suggested by Rogers et al. (2006) involves immersing student teachers in community-based environments and providing spaces for dialogue. This offers a promising way to complicate and deepen pre-service teachers' understandings of language and literacy.

Changes like the above will require schools and school systems to be prepared to critique practices that are inappropriate. Just as individual teachers have a responsibility to understand and respond to the diversity of the families they teach, schools also need to respond to community diversity. The work of Cairney and Ruge (1998) has shown that effective schools share a number of key characteristics. Staff are actively involved in ongoing professional development, there are some key agents for change in the school, resources are being applied to the needs, family and community diversity is not seen as a difficulty or a deficit but richness that is a valuable resource, literacy is seen as a complex set of changing practices and communities and families are engaged as partners. One critical area of policy consideration is the way we treat students who have two or more languages. Cummins, Chow, and Scheeter (2006) suggest that there are good grounds for arguing for increased importance to be placed on community languages based on evidence that suggests the strong positive relationship between language learning in two or more languages. This book also provides support for the importance of valuing community languages and the family literacy practices that are related to them.

What is critical to all of the changes suggested in this chapter is the need to transform the forms of engagement that are fostered between schools and their communities. Barton, Drake, Perez, St. Louis, and George (2004, p. 3) have argued for "a shift from focussing primarily on what parents do to engage with their children's schools ... to also considering how parents understand the hows and whys of their engagement." They concluded that parent involvement is a dynamic, interactive process in which parents draw on experiences and resources to define the way they interact with schools and their staff. In effect they propose an ecological view of engagement and argue that it is more than an object or outcome. The literature that has been reviewed in this chapter offers great support for this view, the greatest challenge in acknowledging and addressing the needs of minority groups in education is to move beyond tokenistic or simplistic solutions that fail to recognize the wonderful richness and diversity of families who schools serve each day. As Barton et al. (2004, p. 5) suggest school relationships with communities and families is "a set of relationships and actions that cut across individuals, circumstances, and events that are produced and bounded by the context in which that engagement takes place"). The studies described in this book provide insights into the diverse literacy practices of families. As well, they offer guidance on the ways we might change relationships between home and school, as we acknowledge these rich linguistic practices. Finally, they provide guidance on how the literacy practices of classrooms might be changed to reflect more adequately the richness that children experience outside school.

## NOTES

1.  Syncretism is a concept that is defined in varied ways. It was an outcome of anthropological research and was concerned with how cultural units have

contact with and exercise influence over each other. But more recently it has been used to refer to the study of "mundane practices of everyday life" (see Volk & de Acosta, 2003, for a full discussion).

2. Intergenerational initiatives seek to influence the literacy of one generation by offering help in literacy to another generation. This typically involves offering adult literacy programs in poor communities in the hope that this will lead to increase in the literacy standards of children as well.

3. The relationship between new language forms such as SMS messaging and everyday classroom practices is one new area of interest that is explored in Sutherland et al. (2004, pp. 413-425).

## REFERENCES

Au, K. (1993). *Literacy instruction in multicultural settings.* Fort Worth, TX: Harcourt Brace Jovanovich.

Au, K. (1995). Multicultural perspectives on literacy research. *Journal of Reading Behaviour, 27*(1), 85-100.

Baker, C., & Luke, A. (1991). *Toward a critical sociology of reading pedagogy.* Philadelphia: John Benjamins.

Barton, D. (1991). The social nature of writing. In D. Barton & R. Ivanic (Eds.), *Writing in the community* (pp. 1-13). London: Sage.

Barton, D. (1994). *Literacy: An introduction to the ecology of written language.* Oxford, England: Blackwell.

Barton, A. C., Drake, C., Perez, J. G., St. Louis, K., & George, M. (2004). Ecologies of parental engagement. *Educational Researcher, 33*(4), 3-12.

Barton, D., & Hamilton, M. (1998). *Local literacies: Reading and writing in one community.* London: Routledge.

Bloome, D. (1986). *Literacy and schooling.* Norwood, NJ: Ablex.

Cairney, T. H. (1987). Supporting the independent learner: Negotiating change in the classroom. In J. Hancock & B. Comber (Eds.), *Independent learners at school* (pp. 78-96). Sydney, Australia: Methuen.

Cairney, T. H. (1995). *Pathways to literacy.* London: Cassell.

Cairney, T. H. (2002). Bridging home and school literacy: In search of transformative approaches to curriculum. *Early Child Development and Care, 172*(2), 153-172.

Cairney, T. H. (2003). Literacy in family life. In N. Hall, J. Larson & J. Marsh (Eds.), *Handbook of early childhood literacy* (pp. 85-98). London: SAGE.

Cairney, T. H. (2005). Literacy diversity: Understanding and responding to the textual tapestries of home, school and community. In J. Anderson, M. Kendrick, T. Rogers, & S. Smythe (Eds), *Portraits of literacy across families, communities and schools: Intersections and tensions* (pp. 41-61). London: Erlbaum.

Cairney, T. H., & Ashton, J. (2002). Three families, multiple discourses: Parental roles, constructions of literacy and diversity of pedagogic practice. *Linguistics and Education, 13*(3), 303-345.

Cairney, T. H., & Langbien, S. (1989). Building communities of readers and writers. *The Reading Teacher, 42,* 560-567.

Cairney, T. H., & Munsie, L. (1993b) *Effective partners in secondary literacy learning Program*. Sydney, Australia: UWS Press.

Cairney, T. H., & Munsie, L. (1995a). *Beyond tokenism: Parents as partners in literacy.* Portsmouth, NH: Heinemann.

Cairney, T. H., & Munsie, L. (1995b) Parent participation in literacy learning. *The Reading Teacher, 48*(5), 393-403.

Cairney, T. H., & Ruge, J. (1998). *Community literacy practices and schooling: Towards effective support for students.* Canberra, Australia: Department of Employment, Education & Training.

Cairney, T. H., Ruge, J., Buchanan, J., Lowe, K. & Munsie, L. (1995) *Developing partnerships: The home, school and community interface* (Vols. 1-3). Canberra, Australia: Department of Employment, Education & Training.

Collins, E., & Green, J. (1992). Learning in classroom settings: Making or breaking a culture. In H. Marshall (Ed.), *Redefining student learning: Roots of educational change* (pp. 59-86). Norwood, NJ: Ablex.

Compton-Lilly, C. (2004). *Confronting racism, poverty, and power: Classroom strategies to change the world.* Portsmouth, NH: Heinemann.

Cook-Gumperz, J. (1986). Literacy and schooling: An unchanging equation? In J. Cook-Gumperz (Ed.), *The social construction of literacy* (pp. 16-44). New York: Cambridge University Press.

Cope, B., & Kalantzis, M. (2000). *Multiliteracies: Literacy, learning and the design of social futures.* Melbourne, Australia: Macmillan.

Cummins, J. (1986). Empowering minority students: A framework for intervention. *Harvard Educational Review, 56,* 18-36.

Cummins, J., Chow, P., & Scheeter, S.R. (2006). Community as curriculum. *Language Arts, 83*(4), 297- 309.

Delgado-Gaitan, C. (1992). School matters in the Mexican-American home: Socialising children to education. *American Educational Research Journal, 29,* 495-516.

Deyhle, D., & LeCompte, M. (1994). Cultural differences in child development: Navajo adolescents in middle schools. *Theory Into Practice, 33*(3), 156-166.

Epstein, J. L., & Dauber, S. L. (1991). School programs and teacher practices of parent involvement in inner-city elementary and middle schools. *Elementary School Journal, 91,* 289-305.

Erickson, F. (1993). Transformation and school success: The politics and culture of educational achievement. In E. Jacob & C. Jordan (Eds.), *Minority education: Anthropological perspectives* (pp. 27-51). Norwood, NJ: Ablex.

Fairclough, N. (1989). *Language and power.* London: Longmans.

Fairclough, N. (1992). *Discourse and social change.* Cambridge, England: Polity Press

Gee, J. (1990). *Social linguistics and literacies: Ideology in discourses.* London: The Falmer Press.

Gonzalez, N., Moll, L. C., & Amanti, C. (2005). *Funds of knowledge: Theorizing practices in households, communities, and classrooms,* Mahwah, NJ: Erlbaum.

Gumperz, J. J. (Ed.). (1982). Conversational code-switching. In *Discourse strategies* (pp. 59-99). Cambridge, England: Cambridge University Press.

Harry, B. (1992). An ethnographic study of cross-cultural communication with Puerto Rican-American families in the special education system. *American Educational Research Journal, 29,* 471-494.

Heath, S. B. (1982). What no bedtime story means: Narrative skills at home and at school. *Language in Society, 11,* 49-76.

Heath, S. B. (1983) *Ways with words: Language, life and work in community and classrooms.* Cambridge, England: Cambridge University Press.

Howard, D. (1994). Culturally responsive classrooms: A way to assist Aboriginal students with hearing loss in urban schools. In S. Harris & M. Malin (Eds.), *Aboriginal kids in urban classrooms* (pp. 37-50). Wentworth Falls, New South Wales, Australia: Social Science Press.

Hymes, D. (1962). The ethnography of speaking. In T. Gladwin & W. C. Sturtevant (Eds.), *Anthropology and human behavior* (pp. 13-53). Washington, DC: The Anthropology Society of Washington.

Ladson-Billings, G. (1995a). Introduction to themed issue on culturally relevant teaching. *Theory Into Practice, 34*(3), 150-151.

Ladson-Billings, G. (1995b). Toward a theory of culturally relevant pedagogy. *American Educational Research Journal, 32*(3), 465-491.

Lankshear, C. (1997). *Changing literacies.* Buckingham, England: Open University Press.

Li, G. (2002). *"East is East, West is West"? Home literacy, culture, and schooling.* New York: Peter Lang.

Li, G. (2004). Family literacy: Learning from Asian immigrant family. In F. B. Boyd, C. H. Brock, & M. Rozendal (Eds.), *Multicultural and multilingual literacy and language: Contexts and practice* (pp. 304-321). New York: The Guildford Press.

Li, G. (2006). *Culturally contested pedagogy: Battles of literacy and schooling between mainstream teachers and Asian immigrant parents.* Albany: State University of New York Press.

Li, G. (2008). *Culturally contested literacies: America's "rainbow underclass" and urban schools.* New York: Routledge.

Louden, W., Rohl, M., Barratt-Pugh, C., Brown, C., Cairney, T. H., Elderfield, J., et al. (2005). In teachers' hands: effective literacy teaching practices in the early years of schooling. *Australian Journal of Language & Literacy, 38*(3), 175-249.

Luke, A. (1993). Stories of social regulation: The micropolitics of classroom narrative. In B. Green (Ed.) *The insistence of the letter: Literacy studies and curriculum theorising.* London: The Falmer Press.

Luke, A. (1995, April). *When literacy might/not make a difference: Textual practice and capital.* Paper presented at the American Educational Research Association annual conference, San Francisco.

Makin, L., & Jones-Diaz, C. (2002). *Literacies in early childhood: Challenging views, challenging practice.* Sydney, Australia: Maclennan & Petty.

Malin, M. (1994). Make or break factors in Aboriginal students learning to read in urban classrooms: A socio-cultural perspective. In S. Harris & M. Malin (Eds.), *Aboriginal kids in urban classrooms.* Wentworth Falls, New South Wales, Australia: Social Science Press.

Marsh, J. (2006). Global, local/public, private: Young children's engagement in digital literacy practices in the home. In K. Pahl & J. Rowsell (Eds), *Travel notes from the new literacy studies* (pp. 19-38). Toronto, Ontario, Canada: Multilingual Matters.

May, S. (1995). Deconstructing traditional discourses of schooling: An example of school reform. *Language and Education, 9*(1), 1-29.

Mattingly, D. J., Prislin, R., McKenzie, T. L., Rodriguez, J. L., & Kayzar, B. (2002). Evaluating evaluations: The case of parent involvement programs. *Review of Educational Research, 72*(4), 549-576.

Moll, L. (1993, April). *Community-mediated educational practices.* Paper presented at the American Educational Research Association annual conference, Atlanta, GA.

Moll, L., Amanti, C., Neff, D., & Gonzalez, N. (1992). Funds of knowledge for teaching: Using a qualitative approach to connect homes and classrooms. *Theory Into Practice, 31*(2), 132-141.

Mulhern, M. (1995, April). *A Mexican-American child's home life and literacy learning from kindergarten through second grade.* Paper presented at the American Educational Research Association Annual Meeting, San Francisco.

Nickse, R. (1993). A typology of family and intergenerational literacy programmes: Implications for evaluation. *Viewpoints, 15,* 34-40.

Ogbu, J. (1992). Adaptation to minority status and impact on school success. *Theory Into Practice, 21*(4), 287-295.

Ogbu, J. (1993). Frameworks—Variability in minority school performance: A problem in search of an explanation. In E. Jacob & C. Jordan (Eds.), *Minority education: Anthropological perspectives* (pp. 83-111). Norwood, NJ: Ablex.

Pahl, K., & Rowsell, J. (2005). *Literacy and education: Understanding the new literacy studies in the classroom.* London: Paul Chapman.

Rogers, R. (2003). *A critical discourse analysis of family literacy practices: Power in and out of print.* Mahwah, NJ: Erlbaum.

Rogers, T., Marshall, E., & Tyson, C.A. (2006). Dialogic narratives of literacy, teaching, and schooling: Preparing literacy teachers for diverse settings. *Reading Research Quarterly, 41*(2), 202-250.

Ruis, R. (1988). Orientations in language planning. In S. McKay & S. L. Wong (Eds.), *Language diversity: Problem or resource?* (pp. 3-25). New York: Newbury House.

Santa Barbara Classroom Discourse Group. (1992). Constructing literacy in classrooms: Literate action as social accomplishment. In H. Marshall (Ed.), *Redefining student learning: Roots of educational change* (pp. 119-150). Norwood, NJ: Ablex.

Siegel, M. (2006). Rereading the signs: Multimodal transformations in the field of literacy education. *Language Arts, 84*(1), 65-77.

Stein, P., & Slonimnsky, L. (2006). An eye on the text and an eye on the future: Multimodal literacy in three Johannesburg families. In K. Pahl & J. Rowsell (Eds.), *Travel notes from the new literacy studies* (pp. 118-146). Toronto, Ontario, Canada: Multilingual Matters.

Street, B. (1984). *Literacy in theory and practice.* Cambridge, England: Cambridge University Press.

Street, B., Baker, D., & Tomlin, A. (2005). *Navigating numeracies*. The Netherlands: Springer.

Street, B. V. (1995). *Social literacies: Critical approaches to literacy in development, ethnography and education*. London: Longman.

Sutherland, R. V., Armstrong, S., Barnes, R., Brawn, N., Breeze, M., Gall, S., et al. (2004). Transforming teaching and learning: Embedding ICT into everyday classroom practices. *Journal of Computer Assisted Learning, 20*(6), 413-425.

Trudgill, P. (2000). *Sociolinguistics*. London: Penguin.

Volk, D., & de Acosta, M. (2003). Reinventing texts and contexts: Syncretic literacy events in young Puerto Rican children's homes. *Research in the Teaching of English, 38*(1), 8-48.

Vygotsky, L. (1978). *Mind and society: The development of higher mental processes*. Cambridge, MA: Harvard University Press.

Welch, A. R., & Freebody, P. (1993). Introduction: Explanations of the current international 'Literacy Crises.' In P. Freebody & A. Welch (Eds). *Knowledge, culture & power: International perspectives on literacy as policy and practice*. London: Falmer Press.

Zentella, A. C. (Ed.). (2005). Premises, promises, and pitfalls of language socialization research in Latino families and communities. In *Building on strengths: Language and literacy in Latino families and communities* (pp. 000-000). New York: Teachers College.

# PART II

## MULTICULTURAL FAMILIES
## AND HOME LITERACY PRACTICES

# AFRICAN AND AFRICAN AMERICAN FAMILIES

CHAPTER 2

# LITERACY PRACTICES OF AFRICAN AMERICAN CHILDREN

## Three Case Studies

### Catherine Compton-Lilly

This chapter presents the stories of three African American children: Alicia, Peter, and Jermaine. Specifically, I explore the ways their literacy practices are situated within home contexts that feature not only activities related to reading and writing but rich relationships that accompany those practices and expansive social and historical roots that led to these literacy practices. Recognizing and understanding that literacy practices of African American students, and all students, are contextualized within rich literacy contexts is the first step in enabling teachers to create instructional practices that build on the resources that children bring to classrooms. In this chapter I present two types of literacy practices that children and parents shared over the course of the research project: (1) literacy practices that parents use to teach children to read; and (2) the literacy practices children share with their siblings and peers. First I will review theoretical insights related to literacy practices in African American homes, then I will discuss the methodology used in this 8-year longi-

*Multicultural Families, Home Literacies, and Mainstream Schooling*
pp. 29–49

tudinal study, and introduce each of the three students and their families. Data from this study revealed that the literacy practices in these three African American homes are uniquely integrated into rich networks of literacy practices at home and school, and involve people in both the present and the past.

## LITERACY PRACTICES AND PEOPLE'S LIVES

In 1983, Heath published her classic account of language and literacy in the Piedmont Carolinas. As part of that study she explored language and literacy in Trackton, a working-class Black community. Her work documents a range of literacy events that she encountered in this community including the reading newspapers, brochures, advertisements, church materials and homework, as well as everyday uses of print in the forms of food labels, house numbers, name brand logos, calendars, and messages on television. Heath emphasizes that in Trackton reading is considered a social activity and that text reading often involves commentary, the telling of related narratives, humor and the negotiation of the text's meaning. Solitary reading practices are discouraged and those who read alone are sometimes considered antisocial. As Heath explains, people in Trackton, are literate; however, reading is generally a means for action and accomplishing goals rather than being an end in itself.

Taylor and Dorsey-Gaines (1988) focused their study on Black children growing up in an inner-city area referred to as Shay Avenue; the children were considered by their parents to be successful in learning to read and write. On their visits to children's homes, Taylor and Dorsey-Gaines collected children's drawings of significant people and places and the cards that they created for family members and friends, while documenting children's interactions with books. These home reading, writing, and drawing activities coexisted alongside texts from school which included dittos to be completed as homework, exercises completed at school that appeared to have been copied from the board, and workbook pages that had been corrected by the teacher. These school literacy activities informed the children's self-selected home literacy activities in various ways, including when children played school at home. Taylor and Dorsey-Gaines write of the concentric worlds of childhood and question whether the home and school worlds of children are encountered as cohesive and meaningful sites or as fragmented experiences characterized by disjuncture and tension. Like Heath, they recognize the practical and utilitarian uses and purposes of reading and writing in this community; unlike Heath, they highlight the need for families to read and write in order to deal with public agencies in the course of managing their lives.

Gadsden (1992) situates literacy within African American families and describes rich historical tapestries that entail people and policies. She explains that the association between literacy, access, and opportunity are powerfully played out in many African American homes as African American elders pass their beliefs about literacy and possibility on to future generations.

Efforts to document literacy activities in African American homes and communities has led to efforts to understand how home literacy activities intersect with school success. For example, Purcell-Gates (1996) examines the literacy activities present in 20 low-income homes; 10 of the participating families were African American. While her study generally supported the contention that children from literacy-rich homes fared better in school, more importantly her study documented the wide range of literacy activities that exist in low-income households.

In recent years, interest in family literacy practices has turned, more specifically toward the intersection between home and school literacy practices (Compton-Lilly, 2003) and the propensity of the school to recognize and acknowledge the literacy practices children bring to school (Moll, Amanti, Neff, & Gonzalez, 1992).

Street (2003) uses the term literacy practices to acknowledge the ways people conceptualize particular literacy events and the social models that people use to make sense of literacy events.This definition of literacy practices recognizes these practices are a broad "cultural conception of particular ways of thinking about and doing reading and writing in cultural contexts" (Street, 2003, p. 79). Street argues that we need to shift away "from observing literacy events to conceptualizing literacy practices" (p. 79). Street describes overlapping relationships that exist between home and school literacies. He notes that literacy crosses boundaries and moves through different settings.

The children in this study are not from Trackton and they are not growing up in a rural working-class community. They are not living on Shay Avenue and not all of the children in this study are perceived by their parents as being successful in learning to read. Each of the three children described in this chapter brings a unique story to his/her classroom that is grounded in their unique experiences at home. Their stories are part of the vast range of experiences and practices that collectively constitute the literacy practices of African American children. However, despite the uniqueness of what each child brings, similarities exist. All of the children are African American and race is part of their stories. All of the children attend high-poverty, inner-city schools; this part of the story matters as well. Finally, all of the children and their families have participated in an eight-year longitudinal research project that has enabled this researcher to document their literacy practices from a rich textured perspective. Thereby, enabling me to capture the diverse literacy practices present in each home, the ways in which parents support their children with literacy, and the roles of peers and siblings in the literacy practices of three African American children.

## METHODOLOGY

The study is part of an 8-year longitudinal study of nine urban families. Longitudinal qualitative research has particular relevance when working with African American families because it has the potential to reveal cumulative effects of racism, classism, and/or sexism by following individual students and groups of students across time and revealing the processes that contribute to the long-term effects of under-funded schooling, racist/classist/sexist educational policies, well-intended but discriminative practices of educators, and negative assumptions held by educators about various groups of students.

At its inception, this 8-year longitudinal study focused on my students' and their parents' conceptualizations of reading. While the study began with a particular focus, over time it has grown to include a range of other issues, including issues related to reading identity, official definitions of reading success, and assumptions made about urban families,

The qualitative longitudinal study that is described in this chapter incorporates three phases of research occurring 4 and 3 years apart. The collective case study began when the researcher was the children's first grade teacher and extended to when the children were in Grades 7 and 8; three of the nine children are the focus of this chapter. While the initial study involved a rich range of data sources including interviews, classroom observations, audiotaped class discussions, and student portfolios; the next two phases of the research focused primarily on parent and child interviews along with writing samples and reading assessments.

During the initial phase of the project the children attended a large urban school that served children from the lowest socioeconomic neighborhood of a mid-size northeastern city; 97% of its students qualified for free or reduced lunch. Consistent with the high mobility rate at this school, several of these students now attend other schools in the same district. During the initial phase, data was coded across cases so that general themes could be identified.

In more recent phases of the project, each family was initially treated as a separate case. Data from each family was coded separately and an index was created for each case to assist the researcher in locating topics within the data sets. Coded data was grouped into categories for each family. Case studies were outlined for each family and recurring themes within families were noted. Cases that shared strong similarities or intriguing differences were linked and became the basis for several papers, articles, and chapters such as this one. The cases in this chapter were chosen because they capture a range of literacy practices and include children of different genders.

In the following section, I introduce each of the families. Then, I examine two issues related to literacy practices that occur in each family: (1) the teaching practices of mothers and (2) the role of siblings and peers in the literacy practices of children. Next I present three findings from the study. Finally, I share conclusions about literacy practices in African American families.

## The Families' Stories

Each of the families described in this chapter participate in rich literacy practices. These practices are unique and are uniquely situated within particular family structures and economic contexts.

### Alicia's Story

When Alicia was my first grade student, she was an enthusiastic and engaged African American 6-year-old. I remember her as always smiling and constantly surrounded by other children. Alicia's mother, Ms. Rodriguez, worked as an assistant in a daycare. While Ms. Rodriguez worked full-time, the family struggled at the poverty line. They no longer received welfare benefits, but still relied on government programs for health care and their housing stipend. I had taught Alicia's older brother, Tyreek, a few years earlier. Alicia has three other older brothers and a younger sister.

When I asked Alicia about her favorite books in first grade, she named books from our basal reading program. By fifth grade, Alicia was a fan of the *Baby-Sitter's Club* Series (Martin & Lerangris, 1986-2000). In eighth grade, Alicia reported that she still enjoyed the Baby-sitter books but that she was also reading what she referred to as "love novels." She shows me a book called *Ruby* written by Rosa Guy (2005) and explains that she stole it from her brother. She also reports reading a love story that she got from the lady next door. Alicia was reading at grade level until her eighth grade year; when she only read at a seventh grade level with poor comprehension.

### Peter's Story

Peter was a polite, thoughtful young man who participated willingly and actively in all first grade tasks. As his mother explained, he is a "model student." Ms. Horner provided customer service for the local phone company. When I first met the family, they were living in a housing project designed to meet the needs of young mothers and provide them with assistance in becoming independent. A few months into the school year, the family moved out of the project and into their own apartment. When Peter was in fifth grade, his mother married and the family had bought a house; they no longer needed public assistance. Peter has a brother who is 2 years younger than him.

When asked in first grade what kinds of things he read, Peter reported that he read books and the words on the boxes of his video games. By fifth grade, Ms. Horner reported that both her boys went "Pokemon crazy" and that they read the magazines that accompanied the cards and games. Peter told me that he liked to read horror and mystery books; he named R. L. Stine as his favorite author and traded *Goosebumps* books (Stine, 1992-1997) with his friends. He excitedly told me the plot of the *Goosebumps* book he had just finished. By eighth grade, Peter explained that he was "really into" the *Lord of the Rings* Books (Tolkien, 1954-1955). He had also recently read *Scorpions* (Myers, 1988) a book about two African American brothers and gang life.

By the end of first grade, like Alicia, Peter was reading at an early second grade level. In fifth grade he successfully read a seventh grade text and at the end of eighth grade he read a ninth grade text with good comprehension.

### Jermaine's Story

Jermaine was a quiet child who often chose to work alone and resisted academic tasks. In first grade, he qualified for Reading Recovery services. His father, Mr. Hudson, was a retired nurse and his mother, Ms. Hudson, was on disability due to chronic back pain; she had previously worked as a health care professional. Economically, the family struggled; they survived by weaving together retirement benefits, disability income, and welfare benefits.

In first grade when I asked Jermaine what he read, he told me he read words and listed, "down," "in," and "with" as examples. When I asked the same question in fourth grade, Jermaine listed topics that interested him: animals, tornados, science, spiders, snakes, raccoons, airplanes and even fire hydrants. He also mentioned books that are also television series': the *Arthur* Series (Brown, 1976-present), *Blues Clues* (Simon & Schuster, 1996-present), and *Clifford the Big Red Dog* (Bridwell, 1987-present). In seventh grade, Jermaine spoke in detail about *Fredrick Douglass and the Fight for Freedom* (Miller, 1993). He recounted the information in the first few chapters. Jermaine also mentioned Harry Potter (Rowling, 1997-present),

*Maniac Magee* (Spinnelli, 1990), and *Freak the Mighty* (Philbrick, 2001) as well as its sequel *Max the Mighty* (Philbrick, 1989).

By the end of first grade, Jermaine was reading at a late first grade level. In fourth grade he successfully read a second grade passage and at the end of seventh grade he read a fifth grade text with several errors and marginal comprehension. Jermaine was retained in second grade and started receiving resource services in fourth grade. He was classified as having a "disorder of written language."

While literacy practices are sometimes conceptualized as practices that families engage in apart from formal schooling, I suggest that home literacy practices are uniquely meshed with school literacy practices, parents' and children's school experiences, and their perceptions of school literacy. Specifically, I present practices described by parents and children that occur at home to support children with literacy and schooling. Then, I examine the powerful role the literacy practices of siblings and peers play in the literacy development of my former first grade students. In contrast to conceptions of literacy practices as activities that are unique to particular families or individuals, I maintain that literacy practices are sets of hybrid practices that entail home practices, intergenerational family practices, sibling practices, peer practices and schooling practices in unique and complex ways.

The literacy practices featured in the stories I tell about Alicia, Peter, and Jermaine are not just their stories. Their stories are contextualized within the lives and experiences of the people they love and the worlds they inhabit. In turn, the literacy practices of Alicia, Peter, and Jermaine push back upon their loved ones and their worlds. Thus, just as parents' literacy practices affect children, children's literacy practices affect the practices of parents, siblings, and peers. In this section, I identify two sets of literacy practices for each family: (1) practices of parents that involve the teaching of literacy, and (2) sibling and peer literacy practices.

## LITERACY PRACTICES INVOLVED IN TEACHING CHILDREN

Parents and children identify a range of literacy practices that they use to help their children with literacy. I suspect that some of these reflect parents' own school experiences while others reflect literacy practices that existed in parents' homes when they were growing up; some reflect mainstream notions of reading and learning to read. Although these practices change over time, parents are consistent in supporting their children. Table 2.1 presents a sampling of the literacy practices that were described in Alicia's, Peter's, and Jermaine's homes when the children were in my first grade class.

### Table 2.1.   Parent Teaching Practices in Grade 1

|  | Ms. Rodriguez | Ms. Horner | Ms. Hudson |
|---|---|---|---|
| Grade 1 | We start out with little baby books and we learn like "I" and "be" and "is" and stuff like that. Then we work our way up because when she gets the two letter words then [we work on three letter words].<br><br>When she's reading along, she comes to me. And if she don't come to me she goes to one of her brothers. And we tell her the same thing. Sound it out! (laughs)<br><br>So it's like when you say this is a window and you spell window and then you spell door and stuff like that. It's simple but as they grow up they be looking at it like, I learned how to read early. Yeah and I learned how to spell early. | Ummm, I know my mother she always bought me books and that was a definite. Uh I've always been surrounded by books.<br><br>[Like for the word] "around." I cover it up, "round" [I] let him say it's "a" and then I cover up the "a" and let him say "round" because the thing was is that "round" looks familiar to him. Um, cause he might be familiar with that but having the two put together.<br><br>It gives them a variety of words um to listen to, to sounds and I read to my kids a lot. I have a book wide open so they can. I can point out so they can see the words along with me. | He said "We didn't read this book." I said "I know this is why she [the teacher] sent it home." So I read all the way through the book fast and then he a read a page and then I read a page and then he read a page and I read a page. So we did a lot of that there. Then I made him go all the way back and we did that there. I waited a while, the next day I brought the same book back out. And let him read it by himself.<br><br>I try to get Jermaine to like sound it [the word] out. Like what word he had trouble with? Uhh, "always" ... I said, "Jermaine that's 'always.' Don't you see the 'a'?" [That's] what I do with always, I do "al" first right? Then I spread it out. And then he get it. |

As Table 2.1 suggests, a range of literacy practices existed in these three homes. Ms. Rodriguez describes having Alicia learn to read by reading little words and spelling the names of familiar objects. Ms. Rodriguez and Ms. Hudson describe encouraging their children to sound out words, while both Ms. Horner and Ms. Hudson describe dividing words into parts. Book reading is mentioned by all three parents. It is notable that in all three cases the mothers describe helping children to focus on words and letters as a means to help them learn to read. While these parents could be understood as adopting skill-based models of reading, they can also be understood as being responsive to the literacy expectations that they assume children will face in school.

It is sometimes suggested that parents become less involved with their children as learners as the children grow older. While the ways in which parents are involved in their children's educations appears to change, the

**Table 2.2.   Parent Teaching Practices in Grades 4/5**

|  | Ms. Rodriguez | Ms. Horner | Ms. Hudson |
|---|---|---|---|
| Grade 4/5 | They're not going to push your child through school when they don't know anything … [You have to] write letters, show up at school meetings and talk to the teachers. | Um ever since um when Peter was in kindergarten um, that's when I had to work the late hours and everything, so Peter basically had to do a lot on his own. So, just ever since then, he's just been | Sometimes, when he don't, he don't, can't pronounce [words] … I tell him to sound it out. |
|  | (Ms. Rodriguez is pointing to Alicia's report card from earlier in the year) So she know if she don't bring her grades up by next quarter, no more Step team. | that way. I don't have to get on him about when he comes home from school, "Go do your homework." Um his homework is always done um when I come home from work. | I got him with the tutoring computer, but he don't ever use it.<br><br>But I'm going through hell with the City School District right now I called my lawyer and everything. I called my lawyer in that civil action against [the district to get Jermaine special services] |
|  | [I said to the teacher, "My baby needs help more in reading not in math. Can you send her more reading homework." She started for a little while and then when she stopped, I went and I got her a tutor [at the local community center].<br><br>I thought he [one of Ms. Rodriguez's sons] needed more help in his English and writing and what I did was I asked around to his friends … (laughs) and the one's that was good in English, I asked him to help him with the English.<br><br>Alicia is more, not sounding out her words…. Tyreek was helping her with that mostly, the sounding part. | **Ms. Horner:** Well, whenever he um comes across a word that he's not able to pronounce or he needs to know um the meaning you know to, then I help him with that.<br>**CL:** And what do you do to help?<br>**Ms Horner:** Um, mainly, I direct him to his dictionary. (Both laugh) | **Ms. Hudson:** (Shakes head) He hates reading.<br>**Jermaine:** No I don't.<br>**Ms. Hudson:** Yes you do. When I be trying you be um like, Jermaine uh go upstairs put your math made easy tape in and when you get through do some reading what you do? What, what attitude do you be giving me? What you be doing? (Jermaine growls playfully at mom) |

data from this study suggests that parents remain involved with their children as readers, writers, and learners. Table 2.2 presents a sampling of ways parents participate in their children's literacy and schooling experiences in Grades 4 and 5. In Grades 4 and 5 parents continue to access a variety of means to support their children as readers. Ms. Rodriguez expresses her belief that she needs to stay in touch with her children's teachers so that her children do not get pushed through school without learning. She approaches Alicia's teacher when she believes Alicia needs more reading work and is able to access tutoring services for her other children outside of school including arranging for Tyreek to help his sister with word solving. Ms. Horner helps Peter by monitoring his homework and helping him pronounce difficult words. Ms. Hudson tells Jermaine to sound out words and has purchased a tutoring computer and a set of math tapes to support him in school. Like Ms. Rodriguez, she intervenes with school personal when needed; in her case, Ms. Hudson has secured the services of a lawyer when the school district threatened to deny Jermaine special education services. While in first grade, most of the roles fulfilled by parents involved helping children to maneuver letters and sounds, in fourth and fifth grade parents' advocate for their children by making sure children are not pushed through school, requesting more work, engaging tutors, and rallying for special services. This trend toward more global involvement in children's education continues into middle school as demonstrated in Table 2.3

By seventh and eighth grades, all three parents report that they no longer need to help their children with reading: Alicia uses the dictionary on her computer, Peter does not need help, and Jermaine gets help from his brother but generally in math. Parents do not help with specific reading tasks such as sounding out words or breaking words into parts; as Ms. Rodriguez explained, "[She] don't need me no more." However, parents still intervene when problems occur with teachers or in reference to school district policies. Jermaine's mother continues to monitor his homework and subscribes to a magazine in the hope that it would interest Jermaine; these efforts to help Jermaine may be in response to his continued difficulties in school.

Based on the comments made by parents and children, it appears that the children in this study receive a wealth of assistance from their mothers. Unlike depictions that characterize parents as becoming less involved with their children's academic lives as children grow older, it appears that at least until eighth grade parents continue to play important roles in their children's lives although those role are increasingly characterized by advocating for children rather than in assisting them with word analysis and solving (Nieto, 2002). They supervise homework, intervene with teachers and administrators, and they work through complex procedures

**Table 2.3.   Parent Teaching Practices in Grades 7/8**

| | *Ms. Rodriguez* | *Ms. Horner* | *Ms. Hudson* |
|---|---|---|---|
| Grade 7/8 | Last year, I had a problem out of one of her teachers and I went to school and I got that straight. And so far [this year] I haven't had no problems out of none of their teachers.<br><br>**CL:** Does she ever get stuck on a word?<br>**Ms. Rodriguez:** She goes to the computer and looks it up on the dictionary.<br>**CL:** Really?<br>**Alicia:** Yeah!<br>**Ms. Rodriguez:** Don't need me no more.<br><br>**CL:** Does she ever show them [her poems] to you?<br>**Ms. Rodriguez:** No. She say I criticize too much and she's holding out.<br>**CL:** You criticize too much? Do you?<br>**Ms. Rodriguez:** (nods)<br>**CL:** (laughs) What kind of …<br>**Ms. Rodriguez:** If you do it, do it right. | **Ms. Horner:** So it was definitively just living in New York City. It had a big affect on his, um on his um schoolwork. But now yes, he's bringing up his grades and um, he's doing well …<br>**CL:** Is that the reason you came back [from New York]?<br>**Ms. Horner:** Um part of the reason why.<br><br>It took about a week. [to get Peter registered at his former school]. I went down there maybe like about four times … for starters I took them to Charlotte and then Charlotte tells me well sorry but you have to go down to Central. Okay? And then uh, taking them down to Central, um, I said well okay yes he's my son but he doesn't live with me. Okay? But I need to get him enrolled into school.<br><br>**CL:** Do you ever have to help him with his reading?<br>**Ms. Horner:** No. | **CCL:** Do you have to help him with his reading sometimes?<br>**OB:** (shakes head).<br>**CCL:** No.<br>**OB:** His brother might. His brother helps him with his math, math once in a while.<br><br>Mr. Dennis was calling me and telling he had homework and if he had homework then I say well I'll be at the school. I'll come and pick it up and I bring it, cause when he had that Easter vacation off? He had a lot of homework to do. Cause I went to school and got it. Okay? To make sure he got it did while he was off.<br><br>**OB:** Then I had another one [a magazine] I got just especially for him. What was it? Um, I, oooh, I it was something about history. [I] ordered that magazine just especially for him to look through. [Jermaine said,] "Mom, what I'm going to look at this for? "Jermaine this is about the history of what's going on the world." |

for getting children registered in school. In addition to helping children, playing these roles exhibits a general wariness of schools; the perceived need for parents to go to school, arrange tutors, and work through red tape suggests that parents do not trust the school system to do these things and thus feel the need to monitor their children and advocate for them.

One fascinating finding from this study was that not only do mothers play important roles in children's literacy experiences but grandmothers and great-grandmothers, even though they may not be physically present, are also significant actors in the literacy learning of my students:

> Ms. Rodriguez:   Or like we used to do [when I was little]. We lived in the city we'd read in the train, on the bus, so you can, you can always make time.

> Ms. Horner:   I always wonder about how Peter can bring home these little books and he can read them off to me. And I was like, because that's exactly what I used to do when I come to think about it. That's what I used to do. I don't remember exactly how she [her mother] got me to do that because there was this fun book, I just loved it to death—*This Is the House That Jack Built.* And I knew that book, front-wards and backwards. I used to love to read it to her.

> Ms. Hudson:   With my mother, we did a lot of reading.
> CL:   Do you remember if it was easy for you to learn to read, or
> Ms. Hudson:   Yeah, it was easy.

The literacy teaching practices of my students' grandparents are not identical to those used by the children's parents yet they feed into the literacy/reading teaching practices that parents bring to their children. Just as Ms. Rodriguez plays spelling games with her children, her mother made a game of reading signs on the trains as they traveled through New York City. Ms. Horner remembers memorizing favorite stories and watched as Peter did the same thing. Like her mother, Ms. Hudson is tough on her children and read to Jermaine when he was little.

Yet legacies of literacy practices are not limited to parent and grandparents. Ms. Horner tells of the lessons she learned from both Peter's great aunt and great grandmother.

> Ms. Horner:   In second grade [the person who helped me most with reading] became my aunt. Cause she had all these books … they were so interesting. So I would always go up to my aunt's house to go read books. She was my library.

Ms. Horner:    My grandmother told me (laughs) she told me when Peter was a little baby, she says "You say the abc's to him and you count to him one to twenty every single day and maybe even a couple of times a day so that as he gets older he will be up a little, you know. He'll be familiar with the letters and the numbers." So that's what I did with him. That's what I did with him and at a young age he was able to count, he can say his abc's.

These stories of family members who contributed to her life as a reader bring to mind the research of Gadsden (2000) in which she challenges deficit views of intergenerational literacy in African American families by documenting the way intergenerational literacy in African American homes often brings a rich history of valuing and respecting literacy abilities and that this commitment to literacy learning breeds vision and purpose for children as they learn to read.

It is important to note that the literacy practices and needs of children affect the literacy practices of their parents. These effects include the adoption of pedagogic literacy teaching practices as their children learn to read, and the changes in their own literacy practices that occur when women become parents. Although Ms. Rodriguez and Ms. Horner say that they love to read, both report that they do not read as much as they did due to the strain of working and raising children. Parents also report reading to their children and sometimes the texts they read reflect their children's reading preferences; Ms. Rodriguez read Tyreek's book about Martin Luther King to Alicia and Quanzaa. Parents also report reading "baby books" and books sent home from school. Ms. Horner noted that Peter's experiences with reading have affected her in a positive way. She explains, "I find myself wanting to read more you know because I see my son always wanting to read and write." The effects that children have on adults' literacy practices are closely related to parents' roles as teachers.

Literacy practices change in other ways. Ms. Rodriguez reports that her work in child care has changed her literacy practices, "Right now I'm into reading all these childcare books because I have to prepare for the daycare and making sure that I get all my work done, because now we've got to do portfolios and stuff like that." She explains "I haven't had time to read novels." During some of my visits, such as the visits I made when Alicia was in fifth grade, Ms. Rodriguez reported that she was regularly reading novels, at other interviews she was not. The literacy practices of parents are not static; they change and develop over time in relation to changing situations.

## SIBLINGS' AND PEERS' LITERACY PRACTICES

The literacy practices of parents and children intersect across the generations and access both home and school literacy practices. In this section, I maintain that exchange and influence also occur within the children's generation as siblings and peers, and that home and school combine and contribute to the literacy practices of children.

### Sibling Literacy Practices

All three children described playing school with siblings or cousins. Alisa, who has several big brothers, took this opportunity to play teacher and boss her brothers around. She described an entire morning of activities that included naps, recess, playing with toys, and reading,

> I be calling people up to the rug like you do [speaking to the teacher researcher] ... because my brothers ... read with me ... and then when they got to use the bathroom I say wait 'til we done with the story and then when they done with the story, they go downstairs and use the bathroom.

Peter plays school with his cousin. He teaches his cousin how to trace letters and copy words that he has written. He also teaches his student not to fight or run in the hallway. He shows them "how to be nice and not kicking and stuff." Jermaine reported playing school with his baby niece. He described writing on the chalkboard and telling his niece to go to lunch, read books, or sit in the corner.

Playing school is a quintessential game, that I suspect many readers remember playing. What is compelling about this game is the intersection of the real with the imagination, the transplanting of the school context into the home, the identity shift from child to teacher, and the child's use of school literacy practices at home. Playing school is perhaps the activity where we can best observe how children understand school and teachers.

Perhaps it is because Alicia has four brothers and a sister while the other children have only one sibling or adult siblings that Alicia's case features the richest web of literacy practices involving her siblings. While all of the literacy practices listed in the Table 2.4 do not involve Alicia directly, they surround her and characterize the literacy practices that occur in her family creating the context in which Alicia reads and writes. Alicia's family participated in a rich range of literacy practices. When Alicia was in first grade, her mother explained that her older brother often helped her with her reading. Likewise, Alicia describes her intentions to help her little sister. When Alicia was in fifth grade an older brother

## Table 2.4.   Sibling Literacy Practices

| *Alicia* |
|---|

| | |
|---|---|
| Grade 1 | **CL:** What prevents you from reading to your children more or do you do that?<br>**Ms. Rodriguez:** I don't have to. They got brothers for that. They brothers read to them.<br><br>**CL:** What are you going to do to help her [ your little sister]?<br>**Ms. Rodriguez:** I want to help her listen to the word and don't p-, if you don't pay attention she won't learn how to read. |
| Grade 4/5 | **Leon:** The last book I read was … it was *Taming of the Shrew.*<br>**CL:** You like Shakespeare?<br>**Leon:** Yeah. I like Shakespeare, *Taming of the Shrew.* I read that one, *The Rose for Emily,* read it um *Raisin in the Sun.*<br><br>**Ms. Rodriguez:** They'll all be about the same, like magazines. Like, my older son likes *Sports Illustrated.* He still has *Sports Illustrated* come to the house.<br>**Ms. Rodriguez:** And Jez is more of —he read music. It's got to do something with music. Jez loves music.<br><br>**Older Brother:** Oh yeah. What's the book you reading now. You still reading *Mama* [McMillin, 1987]?<br>**Ms. Rodriguez:** I finished *Mama.* I finished my book, you're welcome to it.<br>**Older Brother:** I need more books. That's why I called Roberta [a family friend].<br>**Ms. Rodriguez:** Yep, I need books.<br><br>**Ms. Rodriguez:** She goes in her room [to study], close the door, and then she start looking through her books and her papers and if she needs to be tested, she always call her brother. Tyreek test me on this.<br>**CL:** Good. It's a nice thing [she has] a bunch of brothers to do that.<br><br>**CL:** Do you still like to read?<br>**Tyreek:** Yeah<br>**CL:** Do ya?<br>**Quanzaa:** I read more than him.<br>**CL:** Really?<br>**Tyreek:** No you don't.<br>**Quanzaa:** I read at school. I read *Goosebumps.*<br>**CL:** You like *Goosebumps*? Do you read *Goosebumps* Tyreek?<br>**Tyreek:** Yeah<br><br>**Quanisha:** Right mom, my mom read Dr. Martin Luther King that's his [Tyreek's] book [to me and Alicia]. |
| Grade 7/8 | **Ms. Rodriguez:** Like Quanzaa, she need help in math, her brother Jez came other and said anytime you need help I did it before. Give me a call.<br>**CL:** Yep.<br>**Ms. Rodriguez:** I'll help you.<br>**CL:** That's good. She has help when she needs it.<br>**Ms. Rodriguez:** Oh yeah. She gets a lot of help. |

speaks of the classics he reads in school. Ms. Rodriguez describes the various magazines her sons read and Alicia's older brother wonders if his mother has finished reading her most recent novel, so he can read it next; he reports that he recently called his mother's friend to get more books. Tyreek helps Alicia study for tests and Tyreek and Quanzaa both report reading books from the *Goosebumps* series (Stine, 1992-1997). When Tyreek brings home a book about Martin Luther King, Ms. Rodriguez reads it to Alicia and Quanzaa. Reading together and sharing books is a common practice in this household.

While not all the children enjoy the number of literacy practices that Alicia enjoys, they all participate in literacy practices with their siblings. Peter reads to his younger brother and sister and Jermaine's older brother sometimes helps him.

## Peer Literacy Practices

By eighth grade, Alicia's, Peter's and Jermaine's literacy practices have become increasingly intertwined with the literacy practices of their friends. Sometimes, choosing not to read is a part of those practices. While Alicia's literacy practices and her writing of poetry continue at home, she does not share these practices with her friends. In contrast, Peter describes playing a "Lord of the Rings" board game with friends that share his interest in the books. He reports that his friends read other books too; he tells me that boys prefer books about sports and that girls enjoy fictional stories that deal with "feelings" and "relationships." He says that he usually gets his books from the school library. Although Peter's friends are readers, Peter reports that only a few of the students at his school read. Like Alicia, he says that when kids get together they sometimes read magazines; he mentions *Jet* and *Ebony*. He suspects that reading about African American characters is important to his friends saying, "They just pay attention more to that kind of stuff."

Jermaine reports that most of the kids do not like to read, but that the smart kids carry big books. Some of Jermaine's friends do read; Jermaine says they enjoy mystery books. He mentions, "Horror books like *Goosebumps* [and] *Harry Potter*." He describes the ways in which he and his friends get books from the library that contain information about the video games they play. He calls these book "cheat codes" and says that they also find books about Pokemon that have pictures of the various Pokemon characters featured on the cards they collect.

While reading books is not a universal practice in middle school, my former students do engage in a variety of reading and writing practices with their peers. Their book choices (i.e., *Goosebumps*, *Lord of the Rings*,

**Table 2.5.   Alicia's Perceptions of Her Peers Literacy Practices**

| | |
|---|---|
| Grade 7/8 | **CL:** Alicia do most of your, the kids at your school like to read?<br>**Alicia:** No.<br>**CL:** No? Why not.<br>**Alicia:** Cause they just not into it.<br>**CL:** Mmm. What kind of things do they do instead.<br>**Alicia:** Goof around.<br><br>**CL:** Is there anything they do like to read like magazines or …<br>**Alicia:** Yeah, they, they read magazines. I know that.<br>**CL:** What kind of magazines do they read?<br>**Alicia:** All kinds of magazines …<br>**CL:** What about their school books?<br>**Alicia:** I don't think so.<br><br>**CL:** Is reading fun?<br>**Alicia:** No.<br>**CL:** No? Then why do you do it?<br>**Alicia:** Cause it's when I'm bored … That's something to do. |

Pokemon books) and their reading of popular magazines suggest that these literacy practices are separate from school.

## THREE FINDINGS

In this section, I will highlight three findings from the case studies: the intersections between children's and parents' reading preferences, interests in texts that depict African American characters and issues, and issues related to identity.

### Intersections Between Parents' and Children's Reading Preferences

One interesting piece of information evident in all three cases, and in other cases from this study, is the children often report enjoying reading texts that are similar to the books read by their parents. Like his mother, Peter prefers horror novels and mysteries. Jermaine's interest in Frederick Douglass echoes his mother's interest in *Roots* (Haley, 1976) and father's interest in local African American history. Alicia's reading of the books from the baby sitter's club series reflects her mother's preference for series novels or novels written by favorite authors (i.e., Donald Goins or Terry McMillan).

## Interests in Texts That Depict
## African American Characters and Issues

All of the children and their parents display an interest in reading about African American characters and issues. Ms. Rodriguez reads novels by African American authors (Goins, McMillan) while Alicia talks about reading *Ruby* (Guy, 1991) a coming of age novel about an African American girl. Alicia and her mother share their interest in Tyreek's book about Martin Luther King; Jermaine's reading about Frederick Douglass reflects his mother's interest in African American history and Peter talks about reading *Ebony* and *Jet* with his peers. These texts that portray African American people and reflect the values the children and their parents place on the shared histories of African American people. These effects are not just matters of personal preference or interest. These preferences are related to others in complex ways and reflect the positionings that children assume as they move through school.

## Issues Related to Identity

Literacy practices are one way of playing out identity (Ferdman, 1990). Children, and adults, access literacy practices to play out various identities. What they read and what they do not read speaks to alliances with groups of people and types of people. Peter's reading of *Goosebumps*, references his mother's interest in horror, but also closely aligns him with his male peers whom he exchanges books with at school. Likewise, reading teen magazines is a reading practice that Alicia shares with her friends. Unlike reading books, reading magazines is an acceptable literacy practice among her peers. Notably, many of the reading practices shared among peers, reading *Goosebumps* books, *Lord of the Rings* books, Pokemon books, and popular magazines, do not align with school literacy expectations. Race, gender, age, and social affiliations affect the literacy practices that children and their families adopt. Literacy and literacy practices are one way of enacting identity (Ferdman, 1990) and these identities relate to macro issues such as racism, socially shared values, and power.

## CONCLUSIONS

Perhaps the most striking aspect of the stories presented in this chapter is the diversity of literacy learning practices in each of the three families. Alicia's family practices spelling games to help children learn words, exchanging novels, reading popular magazines (i.e., *Sports Illustrated* and music magazines), and reading books from the school library (i.e., Martin Luther King book). Peter's family's reading practices include teaching Peter the alphabet, reading books from school, and reading *Goosebumps* and *Lord of the Ring* books that Peter shares with his friends. Jermaine's family talks about reading books that Jermaine brought home from school as well as books that relate to televisions shows (i.e., *Arthur* stories on PBS and mini-series like *Roots*), using a "tutoring computer," and reading Pokemon books with his friends. These home reading practices are unique for each family and differentially interact with the school practices and expectations.

The literacy teaching practices that parents describe are literacy practices that have the specific goal of helping children to become literate. Literacy teaching practices are enmeshed in the parents' understandings and experiences of learning to read and their beliefs about what schools expect and value. For example, sounding out words, locating word parts, spelling words aloud, and asking for extra papers for children to do at home are all practices that involve school practices occurring at home. In their playing school, children also describe this transposition of school practices into homes; using a chalkboard, copying words, tracing letters, taking naps, playing recess, having children come to the rug for storytime and fussing at children are all school practices that have crossed over into homes as children play school. Unlike conventionally identified literacy practices (i.e., reading the Bible, reading the newspaper, paying bills, surfing the net], literacy teaching practices are linked with the school experiences, expectations and understandings of parents.

Apart from literacy teaching practices, rich interactive relationships are evident in the reading preferences of children. Children's reading preferences are contextualized with the reading preferences of their parents, siblings and peers and the reading that they are assigned in classrooms. Sometimes this effect involves children developing similar reading preferences to family members (i.e., Alicia's brother sharing novels with his mother). At other times these practices involve not reading particular texts within peer groups (i.e., Alicia and her friends not reading school books, but reading magazines). At other times, it involves children and their peers reading books that involve their shared interests (i.e., Alex and his friend reading books about Pokemon characters). Once again, the borders between home and school, family and peer group are crossed as student engage in rich sets of hybrid literacy preferences that are complexly situated within children's lives.

The home teaching practices of parents incorporate information from family histories, parents' school experiences, children's school experiences, and school expectations. This hybridization of home and school literacy teaching practices raises the question to what degree do school literacy practices and expectations affect home literacy practices? Does schooling affect home reading? If is does, how does this occur and what might this merging of home and school literacy practices entail? Conversely, how might home literacy teaching practices and literacy practices in general affect literacy practices at school? These are questions that await further work and challenge the assumption that school literacy can be taught apart from the experiential and social histories that children bring to classrooms.

All of the families described in this chapter enjoy rich literacy experiences. It is essential that educators recognize the rich literacy experiences of all three children and view these experiences as valuable resources that can be developed in classrooms. However, not all of the children are equally successful in school. Peter's success is notable. Considering Peter's success suggests two important considerations for teachers. First, Peter's reading practices align more closely with school expectations. While reading the Lord of Rings series may not reflect school approved reading texts, Peter reads these texts compulsively and the content of these books are closer to the types of texts that children often read in school. Alicia's reading of love stories may not align as well with school expectations for reading and analyzing literature. Jermaine talks about reading a book about Frederick Douglass, but this is the only book he talks about and it was a book that was assigned in school. Second, Peter's reading is deeply enmeshed in his relationships with peers, unlike Alicia who reads books when her friends are not around. I suspect that this meshing of books and social relationships relates to the ways Peter views himself as a reader and fuses reading to a developing reading identity that serves him well in school.

This chapter has explored the ways a small set of literacy practices are mutually constructed across time and are impacted by the experiences of children, their parents, their siblings, and their peers. Home literacy practices are not only impacted by school practices but also by the literacy practices of children and their peers; the same is true of school experiences. What children read and when they read is uniquely contextualized within personal relationship involving parents, teachers and peers and is impacted by the histories that families live and bring. While home and school literacy practices are often viewed as separate practices, This chapter suggests that these practices are situated not only in interaction with each other but also in dynamic relationships with the histories of families, the learning experiences of parents, the experiences and expectations of school, and relationships with peers.

## REFERENCES

Bridwell, N. (1987). *Clifford series*. New York: Scholastic Press.

Brown, M. (1976). *Arthur series.* New York: Little, Brown Young Readers.

Compton-Lilly, C. (2003). *Reading families: The literate lives of urban children.* New York: Teachers College Press.

Ferdman, B. (1990). Literacy and cultural identity. *Harvard Educational Review, 60*(2), 181-204.

Gadsden, V. (1992). Giving meaning to literacy, intergenerational beliefs about access. *Theory Into Practice, 31*, 378-385.

Gadsden, V. (2000). Intergenerational literacy within families. *Handbook of the National Reading Conference Yearbook, 43*, 871-887.

Guy, R. (1991). *Ruby.* East Orange, NJ: Just Us Books.

Haley, A. (1976). *Roots.* New York: Doubleday.

Heath, S. B. (1983). *Ways with words: Language, life, and work in communities and classrooms.* New York: Cambridge University Press.

Martin, A. M., & Lerangris, P. (1986-2000). *The babysitter's club series.* New York: Scholastic Press.

McMillan, T. (1987). *Mama.* Boston: Pocket Books.

Miller, D. (1993). *Frederick Douglass and the fight for freedom.* New York: Facts on File.

Moll, L., Amanti, C., Neff, D., & Gonzalez, N. (1992). Funds of knowledge for teaching: Using a qualitative approach to connect homes and classrooms. *Theory into Practice, 31*(2), 132-141.

Myers, W. D. (1988). *Scorpions.* New York: HarperCollins.

Nieto, S. (2002). *Language, culture, and teaching: Critical perspectives for a new century.* Mahwah, NJ: Erlbaum.

Philbrick, R. (1989). *Max the mighty.* New York: Scholastic.

Philbrick, R. (2001). *Freak the mighty.* New York: Scholastic.

Purcell-Gates, V. (1996). Stories, coupons, and the TV guide: Relationships between home literacy experiences and emergent literacy knowledge. *Reading Research Quarterly, 31*, 406-428.

Rowling, J. K. (1997-present). *Harry Potter series.* New York: Scholastic Books.

Simon and Schuster. (1996-present). *Blues clues series.* New York: Author.

Spinnelli, J. (1990). *Maniac Magee.* New York: Little Brown Young Readers.

Stine, R. L. (1992-1997). *The goosebumps series.* New York: Scholastic Press.

Street, B. V. (2003). What's "new" in literacy studies? Critical approaches to literacy in theory and practice. *Current Issues in Comparative Education, 5*(2), 77-91.

Taylor, D., & Dorsey-Gaines, C. (1988). *Growing up literate: Learning from inner-city families.* Portsmouth, NH: Heinemann.

Tolkien, J. R. R. (1954-1955). *The lord of the rings series.* Boston: Houghton Mifflin.

CHAPTER 3

# FAMILY MATTERS

## How One Somali Bantu Family
## Supported Themselves and an
## American Teacher in Literacy Learning

### Patricia M. Lynch

One afternoon Hussein and I settled on the couch to read a story about an African boy who scoured his village for discarded pieces of wire to make a toy called a "galimoto." I thought Hussein would enjoy this book because he is so much like the main character, always tinkering with gadgets and figuring out how things work. As soon as I opened the book and started reading, Hussein began to echo-read along with me. I read slowly, tracking as I went, while Hussein examined the colorful illustrations as he turned each page. He pointed to pictures he could identify, calling out "boy," "mother," and "baby," and when we reached the end of the story, he turned to me with a smile and said, "Again." (Field notes, July, 2004)

While reading a book together might seem to be an unremarkable event, Hussein's response to our read-aloud was the first of many literacy learning experiences we shared which surprised and delighted me. This one occurred after 7-year-old Hussein had been in the United States for only a month. He and the rest of his family, Somali Bantus who had immi-

*Multicultural Families, Home Literacies, and Mainstream Schooling*
pp. 51–70

grated to the United States from a refugee camp in Kenya, had arrived just 4 weeks before. Like his parents and siblings, Hussein had never been to school and could not read or write his own language, yet he had already developed a remarkable sense of print awareness and book handling. In just a brief time, Hussein applied what he understood about learning from his home culture to reading aloud—that stories are a part of life, and that learning involves close observation and careful listening. He demonstrated "the remarkable cognitive, cultural, and linguistic flexibility of young children," and underscored the importance of culturally situated, out-of-school literacies, referred to as "'invisible' literacies" (Gregory, Long, & Volk, 2004, p. 2), in the lives of new language learners.

It was my privilege to work with Hussein and his family for their first year in the United States, acting as a home/school liaison and afterschool homework tutor, but more importantly to offer them ongoing and authentic opportunities to learn language, learn about language and learn through language (Halliday, 1978). In the process, they showed me that "whoever teaches learns in the act of teaching, and whoever learns teaches in the act of learning" (Friere, 1998, p. 31).

## A BRIEF HISTORY OF THE SOMALI BANTU

Through the initiative of community and church organizations, a metropolitan area in the southeastern region of the United States became home to a community of Somali Bantu refugees who, as a result of their economic, social, and political history, were denied the rights and privileges afforded ethnic Somalis, including the opportunity to learn to read and write their own language.

Many Somali Bantus trace their origins back to Tanzania, Mozambique, and Malawi. When the rise of industrialization created the need for cheap labor in the nineteenth century, Bantu tribes were abducted and brought as slaves to Somalia. Attempts to free themselves by converting to Islam did little to improve their position in society. Their cultural, linguistic, and physical features served to distinguish them from indigenous Somalis, whose tight clan affiliations afforded them greater status and protection. Ultimately, they settled in the Juba River Valley near the Somali-Kenya border and turned to farming to support themselves. Some migrated to urban areas to work as laborers and semiskilled tradesmen, but they continued to be denied the political, economic, and educational opportunities available to ethnic Somalis.

In 1991, civil war broke out, the economy collapsed, and food became scarce. Somali Bantu farms were raided, and family members were raped, beaten, and murdered in the process. An estimated 10,000 Somali Bantu fled the country for refugee camps in Northern Kenya, where they continued to face discrimination from ethnic Somalis and others. Because the Somali Bantu could not return to their home land for fear of reprisals from those in power, they were recognized by the United States as a special interest group, making them automatically eligible to relocate here (Lovgren, 2003; St. John's Episcopal Church, 2004; Van Lehman & Eno, 2003).

## LITERACY AND THE SOMALI BANTU

The Somali government made little effort to build schools in predominantly Bantu areas of the country, and as a result, estimates indicate that only about 5% of Somali Bantu refugees have been formally educated (Van Lehman & Eno, 2003, p. 22). Even if they were able to attend school, they faced instruction in an unfamiliar language. Somalia has two distinct dialects that are similar in written, but not spoken, form. Af Maay is the language of the Bantu, but Af Maxaa is the official written language of the country, which is used in Somali schools. According to Van Lehman and Eno, "the denial of access to education represents one of the most egregious and detrimental examples of Somali institutional discrimination against the Bantu" (Van Lehman & Eno, 2003, p. 22).

## THE PURPOSE OF THE STUDY

The purpose of this study was to chronicle the experiences of one Somali Bantu family and me as we explored each other's language and culture together. My intent was to identify and investigate the conditions that contributed to the family's emerging literacy in order to support them as they grew in their ability to read the word and the world (Freire, 1987). I used an ethnographic design to investigate how the Ali Noor Osman family, composed of two adults and six children, appropriated the resources at their disposal to learn English, and to chronicle their growth as speakers, writers, and readers. I also investigated how various teaching strategies and learning materials employed in the family's literacy learning supported or constrained their progress. The work evolved out of a single question: What happens when an American educator and a Somali Bantu family explore language and culture together?

My purpose here is to highlight one aspect of the larger study: to describe the ways in which family members, both adult and children, continuously assumed the roles of both mentor and apprentice as they supported each other's language learning. In doing so, I reveal some of the vital, yet often invisible, home literacy practices that are so often over-looked or ignored when children from diverse backgrounds enter school in the United States.

## THE CONCEPTUAL FRAMEWORK

### Sociocultural Perspective on Learning

The framework for this study is shaped by a sociocultural theory of cognitive development, rooted in the works of Vygotsky (1978) and those who have reinterpreted him (Lindfors, 1999; Rogoff, 1990, 2003; Wells, 1986, 1999). A sociocultural perspective sees learners as

> apprentices in thinking, active in their efforts to learn from observing and participating with peers and more skilled members [mentors] of their society, developing skills to handle culturally defined problems with available tools, and building from these givens to construct new solutions within the context of socio-cultural activity (Rogoff, 1990, p. 7).

While my position as an educator and native language speaker initially placed me in the role of teacher/mentor to the family, we all, children and adults alike, assumed both apprentice and mentor roles as we scaffolded each other in learning language and culture together.

### A Syncretic View of Literacy

Gregory et al. (2004) argue that language learners are resourceful and opportunistic, transforming the strategies, resources, and people at their disposal to syncretize, or create, for themselves a unique and personalized way to make sense of language which extends beyond methods and materials. A syncretic view of literacy learning is understood to be "an inter-mingling or merging of culturally diverse traditions [that] informs and organizes literacy activities" (Duranti & Ochs, 1997, p. 172), and is an essential part of the conceptual framework for this study.

## PERSPECTIVES ON CULTURE AND
## LEARNING: A REVIEW OF LITERATURE

### Culture and Literacy

The history of the Somali Bantu discloses the ways in which language and culture can serve as markers to judge, alienate and marginalize some while embracing and empowering others. During the nineteenth century, the notion of literacy became the distinguishing factor between so-called civilized and primitive societies. In writing about the Hmong people of Laos, Duffy (2000) argues that to imply that the absence of reading and writing is "an expression of inherent Hmong practices, preferences, and values" (p. 227); to do so ignores the social, political, economic, and military circumstances that led to the absence of literacy. In this regard, the Somali Bantu and the Hmong are very much alike—they became casualties in the struggle for power in their respective countries. The Somali Bantu were prevented from learning to read and write their own language because it was self-serving for those in power to do so, not because they were in some way intellectually inferior. To presume otherwise is to falsely equate the use of printed language with cognitive ability and logical thinking, while ignoring the rich repertoire of literacies which exist for them outside the written word. Cultural communities like the Hmong and the Somali Bantu have existed for centuries without the written word, reminding us that there are many kinds of literacies, equally important but different, which individuals employ in order to negotiate life in their respective worlds.

## LITERACY IN AND OUT OF SCHOOL

Greenfield (1994) asserts that all cultures embrace distinct value orientations through which culture is transmitted across generations. She identifies independence and interdependence as values that are at once separate and intertwined, just as a person is both a unique individual as well as a member of a cultural group, and suggests that every society creates its own balance between the two. The culture of most American schools espouses an independent, competitive spirit, placing high priority on decontextualized, or abstract, thinking (Donaldson, 1978), and privileges written language over other ways of making and sharing meaning. Nieto (1999) argues that "these value themes characterize and contrast European-American culture with that of African, Asian, Latin American, and Native American societies" (p. 9), which often embrace a more social, collaborative, and contextualized way of life. As a result, "school-based literacy ... undermines an interdependence developmental script" (Greenfield, 1994, p. 15), thereby marginalizing those like the Somali Bantu, whose learning has occurred through oral instruction, observation, and collaborative participation in authentic life experiences.

### Cultural Mediators

With an increased interest in the importance of literacy practices and funds of knowledge situated in the home and community, research has focused on the role of parents and others as mentors in the learning process and mediators of cultural values and information (Gadsden, 2000). Compton-Lilly (2004) found that in spite of commonly held myths about the role of poor and diverse parents in their children's literacy lives, the families with whom she worked nevertheless made many valuable contributions to literacy learning based on common sense assumptions about reading and personal experiences in school. Heath's (1983) work in adjacent but culturally distinct communities highlighted the different roles played by parents, extended family, and other community members in the language and social development of children.

In the case of learning a new language and culture, children often become the language and cultural resources for their parents. This was certainly the case in the Osman family. While parents Ali and Saniya taught their children many things about becoming knowledgeable and respected individuals within their own community, they relied heavily on their children to reinforce those values and for help in learning English.

## WORKING IN TWO LANGUAGES

Strategies for literacy learning employed by siblings appear to vary across cultures and according to the nature of the task. For example, in a case study of Pakistani preschoolers in the United Kingdom, Drury (2004) documented the "code-switching" of one young girl at home. As she played school with a younger sibling, the girl moved back and forth between her native language and English as the need arose. Her remarks reflected the procedural type of talk adults often use with children at school to help develop not only language but social skills as well, and some of the first instances of English language use I encountered with the Osman family children reflected this type of talk. Abdikadirm, the oldest boy in the family, would often erupt into a song his teacher sang at school to signal a transition time, "Clean up, clean up, everybody, clean up" as I gathered my materials in the afternoon, and sometimes Hussein would order, "Quiet, children!" when the household sounded particularly noisy.

## REDEFINING THE ROLES

Gregory (2001) studied Bangladeshi and Anglo families living in London's East End, and examined the critical role of siblings in scaffolding literacy learning. She found that it was not only older siblings who "scaffolded," or supported, younger ones in the learning process, but that the relationship between brothers and sisters of varying ages was much more mutual, interdependent and reciprocal in nature than was expected. Gregory's findings "refer to the interaction between the children as synergy, a unique reciprocity whereby siblings act as adjuvants in each other's learning, that is, older children "teach younger siblings and at the same time develop their own learning" (p. 309). The findings of each of these researchers are consistent with my experience with the Osman family, several of which are described later on in the Findings section of this chapter, and which support the idiosyncratic nature of learning both within and beyond the realm of school.

## METHODOLOGY

Because the study was exploratory in nature (Marshall & Rossman, 1999) I employed an ethnographic methodology in order to "carefully observe, systematically experience, and consciously record in detail" (Glesne, 1999, p. 46) the many aspects of my time and work with the family. "Rather than studying people, ethnography means learning from people" (Spradley & McCurdy, 1999, p. 22).

### Participants

The Ali Noor Osman family consists of Ali, his wife Saniya, and six children. At the time of this study, their three daughters were 16, 11, and 5. Asha, the 16-year-old, attended high school while Batula and Isha were enrolled in fourth grade and kindergarten, respectively. Nine-year-old Abdikadir was actually a grandson whose mother gave him to her parents when they immigrated. Hussein, a 7-year-old second grader, and Abdi Aziz, 3 ½, were the other two boys.

Very little personal information was available about the Osman family, including birth dates, schooling, or employment. When questioned about life in Africa, their answers were often vague or contradictory, and what information I could piece together frequently came from others working with the family, or a Somali translator I periodically employed, Aziz Abdullahu. I learned that before fleeing Somalia, Ali had been a truck driver, while Saniya stayed at home with the children, which included three sons who died before the family left Africa. They lived in Kakuma, a Kenyan refugee camp, for 12 years, where they tended a few goats, and spent most of their time fetching water, gathering firewood, protecting themselves, and trying to survive. Aziz informed me that all Somali Muslims were required to attend religious services in the camp and that attendance or absence was noted. Only Asha had any formal schooling in

Africa. Informal assessments I conducted with her before the start of the school year indicated that she read and wrote enough English to function on an upper elementary level. No one else in the family had any formal education, including the parents, so they could neither read nor write, but the younger children alluded to some kind of informal instruction in the refugee camp, where they learned to sing the ABC song and to count to at least 10. This is a close-knit, religious Muslim family who are devoted to one another and grateful for the opportunities afforded them in their new homeland.

## Data Collection

Every week for the entire 2004-2005 school year, I came to the Osman family home to help with homework and to engage the family in learning invitations which provided additional opportunities to speak, read, and write English. For example, we made get-well cards for a sponsor who had surgery, and went shopping at the Dollar Store for gifts to give during Ramadan. My focus was always on the family's use of English: the circumstances that encouraged it, the materials and/or instructional strategies that supported it, and the growth of vocabulary and conventions.

Because of my dual role as a participant observer, there was little time for "in the midst" (Hubbard & Power, 1999, p. 106) note-taking when I was with the family. I kept a blank tape in my car so that when our homework sessions were over, I could audio-tape my thoughts and impressions on the way home. These tapes became the framework for my "after the fact" (Hubbard & Power, 1999, p. 107) field notes, which I wrote each evening. The notes were organized by date and saved on individual disks according to the months in which they were written. Hard copies were then printed and kept in notebooks for easy access during the analysis phase of the research, along with interviews, photographs, work samples, and other artifacts which documented language development across the year. Although I continued to work with the family for the entire school year, formal data collection occurred from late July, 2004 until March, 2005.

## Modeling, Mini-Lessons, and Play

Halliday (1975) reminds us that literacy learning consists of three interrelated aspects: *learning language, learning about language,* and *learning through language.* The children *learned language* as they used it in practical ways. Throughout the year I *modeled* conventional English through the use of authentic learning invitations, such as cooking, taking pictures, and making books, which provided opportunities for the children to ask questions and talk about the experiences we shared. These experiences generated "here-and-now" language (Gibbons, 2002, p. 2), which gave us all a common reference point for conversation, and the additional visual clues of gesture and facial expression which helped us understand each other. And unlike the "English-only" policy at school, I encouraged the children to code-switch freely between Somali and English at home.

*Mini-lessons* based on the children's emerging literacy were created to help them *learn about language* by applying the skills they learned at school and moving them towards more conventional language use. One mini-lesson took place when Batula, Abdikadir, and Hussein brought home a predictable book in which a series of farm animals all went down a hill to the town below. Initially the children read, "The cow went down," for "The cows went down," but after pointing out that the pictures showed more than one cow, saying the word "cows" with special emphasis, pointing to the -s ending, and asking the children to repeat "cows" in place of "cow," they learned the difference and corrected their miscues. Although I did not use them on a daily basis, direct instruction and repetition were familiar teaching and learning strategies from Africa that the family used to help each other with English and to help me learn words and phrases in their language.

"As in the focus of a magnifying glass, play contains all developmental tendencies in condensed form and is itself a major source of development" (Vygotsky, 1978, p. 102). I capitalized on the value of play when I used guessing games and game-like formats to foster learning through language. After Hussein brought home *Frog and Toad Together* (Lobel, 1971) and we had read the chapter "Cookies," I baked some cookies for an after school snack. I hid them, along with the book and toy Frog and Toad figures, in a brown paper grocery bag with the question, "What is in the bag?" written on it. After the children guessed that there were cookies in the bag, I urged them to predict what else there might be. When I told them there were green animals in the bag, they immediately narrowed their guesses from bears and lions to alligators and crocodiles, and when I said the animal's name started with an "f," they made use of their developing phonemic awareness to guess the correct animal character, Frog.

I found that modeling, mini-lessons, and play were instructional strategies that not only engaged family members in learning language, learning about language and learning through language, they became important vehicles for the family to engage me in their language and culture as well, as I describe in the upcoming findings section.

**Data Analysis**

Using Glaser and Strauss's (1967) constant comparative method of analysis, I continuously reviewed field notes, artifacts, transcriptions and photographs to identify recurring patterns of language use, interactions, behaviors, and theoretical connections which were then used to code future data. These became the basis for developing personal hunches and tentative explanations about what I experienced in the research setting. As my hunches were tested, critical incidents emerged to either confirm and focus the study further or cause me to redirect my observations and thinking. Using Mills and O'Keefe's Responsive Teaching Cycle (Whitin, Mills, & O'Keefe, 1990) as a framework, I *observed* the children's responses to our engagements, *interpreted* what happened based on what I knew, and then *planned* subsequent invitations with that new information in mind.

## FINDINGS

The simple answer to my original question, "What happens when a Somali Bantu family and an American explore language and culture together?" is that all of us grew and changed as individual learners. Gregory et al. suggest that "crucial to a sociocultural approach (to learning) ... is the mediator (a teacher, adult, more knowledgeable sibling or peer) in initiating children into new cultural practices or guiding them in the learning of new skills" (2004, p. 7). Although I initially assumed the role of mediator for the family, it quickly became apparent that as I facilitated language learning through mini-lessons, modeling, and play, the children in turn scaffolded me via their responses. The degree to which I paid close attention to those responses and adjusted my instructional strategies directly affected the degree to which they engaged in my learning invitations.

This section begins with a brief description of how Somali Bantu children are culturally situated to learn from a variety of mediators, and how Ali and Saniya created an atmosphere that supported learning in their home. I then describe three scaffolding strategies I used with the family, and how they appropriated those same strategies to scaffold each other and me.

### Cultural Influences of Learning

"It takes a village to raise a child" seems appropriate in describing Somali Bantu child rearing practices. Parents and other adults in the community serve as role models for the children, and anyone may discipline a child who is misbehaving with a pinch, a verbal rebuke, or deprivation of a privilege for a short period of time. This is intended to help children "stay within their channels," as Ali put it, or to conduct themselves appropriately. Thus, Somali Bantu children have the support and assistance of many people in learning the mature roles of their community, and as a result, they displayed a great deal of responsibility and independence in caring for themselves and each other.

When the children arrived in the United States, they could sing the alphabet song and knew how to count to 10, but could not identify letters or numbers in isolation. I was told they learned these songs in a sort of informal school in Kakuma, but nothing much is known about the circumstances of this instruction or their teacher, although Batula insisted that it was "play, no learning." The children had also memorized passages of the Koran, presumably at the weekly services they were required to attend. So as members of multiple circles of influence, such as cultural and religious communities, extended family, peer groups, and siblings, the children appropriated a variety of resources to learn what they needed to survive and participate successfully as members of the Somali Bantu community.

## PARENTAL SUPPORT OF EDUCATION

Conventional wisdom about "at-risk" children and school frequently assumes that their lack of success is the result of a lack of support at home. However, Auerbach (1997) found that,

> Although beliefs about literacy and its payoffs vary, undereducated parents generally not only value literacy, but see it as the single most powerful hope for their children; even parents who themselves have limited literacy proficiency support their children's literacy acquisition in many ways. (as cited in Taylor, 1997, p. 74)

While Saniya and Ali rarely assisted their children with homework assignments because they could neither read nor write, they nevertheless demonstrated the priority of learning by establishing an afterschool routine for the children and modeling good study habits. As we discussed the homework routine for the year and the use of television afterschool, Ali announced, "Book, sleeping, school—good! No TV!" and as long as we were doing homework, the television was never turned on. Saniya was usually in the kitchen cooking the evening meal when the children arrived, and as they shed their jackets and went off to change clothes, she repeatedly called, "Homework, homework" loud enough for everyone in the house to hear, reminding them to get back to the kitchen and get to work. And every day without fail, Ali and Saniya completed their own homework from English classes they attended each week. This normally consisted of fill-in-the-blank workbook pages and copying letters and numbers for handwriting practice. They both had a book bag that contained work books, paper and pencils, and although Saniya often started before Ali got home in the afternoons, they frequently worked together in the living room after supper.

## Scaffolding Each Other

My data is full of vignettes that reveal the many ways in which the Ali Noor Osman family supported and scaffolded each other's language learning. Choosing just a few was not easy. What follows are selected incidents, or "rich points" (Agar, 1996, p. 31), that I believe reveal the ways in which family members appropriated the instructional, material, and human resources around them to reinvent their own particular ways to support and stretch the learning of language for and with each other.

Soon after school began, reading simple books with predictable patterns became a regular part of the children's homework. One afternoon, Hussein and I read a story which he then volunteered to read to Isha. Modeling what good readers do, Hussein tracked the words as he read them, and reminded Isha to, "Look," "Listen me." Later that day I noticed that Isha picked up the same book and read it to her younger brother, Abdiaziz, modeling the behaviors Hussein used with her.

Books, posters, puzzles, and other educational materials were provided for the family by their sponsors and friends, and Abdikadir was particularly adept at using these environmental print resources when working on homework assignments, which frequently involved supplying the correct vowel or consonant to complete simple words. Hussein was experiencing trouble with one such assignment and said to no one in particular, "*Help me!*" Abdikadir immediately got up, located an ABC placemat someone had given the family, and handed it to Hussein, saying, "Look-a theese right he-ah" (Look at this right here). While it might have been easier for him to simply tell Hussein the answer, Abdikadir understood the value of helping Hussein to become aware of the resources he could use to help himself in the future.

Batula took a more pedantic approach to scaffolding, correcting errors and supplying information to her siblings through her own mini-lessons, often before they had a chance to work things out for themselves. Her exchange with Abdikadir in early December illustrates this.

I had written the question, "What did you do at school today?" to begin a written conversation in Abdikadir's journal. When I read it to him, he replied, "Running." Batula immediately corrected him, saying, "I am running." Here she demonstrates that she knows something about the syntax/ conventions of English, and felt the need for Abdikadir to know the proper way to say it. I tried to solicit his help to spell "running", but Batula blurted out the correct spelling for him before we could finish. (Field notes, December 1, 2004).

An example of scaffolding through play occurred one afternoon while I helped Saniya and Batula prepare supper. Hussein sat on the kitchen floor holding a soccer ball with numbers from 1 to 20 on it. He pointed to a number, challenged Isha to guess what it was, then whispered the answer in Somali in Abdiaziz's ear before telling Isha if her answer was correct or not. We had planned to take the ball outside to kick it around after supper, but Hussein had created another way to play with the ball that helped his younger siblings practice identifying numbers.

One of the most powerful demonstrations of family members scaffolding each another occurred one afternoon as I worked with Abdikadir on the hundreds chart.

I thought that since the children were able to count in Somali, perhaps they could identify numbers in isolation if I asked them in Somali. Abdikadir and I worked together on the hundreds chart and he was able to show me 12 and 20, but could not point out my age, 54. I then tried 10, 20, 30, 40, etc., without success. Ali sat across the room working on his own homework when I realized he was providing Abdikadir with subtle hints about which number came next. In Somali he would say, "Afar iyo zero," and Abdikadir could point to that number. What is extraordinary about this is that "afar iyo zero" is not the Somali word for forty- that word is "afartan." Ali was telling Abdikadir to find the "4 and 0." What is also exciting is that with my minimal grasp of the Somali language, I figured out what Ali was doing! (Field Notes, September, 2004)

These vignettes reveal several culturally situated literacy practices which occurred in the Osman home: scaffolding among siblings as well as parents, the importance of oral instruction, and taking responsibility for the welfare of others. Although Ali's gentle scaffolding of Abdikadir in number identification was a parent-child interaction which might be found in many homes around the world, the children were also actively engaged in teaching what they knew to their younger siblings and strengthening their own learning in the process, just as Gregory (2001) discovered. Having grown up in a culture of interdependence (Greenfield, 1994), which emphasized oral instruction and memorization, the children understood the value of playing close attention to the various teachers in their lives. As a result, they appropriated both the language and instructional strategies they themselves had experienced in order to scaffold each other in learning English. Since it is understood within the Somali Bantu community that children take responsibility for their younger siblings, this instruction occurred without them being asked to do so. They created within their family a supportive environment which was reflective of the interdependence valued in their culture.

## Scaffolding Me

As a result of my relationship and experiences with the Osman family, I am beginning to grasp the truly reciprocal nature of teaching and learning. While I may have provided a degree of expertise with regard to materials, strategies, and the English language, I was completely dependent upon the family's responses to my learning invitations to make more informed and relevant instructional choices with and for them. The more sensitive I became to their purposes and intentions for learning, the more engaged we all became as family members scaffolded me through modeling, mini-lessons, and play.

Just as I modeled English for the family members, they often modeled their own language for me. In the following event, Saniya and Batula expanded my vocabulary by way of a Somali cooking lesson.

> Saniya was sitting on the floor of the kitchen making yeast dough, and later I noticed that Batula was rolling it out on the bottom of a saucepan and frying it. She told me it was called jabaata. She repeated the word until I pronounced it correctly, then I repeated it over and over to remember it. Batula thought that was hysterical- she laughed and laughed at me, then put a piece of jabaata in a zip-lock bag for me to take home. (Field notes, November 9-10, 2004)

As Batula shaped and fried the jabaata, we talked about how she knew when to turn it over and how long to cook it. As my field notes show, she modeled the word "jabaata" repeatedly until she was convinced I had the sound of it, and drew great pleasure from my need to repeat the word until I could pronounce it easily. She even tested me later on to see if I remembered how to say jabaata!

One afternoon in December, I struggled to get Abdikadir to look at a predictable book featuring African animals that he had brought home from school. The scowl on his face let me know that he was not in the mood to read. Surprised that he resisted engaging with content that I thought might be familiar, it suddenly occurred to me that we might connect if I asked him to tell me the animal names in Somali. His face lit up immediately, and he began repeating the words for elephant, lion, rhinoceros, giraffe, and monkey, as well as for the idea of telling someone something. Suddenly the whole family was involved in this mini-lesson as I tried to scribble the words phonetically. They were all amused that hearing the words once or twice was not sufficient for me to remember them. Having grown up with a tradition of oral learning, they were surprised that their "teacher" required the crutch of written words and could not hear language as well as they did.

Here is what I wrote:

> Tiger (tiger) rinoserui (rhinoceros) inshegoi (tells) = the tiger tells the rhinoceros; Liewu = lion; Maroro= elephant; Girre =giraffe, Danyar = monkey; Shawell = tiger; Gawa = snap

> I wonder if in the Somali language, you put the subject and object next to each other, then the verb after them? That's what it looks like from what the children told me.

I wanted to show Ali and Saniya what the children had taught me, so I asked Hussein to get the book and read from my notes as he turned the pages. Ali smiled and nodded, then created a mini-lesson to correct my pronunciation for giraffe:

> He took his job very seriously, looking me in the eye and earnestly repeating the words so I would get them. It seemed to me that it was important for him to teach me. I had been using a soft "g" and a distinctly short "i" sound when I said "girre," (my phonetic spelling) but after repeating the word for me several times, I realized that to say "geri" (correct Somali spelling) correctly, I needed a hard "g" and short "e" instead of "i." (Field Notes, December 7, 2004)

My "What is in the bag?" guessing game became a tool which Batula used to expand my Somali food vocabulary. As I worked with the others at the kitchen table, she brought out a tall plastic pitcher with a lid, and challenged me to guess, "What's in here?" She grinned mischievously as I guessed what I thought the pitcher contained- juice, soda, water- and she shouted, "No!" with delight every time I was wrong. Just as I had done, Batula gave me clues about the mystery substance, such as, "This eating," and "Buh, buh, bas—," to let me know how the word started, but I was clueless. Finally, in exasperation, she removed the lid to reveal uncooked spaghetti noodles, the "basta," or pasta, about which she had hinted. In this event, she not only demonstrated an understanding of how the game worked, she provided meaningful clues to help me narrow my hunches. Batula had appropriated instructional strategies I had used with the family to scaffold my language learning in a playful way.

Each of these incidents demonstrates how the participation in everyday activities fosters language. Modeling vocabulary and conventions occurred naturally as the family and I inquired about each other's lives and communicated with each other. Language learning, then, was not objectified, but was the logical result of our experiences together.

## DISCUSSION

As Delpit (1995, p. xiv) asserts, "We all carry worlds in our heads and those worlds are decidedly different." They are socially constructed cultural frameworks that shape who we become, how we think, and the ways in which we learn about others, ourselves, and the world at large. In this study, I attempted to step out of my world to "reach the worlds of others" (Delpit, 1995, p. xiv) and explore the literacy learning of one Somali Bantu family. They showed me that "families' funds of knowledge and ways of knowing are complexly structured and highly dependent on the cultures to which they belong, the languages they speak, and the social, economic, and political circumstances of their daily lives" (Taylor, 1997, p. 7). Contrary to commonly held assumptions about populations like the Somali Bantu, who have limited material resources and who are culturally and linguistically different from the society in which they live, the Osman family showed me how teaching and learning was woven into the fabric of their daily lives.

Perhaps the most important lesson I learned from this study is that I become the best teacher when I am the most vulnerable learner. From a professional perspective, it became apparent that as I scaffolded language learning through mini-lessons, modeling, and play, the children in turn scaffolded me via their responses. The degree to which I paid close attention to those responses and adjusted my instructional strategies directly affected the degree to which they engaged in my learning invitations. This was important because, as Cambourne (1988) admonishes, "without the learner's engagement with the demonstrations which are made available by the person or artifacts which surround/immerse him, they will wash over him and pass him by" (p. 51). And as they became comfortable with them, the children used some of those same scaffolding strategies to help me learn their language and culture. I found that embracing my vulnerability as a learner not only benefited me, but positioned all of the family members as experts and teachers, roles I suspect they seldom experienced when negotiating the cultural and linguistic landscape of America. Wells (1999) was right when he said that "as an opportunity for learning with and from others, the ZPD applies potentially to all participants and not simply to the less skillful or knowledgeable" (p. 331).

## IMPLICATIONS OF THE STUDY

I believe the improvement of public education requires a commitment on the part of classroom teachers to humanize the process of teaching and learning, to see each child as his or her unique and particular self. One compelling implication of this study is the need to "question assumptions and challenge stereotypes" (Gregory et al., 2004, p. 225) which currently dominate thinking in public schools today, and to consider the ways in which "impediments to our freedom are more the products of social political, economic, cultural, historical, and ideological structures than of hereditary structures" (Freire, 1998, p. 20). The study shows that instructional decisions are a direct reflection of personal and institutional priorities, and joins the voices of many respected educators who urge teachers to "open up possibilities for improving the quality of life in their classrooms" (Mills, O'Keefe, & Jennings, 2004, p. x). This requires being aware of students' lives both in and out of school, and learning to appreciate and value their particular ways of knowing which may differ from our own. Eisner (1994) believes that defining school curriculum in terms of language also defines what kinds of opportunities students have to encounter other forms of communication, or sign systems, that relate to their interests and abilities. "When we limit ourselves to language, we cut ourselves off from other ways of knowing" (Berghoff, Egawa, Harste, Hoonan, 1994, p. 4). Making and sharing meaning through the visual and performing arts, as well as through written and spoken language, creates an inclusive experience which expands the possibilities for learning and allows all students to participate regardless of their cultural, cognitive, or social status. Reaching out to families in these ways demonstrates a desire to humanize the educational process and a willingness not only to teach, but to learn with and from others.

## ADDITIONAL IMPLICATIONS FOR RESEARCH

This study reveals that learning is an idiosyncratic process, and each of us carves our own paths to literacy by transacting with the human, material, and environmental resources at our disposal. It always involves a measure of risk, but "learning is welcome when it affirms a continuing sense of self" (Bateson, 1994, p. 79). It seems to me that that is the goal of public education—to teach our children in such a way that they experience a "continuing sense of self." With that in mind, I suggest the following topics merit further investigation:

- How might learning about culture, learning culture and learning through culture strengthen the relationships between teacher, students, and their families, and support the multiple literacies in which children participate?
- How do decisions that teachers make regarding materials and instructional strategies serve to support or constrain the learning of children from diverse cultures?
- What other ways of teaching, learning and knowing might students' families and backgrounds contribute to their growth and success in school?

## CONCLUSION

This study helps demonstrate that the pathway to literacy is a syncretic process in which individuals make use of existing resources from home, school and community to create a form of learning which is uniquely personal. The Osman family's resourcefulness in the face of many obstacles to their literacy learning helps dispel the myth that literacy and cognitive ability necessarily go hand-in-hand. The study also provides evidence that encouraging new language learners to use their native language supports them in the process of learning to speak, read, and write a second language, and that siblings and parents, as well as peers and those outside the immediate family, may all serve as mediators of language and culture for one another. It underscores the fact that literacy learning can no longer be considered a unidirectional process from adults to children, but a multigenrational, multidirectional process. Given the rapidly changing demographics in our country, it is imperative that educators, administrators, and policy makers reposition themselves to learn from, as well as teach, those whose cultures are different from mainstream America, because, as Gibbons (2002) asserts,

> Second language learners are not a homogeneous group, but are as varied in terms of their background, experiences, language, expectations, values, cultures and socio-economic status as any other group of students. More important, they can no longer be thought of as a group apart from the mainstream—in today's culturally and linguistically diverse classrooms, they *are* the mainstream. (p. 13)

## REFERENCES

Agar, M. (1996). *The professional stranger: An introduction to ethnography.* San Diego, CA: Academic Press.

Auerbach, E. (1997). Reading between the lines. In D. Taylor (Ed.), *Many families, many literacies* (pp. 71-81). Portsmouth, NH: Heinemann.

Bateson, M. (1994). *Peripheral visions: Learning along the way.* New York: Harper-Collins.

Berghoff, B, Egawa, K., Harste, J., & Hoonan, B. (2000). *Beyond reading and writing: Inquiry, curriculum, and multiple ways of knowing.* Urbana, IL: National Council of Teachers of English.

Cambourne, B. (1988). *The whole story: Natural learning and the acquisition of literacy in the classroom.* Auckland, New Zealand: Ashton Scholastic.

Compton-Lilly, C. (2004). *Confronting racism, poverty, and power: Classroom strategies to change the world.* Portsmouth, NH: Heinemann.

Delpit, L. (1995). *Other people's children.* New York: The New Press.

Donaldson, M. (1978). *Children's minds.* New York: W.W. Norton.

Duranti, A., & Ochs, E. (1997). Syncretic literacy in a Samoan-American family. In L. B. Resnick, R. Saljo, C. Pontecorvo, & B. Burge (Eds.), *Discourse, tools, and reasoning: Essays on situated cognition* (pp. 170-201). Berlin: Springer-Verlag.

Drury, R. (2004). Samia and Sadaqat play school: Early bilingual literacy at home. In E. Gregory, S. Long, & D. Volk (Eds.), *Many pathways to literacy: Young children learning with siblings, grandparents, peers, and communities* (pp. 40-51). New York: Routledge Falmer.

Duffy, J. (2000). Never hold a pencil: Rhetoric and relations in the concept of "preliteracy." *Written Communication*, *17*(2), 225-257.

Eisner, E. (1994). *Cognition and curriculum reconsidered.* New York: Teachers College Press.

Freire, P. (1998). *Teachers as cultural workers: Letters to those who dare to teach* (D. Macedo, D. Koike, & A. Olivera, Trans.). Bolder, CO: Westview Press

Gadsden, V. L. (2000). Intergenerational literacy within families. In M. L. Kamil, P. B. Mosenthal, P. D. Pearson, & R. Barr (Eds.), *Handbook of reading research* (Vol. 3, pp. 871-887). Mahwah, NJ: Erlbaum.

Gibbons, P. (2003). *Scaffolding language, scaffolding learners: Teaching second language learners in the mainstream classroom.* Portsmouth, NH: Heinemann.

Glaser, B., & Strauss, A. (1967). *The discovery of grounded theory: Strategies for qualitative research.* Chicago: Aldine.

Glesne, C. (1999). *Becoming qualitative researchers: An introduction.* New York: Longman.

Greenfield, P. M. (1994). Independence and interdependence as developmental scripts: Implications for theory, research, and practice. In P. M. Greenfield & R. R. Cocking (Eds.), *Cross-cultural roots of minority child development* (pp. 1-37). Hillsdale, NJ: Erlbaum.

Gregory, E. (2001). Sisters and brothers as language and literacy teachers: Synergy between siblings playing and working together. *Journal of Early Childhood Literacy*, *1*(3), pp. 301-322.

Gregory, E., Long, S., & Volk, D. (2004). *Many pathways to literacy: Young children learning with siblings, grandparents, peers, and communities.* New York: Routledge.

Halliday, M. A. K. (1978). *Language as social semiotic: The interpretation of language and meaning.* Baltimore: University Park Press.

Heath, S. (1983). *Ways with words: Language, life and work in communities and class-rooms.* Cambridge, United Kingdom: Cambridge University Press.

Hubbard, R., & Power, B. (1999). *Living the questions: A guide for teacher researchers.* Portland, ME: Stenhouse.

Lindfors, J. (1999). *Children's inquiry: Using language to make sense of the world.* New York: Teachers College Press.

Lobel, A. (1971). *Frog and Toad together.* New York: HarperCollins.

Lovgren, S. (2003). Refugees in the U.S.: One family's story. *National Geographic News.* Retrieved April 21, 2004, from http://news.nationalgeographic.com/news/2003/0620_030620_banturefugees.html

Marshall, C., & Rossman, G. (1999). *Designing qualitative research.* Thousand Oaks, CA: SAGE.

Mills, H., O'Keefe, T., & Jennings, L. (2004). *Looking closely and listening carefully: Learning literacy through inquiry.* Urbana, IL: National Council of Teachers of English.

Neito, S. (1999). *The light in their eyes: Creating multicultural learning communities.* New York: Teacher's College Press.

Rogoff, B. (1990). *Apprenticeship in thinking: Cognitive development in social context.* New York: Oxford University Press.

Rogoff, B. (2003). *The cultural nature of human development.* Oxford, England: Oxford University Press.

St. John's Episcopal Church. (2004). *Somali Bantu resettlement information.* Retrieved April 21, 2004, from http://www.stjohnscolumbia.org/somalibantu/history.htm

Spradley, J., & McCurdy, D. (1999). *Conformity and conflict: Readings in cultural anthropology.* Boston: Allyn & Bacon.

Taylor, D. (Ed.). (1997). *Many families, many literacies: An international declaration of principles.* Portsmouth, NH: Heinemann.

Van Lehman, D., & Eno, O. (2003). *The Somali Bantu: Their history and culture.* Washington, DC: Center for Applied Linguistics. Retrieved April 21, 2004, from http://culturalorientation.net

Vygotsky, L. (1978). *Mind in society: The development of higher psychological processes.* Cambridge, MA: Harvard University Press.

Wells, G. (1986). *The meaning makers: Children learning language and using language to learn.* Portsmouth, NH: Heinemann.

Wells, G. (1999). *Dialogic inquiry: Toward a socio-cultural practice and theory of education.* Cambridge, England: Cambridge University Press.

Whitin, D., Mills, H., & O'Keefe, T. (1990). *Living and learning mathematics: Stories and strategies for supporting mathematics literacy.* Portsmouth, NH: Heinemann.

**ASIAN FAMILIES**

CHAPTER 4

# WRITING IN KOREAN AND ENGLISH

## A Case Study of Parent-Child Interactions in a Korean Family

**Hye-Young Park**

This study has grown out of my desire to understand and help my son in his bilingual and bicultural development. What I learned from observing my son and examining my role as a language minority parent/tutor, along with what I learned from the difficulties I encountered as a mother/researcher are valuable contributions to the field. To preserve and develop my son's Korean literacy and culture while living and studying in the United States, where English monolingualism is the norm (Bernhardt, 2000), I needed to understand the sources of our interactional conflicts. To this end, I investigated our parent-child interactions in each writing context based on our different perspectives and experiences—as child and as mother/researcher—in the areas of language, culture, and stage of psychological development. I examined Danny's perception of the writing events and my role in the process over time. This chapter reports the findings of my investigation and is guided by the following research questions:

*Multicultural Families, Home Literacies, and Mainstream Schooling*
pp. 73–91

1.  What is the nature of our parent-child interactions during English writing and Korean writing respectively? Are there any differences in style between the two interactions?

2.  What are some difficulties that I face, as a language minority mother/researcher in the process of interacting with my son? Do my son and I have different perceptions about the origins of these difficulties?

3.  How does my child perceive my efforts as a writing helper and his writing tasks?

## THEORETICAL FRAMEWORK

My understanding of Danny's bilingual development was situated in two areas of research: language loss and Gee's D/discourse.

### Language Loss

While the number of foreign-born U.S. residents continues to rise, there has also been an increase in the number of immigrants of generation 1.5 (Danico, 2004), who often experience a first-language loss. A growing body of research analyzing first-language loss points to the negative consequences of that loss, including negative self-image and identity crises. Researchers have shown that many language learners adopted a negative view of their own cultural heritage or race in the process of losing their native language (e.g., Gee, 1996, 1999; Kouritzin, 1999; Li, 2002; Tse, 2001; Wong Fillmore, 1991, 2000). Wong Fillmore (1991) documented the pattern of Asian immigrants' heritage language loss. She found that in the United States, where minority languages are not highly valued and a strong emphasis on assimilation exists, children's loss of the first language has profound effects on their relationship with their parents and the community, and this can cause serious social and emotional problems. Tse (2001) also found that young participants in her study had no interest in learning their home language until they realized its value later in life. She concludes that "being accepted and avoiding alienation is perhaps one of the biggest pulls toward English, especially for children and adolescents" (p. 32).

### Gee's Discourses

According to Gee (1999), activities and identities are rarely accomplished through language alone (*discourse with little d*), but rather, they are enacted through language in conjunction with social interactions, non-linguistic symbol systems, and distinctive ways of thinking and feeling at a given time and place (*Discourse with big D*). From a sociocultural perspective, Gee (1996) suggested that when there are tensions between *our primary and secondary Discourses*, these tensions might lead to an "identity crisis." According to him, primary Discourse is the language and socio-cultural practice we are born into and forms our most important social identity, which is closely linked with first language maintenance. People also *learn* many secondary Discourses during their lives such as the schools and the social environments outside home, which also have a set of language and sociocultural practice attached to them. When the individual may experience a conflict between the two different linguistic/cultural D/discourse values and practices, and the social identity attached to a person's primary Discourse is challenged or devalued, s/he will resist his/her first language and identity.

The concept of "cultural models" is also important in the Discourses. Cultural models, a family of connected images shared by people belonging to a specific socio/cultural group, are linked to each other and help organize the thinking and social practices of such groups. Gee (1999) further explains,

> Cultural models can be about "appropriate" attitudes, viewpoints, beliefs, and values; "appropriate" ways of acting, interacting, participating, and participant structures; "appropriate" social, cultural, and institutional organizational structures; "appropriate" ways of talking, listening, writing, reading, and communicating; "appropriate" ways to feel or display emotion; "appropriate" ways in which real and fictional events, stories, and histories are organized and end, and so on and so forth. (p. 68)

Gee's theories of Discourses help me interpret how meanings are situated during my interactions with Danny in each writing context and understand that how our different ways of interacting may in part based on our different linguistic and cultural experiences.

## METHODS

### Research Sites

We live in Urbana-Champaign in Illinois, a Midwestern university town, situated about 140 miles south of Chicago. The rest of our family lives in and around Seoul, Korea, where we visited during the summer of 2004.

## The Bilingual Child: Danny

At the beginning of my study in the summer of 2004, Danny was entering fifth grade in a Champaign public school. Prior to entering U.S. schools, his Korean literacy was above his age level. Initially, I focused on helping him with his English rather than with maintaining his Korean skills. It was not until our 2004 summer trip to Korea that I fully recognized Danny's distress that he could not be understood in Korean and thus the need to bring more linguistic balance into his life. It was about then I started this study.

## Researcher/Mother as a Participant Observer/Observant Participant

I came to the United States with my only son, Danny, in May 2000. At that time, I held a bachelor's degree in English language and literature and a certificate in Teaching English to Speakers of Other Languages (TESOL). After earning a master's degree in science in elementary education at the State University of New York at Potsdam, I am currently pursuing my doctoral degree in language and literacy at the University of Illinois.

Through the study, I saw myself shifting roles between being an "insider," as a mother, and an "outsider" as a researcher. As an insider, I described myself, my son, my own culture, and our shared experiences in the Stake's (1995) form of a case study, whose focus is particularization, not generalization. According to him, the first emphasis is on uniqueness—what the case is and what it does—"that implies knowledge of others that the case is different from" (p. 8). I combined my own experience with that of my son in confessional and interpretive ways (Van Maanen, 1988). I could uncover subtle and sophisticated emotional and cultural elements in my son that only an insider could understand. On the other hand, as a former classroom teacher and doctoral student, I was able to observe what my bilingual son was going through, especially linguistically, in his daily life as an "outsider." This dual position allowed me to make meaning out of what I might have taken for granted from multiple perspectives and to construct my son's and my own stories in a way that would be more relevant and authentic than from either position alone.

## Data Collection

The study lasted from October to December 2004, although I included some data from 2005 and 2006. The data consist of: (1) transcriptions of seven audio and videotaped parent-child interactions; (2) two audio taped semistructured interviews with Danny; (3) Danny's six Korean and eight English writing samples; and (4) reflective journals by Danny and me.

## Design and Procedures

I asked Danny to write personal narratives in both languages at home. Once Danny had written on a topic in English or Korean, we discussed it in a parent-child interaction format to help him improve his first drafts. Seven interaction sessions were videotaped and/or audio taped after first drafts. My focus during the interactions, which lasted 15-20 minutes, was on organization, elaboration, and audience. After each of our parent-child interactions, I asked Danny to write a second draft independently.

In addition, semistructured interviews were conducted in English by me and a friend of mine. They were video and/or audio taped. The interview questions were loosely constructed around Danny's thoughts and feelings related to the writing process.

## Data Analysis

As is common in qualitative inquiry, I used constant comparative analysis (Glaser & Strauss, 1967) as I informally proceeded to identify themes in the data. Analysis began with my transcription of video and audio taped interactions. A large portion of Danny's writing and our P-C interactions were collected in Korean, which I translated into English in a literary version.[1] To increase the validity of my data, I asked a Korean-English bilingual to review my translation. I also allowed Danny to review the transcripts to see if the data reflected his own perceptions of his experiences.

I approached the data in two ways. First, I described the nature of our parent-child interactions and how they were the same or different between English and Korean writing development. Second, I also began to investigate Danny's perception of the interactions with me through two interview protocols. Overall I relied heavily on direct interpretation of my data in the form of Stake's intrinsic case study while embedded the analysis within Gee's theories of D/discourses.

## FINDINGS

My findings suggest that our parent-child interactions around Danny's English writing development proceeded smoothly while his Korean writing development often involved considerable conflicts. Additionally, Danny's perception of his writing tasks and me as a writing helper has

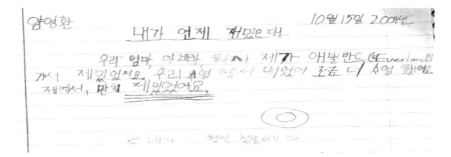

Figure 4.1.   "A time when I felt excited" (10/15/04). Translation: My mom, dad, and I went to Everland and were excited and we swam and ate, and swam a little more, I was very much excited.

changed over time. Last, parent-child interactions during Danny's writing development were clearly helpful to the child's biliteracy development even though there were considerable conflicts. In the following presentation of the detailed findings, I present findings on unsuccessful interactions, successful interactions, and Danny's perceptions of writing.

## Unsuccessful Interactions

### Limited Korean

While I was helping Danny with his Korean writing development, I faced many communication difficulties. Mainly, this appeared to result from differences in linguistic/cultural understanding between us. Our levels of *Discourse* that includes *discourse* were clearly different enough to have frequent communication difficulties. Here, I present the most representative Korean writing event to show the origins of difficulties: the first draft of a personal narrative Danny wrote entitled, "A time when I felt excited," which is the first Korean writing assignment that I gave to him (see Figure 4.1).

Danny finished up his first draft on his impression of his visit to Everland (the Korean version of Disneyland) during our stay in Korea. I was helping him to elaborate on the topic while we were sitting on the floor by the bed. I asked him to speak in Korean as long as he could understand my Korean. We immediately met a communication difficulty, which originated from Danny's limited Korean language, especially his lack of Korean vocabulary. The following is our first discussion about his Korean writing assignment on the Everland trip.

**Vignette 1-1: Fun or Crying? [excerpts from transcript 10/17/04]**

M (Mom): 자, 네가 즐거울때, 행복할때 그지? (Let's see, you had fun, you were happy, uh?)

S (Son): 즐거울때? (I had fun?)

M: 응, 네가 행복할때! (Yes, you were happy!)

S: You said, "즐거울때." ("When I had fun.")

M: 즐거울때도 되고 즐거운게 행복 한것이잖아. (It is OK to say, "had fun" since having fun is being happy.)...

S: 즐거운게 우는것 아네요? (Isn't "Having fun" crying?)

It is clear in this vignette that Danny's lack of Korean vocabulary led to the communication difficulty. Danny did not know the meaning of 즐거울때 (having fun) when I equated it with 행복할때 (being happy). Soon after, we had another difficulty that resulted from Danny's limited Korean:

**Vignette 1-2: Swam or Saw?**

M: ...근데 에버랜드 가서 너 뭘 봤니? 수영만 했어? (And when we went to Everland, what did you see? We only swam there?)

S: 네, 수영 봤어요. (Yes, I saw swimming.)

M: 수영만 했어? 사람들도 봤잖아! (Did you only swim? We also saw people!)

S: 네 (Yes.)

M: 거기서 뭘 봤어? (What did you see there?)

S: You are not making sense. You said, "수영했어? 사람도 봤지! 했어? 봤어?" ("Did you swim? You saw people. Swam? Saw?")

Again, in vignette 1-2, there was a communication conflict. After reading over the transcript, I came to realize that an important part of the communication problem was mine. I was too impatient to wait for him to answer my question, "What did you see?" before asking him another question, "Did you only swim there?" All he could hear seems to be the two verbs, "swim" and "see." He couldn't make connection between the two when he answered like, "Yes, I saw swimming." My fast Korean might have overwhelmed him when his level of Korean proficiency did not catch where I was going. It seems that his lack of Korean language ability led him to interpret my words *literally* and not comprehend them in the overall *context*. For example, in vignette 1-2, in response to "Did you only swim? We also saw people!" Danny should have told me, "No, I swam there and I also saw people swimming" instead of "Yes, I saw swimming."

My intention to help him with elaborating about the event did not go well. In addition to these difficulties due to Danny's limited Korean, we also experienced communication breakdowns due to our growing cultural differences. The next few minutes of dialogue reflect these differences.

## *Different Perspectives*

### Vignette 1-4: Time, Money, Refills?

M: 햄버거 샀는데 안 좋은 점도 있었잖아! 사람이 너무 많아 가지고 얼마나 많이 기다렸니? (We bought hamburgers, but there were some things we didn't like. Think about how long we waited?)

S: 많이 안 기다렸어. (We didn't wait so long.)

M: 응? 많이 안 기다렸어? (Uh? we didn't wait so long?)

S: 네, 뭐 5분.... (No, about 5 minutes....)

M: 쭉 기다렸잖아. 그리고 거기 비싸지 않았니? (We were waiting in line for quite a while. And didn't you think it was expensive?)

S: 아니요, 뭐 거의다 만원 패밀리 팩. (No, it was only about $10 for a family pack.)

M: 음 ... 사람들도 많고 줄도 많이 섰잖아! 리필도 한번밖에 안되고 (Hum... there were lots of people and we were waiting in line for a long time. Besides, we couldn't refill more than once!)

S: 뭐요? (What did you say?) 아니예요. 리필 많이 했어요. 뭐 몰라요? (That's not true. We refilled a lot. Don't you know?) 아빠 (My dad) said he wanted grape juice. So, 제가 가져 왔어요. (I brought it.)

M: 음.... (Hum....) [Thinking that was not right, suppressing my impatience!]

S: 물어보면 되요. (You can ask.) Grape juice 줘보세요, 해서 줘요. (Give me grape juice, and then they will give it to you.)

Here, although my intention was to help him elaborate on his writing, I struggled to let go of my control over the situation. We experienced the same event from different perspectives. Here, there was disagreement on the waiting time, price, and refilling of drinks when we had lunch in Everland. It appeared that I approached the event with adult eyes while my son approached it with the eyes of a child. In Danny's mind, the waiting time seemed to be much shorter than it was, since he was excited to be at Everland. For me, however, it felt like more than one hour. But from looking at my watch, I knew that the actual time was 20 minutes. This difference of perception is probably more due to age (*children's Discourse versus that of adults*) than linguistic or western/ eastern cultural experiences. He was not trying to placate me. He simply expressed his perception of the event.

In terms of the way he responded to me, although he used proper honorific Korean endings, his constant negation of my perception was disagreeable to me. I felt upset and could hear myself thinking, 'How dare he disagree with me? When an adult says something, you had better listen!' My feelings and normative expectations were determined by my Korean Confucian upbringing (*Confucian Discourse*), while his responses seemed to be influenced by his experiences living in the United States. Whereas I was raised under a Confucian value system, in which a linear hierarchy governs family structures and other social institutions, Danny had not fully internalized these cultural norms of Korea. My expectation that he would follow the same Confucian conventions—such as respect for authority, and especially obedience on the part of young people toward their elders—was not fulfilled. On the contrary, his confrontational attitude during our interactions irritated me. The next few minutes of dialogue contained a communication difficulty that came form our different perspective on my role as a wring helper:

### Vignette 1-6: Helping or Being Bossy?

M: You just wrote two lines!

S: 알았어요. (I see.) [But] you said write as much as I could!

M: 엄마가 Blame 하는 것 아니야! 거기 갔더니 뭐 어떤 사람은 뭐하고 또 어떤 사람은 저거하고, 우리가 재미있는 시간을 보냈고, blah, blah, blah.... 엄마가 도와줄께, 알았지? 네가 한번 해 봐! (I am not blaming you! Write some thing like, "When we went there, we saw people were doing this or doing that [all sorts of things], blah, blah, blah.... And we had a good time, right? Write those things! I will help you with your writing of course. Why don't you try?)

He seems to understand my desire to help him elaborate on his writing as a criticism of the amount that he actually wrote, thinking that I changed the instructions. Perhaps, it is the tone of my voice. I wonder if his response is gender related since boys tend to be more goal-oriented. From his perspective, he might have thought that he had finished with what I had asked him to do. Thus, the goal was achieved and he did not understand why we had to talk about it further. The conversation continued:

M: 그리고 먹을때도 줄서서 기다렸다는 것 뭐 이런것 좀 자세히 써야 되지않니?
(For example, when it comes to eating, you should have written about your waiting in line in greater detail, right?)

S: You said I might write as much as I can. I couldn't.

M: 왜 못해? 왜 못써? (Why you couldn't? Why couldn't?)

S: You said I might write as much as I can!

M: 근데 왜 더 못 썼어? (OK, but why couldn't you write more?)

S: That's what I could write!

Perhaps, I had expected a certain amount of writing from him. I might have thought that he simply did not want to write when perhaps he was not able to. After our interaction, he wrote his second draft (see Figure 4.2).

Danny's initial Korean personal narrative writing tended to be list-like, and voiceless. In his second draft, Danny added some facts and added the sentence, "We waited in a line for a long time," which he wasn't in agreement with me in a personal narrative in Korean. I also found that Danny's English writing was better than his Korean writing with the same topic.

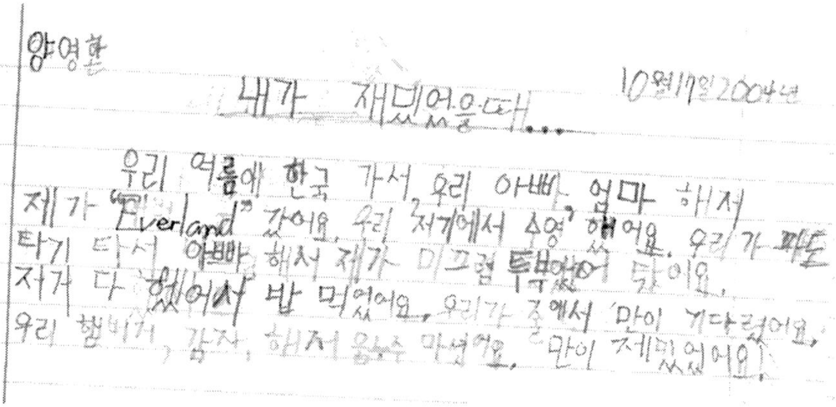

양영훈

내가 재밌었을때...                    10월17일 2004년

제가 "Everland" 우리 여름에 한국 가서, 우리 아빠, 엄마 해서
타기 다시 아빠 해서 제가 그럼 탔어요. 우리가
자가 다 했어서 밥 먹었어요, 우리가 줄에서 '마이 기다렸어요,
우리 형누가 감자, 해서 음수 마셨어요, 마이 재밌었어요.

Figure 4.2.   Danny's second draft. Translation: We visited Korea. And my mom, dad, and I went to "Everland" and we swam there. We rode a wave and Dad and I did water sliding. After that, we ate. We waited in line for a long time. We drank [sic] hamburger, potato, and soft drinks. I was very much excited!

Writing in English was more expressive of his feelings and it contained better and more extensive arguments, making his sentence structure sophisticated and accordingly, the sentences longer, while writing in Korean was flat and fact oriented with limited vocabulary. He wrote in English on the same topic:

A time when I was happy 11/05/04

A time I was happy, exited, and enjoyed at the same time is when my mom, dad, and I went to Everland. Everland is a place where you can do a lot of stuff such as swim, go on waterslides, ride a roller coaster, ride ferries wheels, go to a circus, pet animals, feed them, and even go to gift shops.... We went swimming and we did. First we found lockers, then took a quick shower, after that, we wore our swimming suits. Then we met at a place. Then, we raced to an outside pool and splashed water at each other. After a short while, we heard a "boop boop" and that meant that a great wave would charge at us after the sound. It almost looked like a tidal wave! It was fun because it's like you surfing barefooted, but your legs are buried in the water! After that we went the water slides. We had to ride on these tubes so we would be safe. Sometimes we took the double tubes and sometimes we would go on single tubes. Then, it was a little late. So we began to get our cloths and pack to go home. I thought there would be no day greater than this!!!

In this section, I showed two origins of communication difficulties during Danny's Korean writing development. Danny Korean language use, was not compatible with that of mine. I felt I was superior to Danny, since

I am older and an "expert" at what it means to be a Korean. In addition, Danny's *Children's Discourse* was not compatible with that of mine as an adult. On the other hand, in the English writing context, I seemed to put myself on a more equal footing; we both have a similar level of American linguistic/cultural understanding *(secondary Discourse)*. Next, I demonstrate how freely our parent-child interactions were flowing during Danny's English writing development.

## Successful Interactions

### *Eliciting Advice*

Figure 4.3 represents the English piece that demonstrated Danny's struggle in his American school in the fall of 2003 when we first moved to Champaign. It revealed that he saw a racial barrier between American kids and himself. See Figure 4.3 for his first draft.

This experience was very traumatic for Danny. I tried to help him relieve his emotional conflicts. In the next vignette, we discussed ways of dealing with bullies while sitting on the floor next to each other.

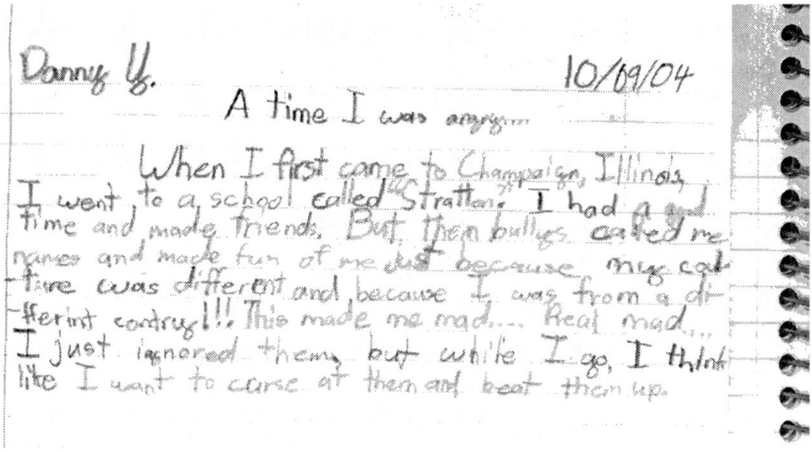
Danny Y. 10/09/04
A time I was angry....
When I first came to Champaign, Illinois, I went to a school called "Stratton." I had a good time and made friends. But then bullies called me names and made fun of me just because my cul-ture was different and because I was from a di-fferint contry!!! This made me mad.... Real mad... I just ignored them, but while I go, I think like I want to curse at them and beat them up.

Figure 4.3. A time I was angry ... (10/09/04). When I first came to Champaign, Illinois, I went to a school called "Stratton." I had a good time and made friends. But then bullies called me names and made fun of me just because my culture was different and because I was from a different country!!! This made me mad.... Real mad.... I just ignored them, but while I go, I think like I want to curse at them and beat them up.

**Vignette 2-1: Why Did They Do? [excerpts from transcript 10/13/04]**

M: But, why did they do?
S: I don't know. They just, like, pick on kids that are smaller than them.
M: They just try to show off or ...?
S: Yeah, and people cry and stuff.
M: Oh so, they want you to feel bad?
S: Well they, yeah, they call me names so, so like they are trying to make people scared of them.
M: But, even if you are not from a different country or culture, they still would make fun of you, right?
S: Yeah, they do.
M: But why did you say, like, because I'm...
S: Well, I mean, from my culture, they call me "ching chong" and stuffs, but other people they say, you know...
M: Different things?
S: Yeah!

We talked about how Danny could deal with his differences from American children. I pointed out to him that the problem was not necessarily a cultural one, but something that happens to new kids in many social situations. Immediate acceptance by peers rarely happens especially in the school setting. It is apparent to the reader that any American mom could be saying the same things to her children, but the differences in race and culture are never far from consciousness. Here is another example of my effort to help Danny deal with bullies. As demonstrated in this conversation, I was a continuous coconstructor through collaborative reasoning (Waggoner, Chinn, Yi, & Anderson, 1995).

**Vignette 2-2: Just Ignore Them**

M: ... So if this kind of thing happens again, how are you gonna act? You said you were really mad.
S: Just tell the teacher, or say, "Stop it!" ... in a mean way ...
M: So actually, if you are mad, that means you make them happy, right? By making you feel mad?
S: Yeah.
M: That is their goal, right? So what are you going to do?
S: Just ignore them, just go somewhere else.
M: Yeah, right! Just ignore them, and don't let them bother you, right?
S: Because if I stop, they feel I am a boring person [since I do not act in the way they expect me to do such as getting mad].

### Sharing Problems

In the following vignette, I tried to indicate a cross-cultural problem that I had experienced, which Danny also was experiencing. It is about my classroom experience. Most of my fellow students in class were white

American or Canadian citizens. I often found myself the only person in class from a different continent.

### Vignette 2-3: I Had the Same Problem

M: ...You know what? I had the same problem. When I was in the elementary education program, all the people in my class were native speakers...
S: Uh huh...
M: All native speaking Americans, except me. In my class, we were assigned to groups of four. In my group, three of the people were Canadians. We were supposed to discuss the issues raised in the class. I tried to listen to them. I tried to show I was listening by saying, "yeah, right," etc. Nodding my head all the time like this (gesturing). But you know what? They just ignored me. They just acted as if I was not there! So I felt really mad and upset! You know what I mean?
S: It's just like you are saying, "Hey, guys! What are you talking about?" And they just keep on talking among themselves.
M: Yeah, I tried to show them I was listening. I was...
S: Cooperating?
M: I felt like I was absolutely ignored.
S: Yeah.
M: I felt tears in my eyes. I went to the bathroom and cried. I cried out of anger and out of sorrow. I wiped my tears and decided to say something to them. I came back and I said clearly, "Are you going to be a teacher? .... What if in your classroom maybe, one of your students comes from a different country...
S: Are you just going to ignore them?
M: ... Are you going to ignore them just like you are ignoring me. Just because they speak or they act differently than you do? What are you going to do as a teacher? And they just remained silent...so I just spoke out... but I didn't want to get mad. I just tried to reason with them while trying to calm down.

Danny could see that I was a person who had similar feelings, coming from the same sociocultural background as he does, and I had faced a similar problem. He felt sympathetic, highly engaged, and even anticipated what I was going to say.

## Coaching Role
Here, I was a writing helper and coached Danny with a conclusion.

### Vignette 2-4: They Will Stop Doing It Because ...

M: In the last part, say what would you do if it happens again? And why? If you see the person like you ...
S: What are you going to do?
M: What is your advice?

S: Maybe like, you guys shouldn't be talking. Because bullies keep on calling names with their throats, their throats run out. Names don't hurt me.

As seen in vignette 2-4, Danny sometimes viewed me as a coconstructor, an advising parent, a person from the same world, and a writing helper. In his second draft, he wrote:

A time I was angry…10/16/04

When I first came to Champaign, Illinois, I went to a school called "Stratton." When I went to the school, most of the people were nice to me. The other people were either people that called me names or … bullies. They beat people up, and pushed people that are younger than them around. They called me certain names "Ching Chong" and stuffs like. They called me certain names just because I was from another country! What they want me to feel is to be afraid of them. But I just ignore them and just walk away. Then the bullies will be bored and walk away! So here is some advice. See a bully calling you a name? Follow my advice.

In Danny's English writing after interaction, he seemed to have internalized the social skills he acquired in oral discussion with me and was able to transfer the schema to written argument independently. Both of Danny's first and final draft narratives entitled *A Time I was Angry* showed that he focused on one topic in sequence and his voice was clear. However, in his first draft, he just expressed his anger toward some of bullies whereas in his second draft, he provided some more details and evaluative comments about helping the people who might experience a similar situation. In his second draft, he also positioned himself in relation to his audience, confirming that my role as a tutor and mother had a positive impact on his writing development.

## Perceptions

In the preceding findings, I focused the differences in style of our parent-child interactions between Korean writing context and English writing context. The following finding section reflects that Danny's perception of the origins of our difficulties is similar to mine. Also, it shows that Danny's perception of his writing tasks and my role as a writing helper have changed over time.

A few days after his second Korean piece, titled *A Time When I was Happy*, I had a chance to interview Danny about his perceptions of his interactions with the writing tasks and me.

**Vignette 3-1: My Interview With Danny [transcript 10/20/04].**

M: How is writing in English and Korean different?

S: Writing in English is easier than writing in Korean because I know English more than Korean. I can't think of the word when I write in Korean sometimes.

M: Do you think that your mom was helpful when she was asking you to write in detail more? Would you speak frankly?

S: A little bit actually one-third out of a whole.

M: In what way did your mom help?

S: When I don't know the word in Korean, my mom tells me and she helps me with elaborating.

I started as an interviewer. Soon after, I shifted into my role as mom by referring to myself as "me" rather than "your mom." The tone of our conversation changed.

**Vignette 3-2: Bossy Mom?**

M: Why did you disagree with me when we talked about writing in Korean?

S: Because you told me to write as much as I could. It could be even one line. But then, you said to do this and that?

M: What are this and that?

S: By saying you should have done this and that.

M: How about in English?

S: You corrected me, and I agreed because it was right.

M: How about in Korean?

S: We got confused because we disagreed on our words.

M: You were not cooperative.

S: How was I not cooperative?

M: You disagreed on whatever I said.

S: Because, what I was saying was true!

M: Do you think I was helpful with writing in Korean?

S: Well … 260 out of 1000."

M: How different was I when I helped with Korean writing and English writing?

S: In English, we cooperated well and we agreed on what we disagreed about. In Korean, we didn't cooperate well and we disagreed on each other's words.

M: Why do you think it happened like that? I felt mad…

S: You and I were mad because you argued about our memory [of events] and words.

This interview reveals an agreement between us and the ways in which we identified the origins of our difficulties. For example, in Danny's response to one of my questions, "You [Mom] and I were mad because you argued about our memory [of events] and words." In addition, this interaction shows a conflict between cultural models and the social hierarchy I expected between us (*Confucian Discourse*). Also, Danny's quantification of the amount of help from me was at odds with the way most Korean children would respond to the question, "Do you think that your mom was helpful?" Typically, they would say, "Yes, you helped me a lot, a little, or you did not help me at all." I speculate that he may have picked up this sort of numerical response from his school: his westernized way of thinking. Despite our different perspectives and the failure of being a dispassionate researcher, the interview protocols reflected that Danny and I were honest and direct about our feelings.

A year and a half later, in an effort to see if Danny would open up more with someone else, I asked my friend, Ted to interview him. The following interview protocol suggests that he was able to appreciate my efforts. Also, it reflects his motivation about Korean writing.

**Vignette 3-3: Ted's Interview With Danny [transcript 04/16/06]**

T (Ted): If you had to continue to work with your mom on your Korean writing, what would you improve the most?
D (Danny): ... when I show it to her, she usually says "write more write more"; or she helps me to elaborate and corrects my spelling and she doesn't say to write more out of expressing anger, but she says it because of me and for my benefit and so I can learn more and increase my language for the future of [for] my benefit.
T: Why do you think it is important to learn to write in Korean?
D: Because I am from Korea and it would be shameful if I didn't know how to write in Korean. If it wasn't [weren't] for the training, I would've still been writing 2 or 3 sentence stories ... I wouldn't be writing 30 sentence stories. But I am doing [that] right now!

## DISCUSSION AND CONCLUSION

In the preceding section, I have illustrated how my interactions with my son during Korean writing were different from those of English writing development and Danny's perception of my efforts and his writing tasks. The findings from the study have some implications for first language maintenance for language minority parents.

As my stories suggest, I have experienced a good deal of frustration and sometimes feel overwhelmed by the difficulty of raising my bilingual son. I have learned from my informal conversations with many Korean, Chinese, and South Asian parents that, like me, this frustration has lead many of them to give up the effort of helping their children develop their first language. Some of the justifications they have given are: (1) "I have done my best and I cannot help it! Enough is enough!" and/or (2) "My children will live in the US and why bother to teach them their native language?" In the first case, we might have done our best according to our own perspective without considering our children's unique cultural/linguistic situation. Throughout my experience in the United States, I have noticed that parents and educators, including me often do not have the ability to recognize the strengths and needs of bilingual children. More often, we feel that we do not have time to deal with them.

In the second case, even though first-language loss is strongly related to negative consequences, many people from language minority homes, including me, often do not see the value in our native languages until we lose it (Kouritzin, 1999). It is really a challenge to bring up our children bilingually/culturally, especially when they are not fortunate enough to be in a school that offers native language support. However, it is also true that we, language minority parents, who communicate on a daily basis with our children, have language resources and a special advantage in bringing them up bilingually in a foreign country. We should take initial action to enable our children to develop biliteracy rather than feel the pain of regret later.

Some of the factors that might be responsible for the difficulty to maintain first language at home come from the fact that bilinguals have almost always been evaluated in terms of monolingual standards (Grosjean, 2002). For example, my expectations for Danny's Korean writing achievement were based on those for a monolingual Korean child. This suggests that depending on which perspective we take, being bicultural/bilingual can be interpreted as an asset or a problem. Grosjean (2002) suggests that we must redefine bilinguals within bilingual standards. Similarly, Pennycook (2001) proposes the notion of "heterosis" when understanding bilinguals, which refers to "the creative expansion of possibilities resulting from hybridity with the notion of synergy as the productive melding of two elements to create something larger than the sum of its parts" (p. 9).

In conclusion, my hope is that this case study will provide some insights about the linguistic and cultural issues surrounding interactions between language minority parents and their children in the United States. However, I do not intend to generalize about parent-child interactions in other Korean, Korean-American, or Asian American families. As Stake (1995) explains:

> We are interested in it [this particular case], not because by studying it we learn about other cases or about some general problem, but because we need to learn about that particular case.... We are often amazed at how much readers will recognize as relevant to their own cases, even though in many ways the studied cases are different. (pp. 3, 7)

I believe more in-depth explorations of the difficulties language minority parents and children encounter around writing in their home settings should be carried out in an effort to provide educators and parents with better understandings of the challenges they might face in home literacy learning and identify specific ways for structuring more effective language and literacy lessons in their school instruction.

## NOTE

According to McCarthey, Guo, and Cummins (2005), literary version is a kind of translation which focuses on the content rather than word for word meaning.

## REFERENCES

Bernhardt, E. (2000). Second-language reading as case study of reading scholarship in the 20th century. In M. Kamil, P. B. Mosentahl, P. D. Pearson, & R. Barr (Eds.), *Handbook of reading research* (Vol. 3, pp. 791-811. Mahwah, NJ: Earlbaum.

Danico, M. (2004). *The 1.5generation: Becoming Korean American in Hawaii.* Honolulu: University of Hawaii Press.

Gee, J. P. (1996). *Social linguistics and literacies: Ideology in Discourses* (2nd ed.). London: Taylor & Francis.

Gee, J. P. (1999). *An introduction to discourse analysis: Theory and method.* London: Routledge.

Glaser, B. G., & Strauss, A. L. (1967). *The discovery of ground theory.* Chicago: Aldine.

Kouritzin, S. G. (1999). *Face(t)s of first language loss.* Mahwah, NJ: Erlbaum.

Grosjean, F. (2002). *An interview of François Grosjean on bilingualism.* Retrieved February 28, 2005, from http://www.unine.ch/ltlp/grosjean.html

Li, G. (2002) *"East is East, West is West?": Home literacy, culture, and schooling.* New York: Peter Lang.

McCarthey, S. J., Guo, Y. H., & Cummins, S. (2005). Understanding changes in Mandarin elementary students' L1 and L2 writing. *Journal of Second Language Writing, 14*(2), 71-104.

Pennycook, A. (2001). *Critical applied linguistics.* Mahwah, NJ: Erlbaum.

Stake, R. (1995). *The art of case study research.* Thousand Oaks, CA: SAGE.

Tse, L. (2001). *"Why don't they learn English?"* New York: Teachers College Press.

Van Maanen, J. (Ed.). (1988). *Tales of the field: On writing ethnography.* Chicago: University of Chicago Press.

Waggoner, M. A., Chinn, C. A., Yi, H., & Anderson, R. C. (1995). Collaborate reasoning about stories. *Language Arts, 72,* 582-589.

Wong Fillmore, L. (1991). When learning a second language means losing the first. *Early Childhood Research Quarterly, 6,* 323-346.

Wong Fillmore, L. (2000). Loss of family languages: Should educators be concerned? *Theory into practice, 39*(4), 203–210.

CHAPTER 5

# FAMILY LITERACY

## Learning From an Asian Immigrant Family

**Guofang Li**

More children from many diverse linguistic, cultural, religious, and even academic backgrounds are attending North American schools (Garcia, 1999; Moll & González, 1994). In fact, the changing demographics in today's schools pose unprecedented need for literacy educators to understand children's outside school literacy experiences (Au, 1993; Valdés, 1998). Important questions arise when many classroom teachers try to understand children from diverse cultural and linguistic backgrounds in order to better facilitate these children's learning in their classrooms. For example, in what ways is the literacy learning of children from diverse backgrounds supported at home? How do their home literacy learning experiences differ from their school experiences? How might children's home experiences inform us about fostering children's literacy learning in school? In order to address these questions, I studied a Chinese immigrant student's (i.e., Yang Li's) home literacy practices, and explored ways his family supported his school learning as he made his cultural and literacy transitions to North American society. Below, I provide a brief biography of Yang Li's family.

*Multicultural Families, Home Literacies, and Mainstream Schooling*
pp. 93–110

## YANG LI AND HIS FAMILY

Six-year-old Yang Li was a first grade student. He moved to Canada in 1997, with his mother to join his father who was a student at a Canadian university. Yang Li's father, Li-yong, a former engineer in China, was pursuing his master's degree in chemistry. His mother, Nie-dong, also a former engineer, was a lab assistant at the University.

Yang Li and his family lived in a crowded one-bedroom second-floor apartment above a Chinese cafe. There were five apartments on the second floor including two one-bedroom apartments and three single rooms. Seven people lived in five apartments and shared two bathrooms. All adults were university students including four Chinese (including the Li family), two East Indians, and one Canadian. I visited the Li family at their apartment weekly for eight months in order to explore their home literacy practices, interactions, and routines, relating to the literacy events in their home. I also asked Yang's parents regarding their beliefs about literacy and Yang's learning in cross-cultural contexts. Additionally, I collected samples of Yang's writing and drawing, and participated in some of the games and activities Yang played with his parents. Below, I describe in detail Yang's home literacy practices.

## FOUR FACETS OF HOME LITERACY PRACTICES

In order to better present Yang Li's home literacy practices and how they differ from school practices, I used Leseman and de Jong's (1998) four interrelated facets of home literacy practices as themes to categorize Yang's experiences at home: (a) literacy opportunity, (b) instruction, (c) cooperation, and (d) socioemotional quality. Literacy opportunity refers to children's interactions with literacy of whatever kind, in whatever form in the home milieu. These interactions include children's direct contact with print, chances to observe parents' reading and writing activities, exposure to media, and opportunities for joint reading and writing practices. Literacy instruction refers to direct or indirect guidance provided by parents to the child through literacy activities. Leseman and de Jong's concept of instruction only includes parents' guidance to a child during shared storybook reading such as parents' procedural utterances, pointing, labeling, repeating and completing, explaining, evaluating, and extending. I extend the concept of instruction to more explicit and deliberate teaching using different texts and strategies in literacy related activities at home. Literacy cooperation involves active participation of a child in the literacy related events. A child's cooperation in literacy activities is reflected in the child's understanding and acceptance of the role s/he plays in activities and how s/he responds to the parents' literacy instructions. Socioemotional quality is an affective factor that includes indicators such as the bond between the parents and the child. In this study, I extended the notion of socioemotional quality to include the pressures from home and school that affected Yang's emotional well-being.

In the following section, I illustrate Yang Li's literacy learning at home and ways his parents supported his literacy development relative to these four facets described above. Although I discuss each facet as a separate category, as Yang's story indicates, these four facets are interrelated and sometimes overlapping.

## Yang's Literacy Opportunities in the Home Milieu

Yang's home environment was characterized by a rich presence of print, media, and other literacy materials such as books and maps. In this positive literacy environment, Yang had opportunities not only to have direct contact with reading and writing, but also to observe his parents' reading and writing in both English and Chinese. In addition, Yang's interaction with literacy also occurred in a variety of settings such as shopping centers, the library, bookstores, and through a variety of media such as flyers and computers.

### Literacy Opportunities Inside the Home

Yang's parents, Nie-dong and Li-yong, made use of their limited space in their one-bedroom apartment to provide Yang with different learning opportunities. There were bookshelves along one side of the wall where Yang had his own book section. Yang's section included several books written in English that were borrowed from the public library such as *Are You my Mother* by P. D. Eastman (1967), *One Day at the Supermarket* by Donna Bryant (1989), *I Want to be an Astronaut* by Byron Barton (1988) and some other books written in Chinese and English that belonged to Yang. The Chinese books included Chinese language arts and math textbooks, and some Chinese storybooks such as *The Collection of Children's Fables* (Beijing Children's Press). The English books he had included *Elephant Family* by Jane Goodall (1991), *Disney's Mulan* by Gina Ingoglia (1998), and *I Can Read About Seasons* by Robyn Supraner (1999). Yang also subscribed to a magazine called *Owl* (Young Naturalist Foundation). Yang's parents also used the space on the wall of their bedroom to help Yang's learning. The other side of the wall displayed a big world map where Yang was taught about world geography whenever they had time. Beside the map, Yang's parents hung an English alphabet with lower and upper cases, and illustrations of the letters so that Yang could look at the chart and learn any time he wanted.

Yang also had multiple opportunities to use paper and pencils. Yang often sat at the desk in one corner of their bedroom drawing pictures, copying textbooks, or studying math. Sometimes he just lay on his bed to draw or write. His finished and unfinished drawings were lying everywhere on the desk and on the beds. Yang was accustomed to reading and writing as his parents often wrote and read at home. His parents read a variety of materials at home. For example, his father read the Chinese newspaper, *China Daily Overseas Edition,* almost daily. He often brought his textbooks, lab manuals, and research papers from school to read at home. Whenever he had time, he studied English using TOEFL (Test of English as a Foreign Language) and GRE (Graduate Record Examination) workbooks and Chinese-English dictionaries. To improve his listening comprehension, he used a Walkman to listen to English tapes. Yang's mother read some Chinese magazines borrowed from friends or downloaded from the Internet. Sometimes she read some English newspapers such as the *National Post.* The English materials she read to improve her English were the Jehovah's Witness monthly publications: *The Watchtower: Announcing Jehovah's Kingdom* and *Awake!* Like her husband, she read chemistry lab materials and wrote some lab reports at home whenever she was busy at work. Therefore, for Yang, reading and writing were inseparable parts of his family's daily life.

Exposure to Western media was also an important part of Yang's home experiences. Yang watched lots of cartoons and movies such as *Mulan, Air Force One* and *Speed,* and different TV programs such as the animated Eddie Murphy show *The JPs, Bug's Bunny, CBC Playground* and *The Simpsons.* Watching TV and videos was considered a learning tool for Yang. The TV was always on with closed captioning, so he could listen and see the words simultaneously. Sometimes, Yang mimicked long English sentences to his mother without understanding what they meant. In Chinese, Nie-dong would ask, "What are you talking about? Say it again?" Yang just smiled, "I just learned from TV." Sometimes, after watching TV programs, he drew pictures of the cartoon characters such as Chippy Go-Road Runner, Penguins, Tweety and Puddy cat.

### Literacy Opportunities Outside the Home

Yang's exposure to reading and writing was not limited to the boundaries of their apartment. Li-yong and Nie-dong made an effort to take Yang to a variety of places where Yang could learn more English. They treated outings as important learning opportunities and made use of whatever "teachable moments" were available. For example, they took Yang shopping with them and showed Yang how to read flyers. Yang's dream was to become president of a country and have a huge house with big computers. When his parents read the flyers for groceries, Yang read the sections for furniture and computers for his future house and office. He liked to look through the flyers of Future Shop or Home Hardware. "I like this one. This is for my office. That one is for mom. Mine is the biggest!" he said in Chinese, "But mine costs a lot of money, lots lots of money. I need to make money first!"

Li-yong and Nie-dong also took Yang to his favorite downtown library to borrow storybooks. Yang learned how to find books he wanted on the computer and then locate them in the library. Once when I was with him in the library, he sat in front of the computer, and entered the book title he wanted with out my help. He scrolled down and selected the book, and then he copied the call number onto a piece of paper. After that, we went together to find the book. When we were ready to go, Yang handed the librarian his card and checked out all his books.

Besides the library, Yang also visited some bookstores in town where his parents bought workbooks to enhance Yang's academic development in either English or math. Whenever there was a book sale somewhere, Yang's parents tried to buy books and magazines to cultivate Yang's interests in science and geography. For example, Yang was first introduced to the children's magazine *Owl* at one of the book fairs where they bought several issues for five cents each.

Some evenings when both of his parents were busy with their work, Yang went with them to their lab where they could work on their experiments and supervise Yang at the same time. During this time, Yang sat for hours in front of a computer playing games. He often shouted and repeated after the voices from the games: "Game over, Man! Game Over!" or "Oops! You missed!"

Although Yang was provided with many different literacy opportunities in a variety of settings inside and outside the home, and his English was improving, his parents did not stop at merely exposing him to the English language. Instead, they took active measures to teach him English and prepare him for Canadian schooling. In the next section, I illustrate the various instructional strategies Yang's parents used to help him learn English.

### Literacy Instructions in the Home Milieu

Yang's parents used the instructional strategies specified by Leseman and de Jong (1998) such as procedural utterances, pointing, and explaining during their parent-child shared story reading. Since these strategies are the same as the mainstream practices, I will not touch upon them in this section. Instead, I focus on Yang's parents' unique instructional practices that are rooted in their Chinese cultural background. These unique practices include explicit instructions using bilingual word lists, worksheets and rote-learning approaches.

Yang attended kindergarten only briefly in China before moving to Canada. When Yang first moved to Canada, he was placed in first grade without even knowing English. He did not understand what the teacher and students said and out of frustration he cried in class almost every day during the first month. The other children called him a "cry-boy." Even when Yang knew a lot about a topic (for example, about animals), he could not make the teacher recognize his ability because of his language difference. His teacher called on other children who were bilingual to help him. Yang often came home and asked his mom if he was stupid and told her that it was not very good to be Chinese.

Yang's English had been a concern for Li-yong and Nie-dong since he began school. Li-yong and Nie-dong used many methods to teach Yang English and prepare him for school. They made flash cards to teach him the English alphabet. After Yang learned the basic alphabet, his parents made bilingual word lists in both Chinese and English from some children's books they borrowed from the public library. Yang read, memorized, recited, and copied (at least twice) all the words every day. For example, Yang's parents made a bilingual word list based on several children's books such as *Daddy* and *Mr. Mugs* from the library. They broke the sentences down into words, and listed the Chinese words on the side of the English words. Sometimes, they made bilingual word lists by themes such as animals and household items (see Figure 5.1). This approach was the way Nie-dong and Li-yong learned English, especially English vocabulary. They liked this approach because they observed that by having Chinese meaning of the words presented there, it was easier for Yang to understand the meaning of the English words. Yang's mother explains:

> Yang learns the meaning of words in Chinese first. Unlike English as first-language learners who, once they learn how to read a word, understand the meaning. For Yang, the procedure is more complicated—he has to internalize the meaning in Chinese after learning a new English word, then he can get the meaning of the English words.

Since Yang attended kindergarten for a short time in China, in order for him to have a sense of language continuity, his parents continued to teach him Chinese characters using simple Chinese poems and stories they downloaded from the Internet in the first couple of months so that he could make a transition to English. As Yang progressed with his English, Li-yong and Nie-dong gradually reduced the teaching of Chinese. They thought that learning Chinese would negatively influence his progress in English, and had already identified strong Chinese interference in his spoken English. For example, Yang had little sense of plural

| | |
|---|---|
| horse | 马 |
| sheep | 羊 |
| bird | 鸟 |
| chiken | 鸡 |
| duck | 鸭 |
| dog | 狗 |
| cat | 猫 |
| pig | 猪 |
| monkey | 猴 |
| fox | 狐狸 |
| rabbit | 兔 |
| bear | 熊 |
| panda | 熊猫 |
| insect | 虫 |
| fish | 鱼 |
| elephant | 大象 |
| tiger | 老虎 |
| giraffe | 长颈鹿 |
| ox | 牛 |
| mouse | 鼠 |
| frog | 青蛙 |

Figure 5.1.   A sample of Yang's bilingual list by theme.

forms or the change of tense in English because there was no tense change in Chinese. They decided not to send Yang to learn Chinese or teach him Chinese themselves until his English had reached fluency. Nie-dong admitted that it was not good to stop his training in Chinese, "But we have no choice. Right now his English is not good enough. If we add Chinese to him, it is not good for his English."

When Yang could read more words in English, Li-yong and Nie-dong progressed using all English materials instead of bilingual word lists. They made working sheets from some of the workbooks that they found in the library for Yang to practice his English. Different from the previously used bilingual word lists, these worksheets focused on individual words (see Figure 5.2 for an example of the work sheets). When Yang could read a simple book without difficulty, his parents did not type the words from the book into a word list but instead asked him to read the

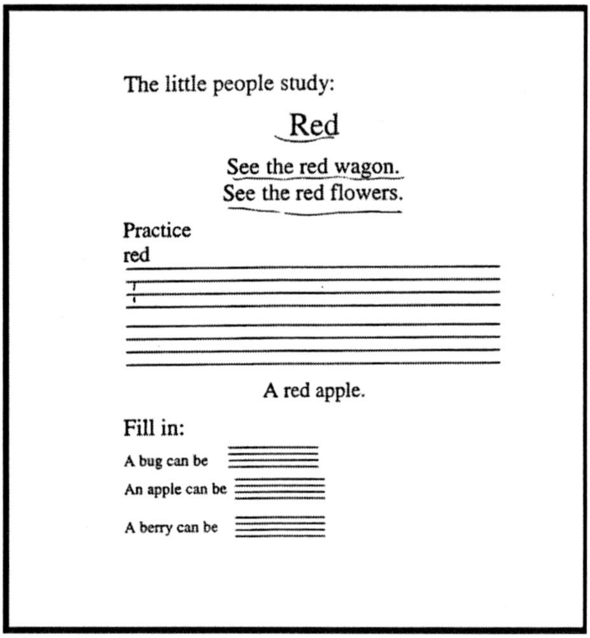

The little people study:

## Red

See the red wagon.
See the red flowers.

Practice
red

A red apple.

Fill in:

A bug can be

An apple can be

A berry can be

Figure 5.2.   A sample of Yang's worksheets.

words several times under their supervision. They made sure that he did not omit reading some of the letters and sounds, especially the ending "t" and "s" sounds. However, they continued to make Yang copy the books down word by word because they firmly believed that copying could help Yang learn the words by heart. Li-yong told me, "It [copying] is based on how I learned Chinese when I was in elementary school. Copying is good for memory. If you read without memorizing, it is no use." Yang read, copied, and memorized over 80 books at home.

Although they focused a lot of effort on reading, Li-yong and Nie-dong did not deliberately teach Yang creative writing skills. They held the traditional Chinese belief that one's writing ability could be improved through continued exposure to texts and through reading/memorizing English texts. As a Chinese saying goes, "If one can memorize 300 Tang Dynasty poems, s/he who did not know how to write poetry can now write poetry." In their view, if Yang increased his vocabulary through reading and copying English story texts, and could speak fluent English, he would be able to write. Yang often gave them notes saying things like "Mom and dad, I love you," which proved to them that if he could speak and read English, he could write too. Occasionally, they created opportunities for him to

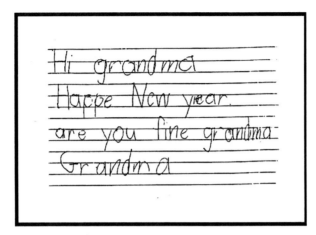

Figure 5.3.   Yang's English letter to his grandma during Chinese New Year.

write. For example, they modeled a letter in English to Yang's grand-mother in China, and asked Yang to copy it. After Yang could write, they encouraged him to write letters by himself. See Figure 5.3 for one of the letters he wrote.

Besides English teaching, Nie-dong and Li-yong also taught other subjects such as geography and math to Yang at home. Therefore, Yang had a very busy schedule at night. However, Yang demonstrated a zest for learning and seldom expressed resistance to his parents' instructions. He understood his role in the literacy activities and was always an active participant. In the next section, I describe how Yang as a young learner participated and sometimes initiated interactions in his joint literacy activities with his parents.

### Home Literacy Cooperation

Yang's cooperative efforts were reflected not only in his active response to his literacy role and the stories during his shared book reading with his parents, particularly with his mother, but also in his constant enthusiasm to retell stories read to him, and his ability to initiate new plays such as his daily "mother-son" talk. He read books with his mother after supper. Usually, Yang read the books first, and Nie-dong listened. If they ran into any new words, Nie-dong checked the dictionary to figure out the meaning in Chinese. Then to have fun, they took turns reading, with Yang reading a page and Nie-dong reading a page. This way, they were both reading and learning. For example, one evening before Halloween, they read *Hallow-een Storybook* that Li-yong had retyped and printed from the computer for

Yang. Yang started to read and they did not know the word pumpkin, so they checked in an English/Chinese dictionary and found out the meaning of "pumpkin" in Chinese. As Yang read, Nie-dong underlined the words that they had problems pronouncing, and asked Yang to repeat the words later. After Yang read it a couple of times, they began to take turns:

> Yang: See the big pumpkin.
> Nie-dong: 该我了[my turn]. The pumpkin is orange.
> Yang: It is round, round, round, round, round...
> Nie-dong (signaling him to stop): Yang!
> Yang (he stops and makes faces to her): 该妈妈了[Mom's turn]!
> Nie-dong: It is a Jack-o-latong.
> Yang: 不是的, 妈妈 [no, mom]. 是 [it's] jack-o-lantern, lantern, 不是 [not] latong!

This kind of mother-child cooperation during their English story reading also occurred during their Chinese story reading. Yang asked his mother to read him a Chinese story every night before he went to bed. Nie-dong told me that Yang had already figured out different functions of English and Chinese, "It is so strange that he knows the difference. It is clear to him that English is something he has to learn, a necessity for school and for talking with other non-Chinese people. But to listen to Chinese stories is a pastime, a relaxing moment." She borrowed some Chinese children's stories from friends, stories from Chinese classics such as *The Monkey King*, and *The Three Kingdoms*. When they ran out of Chinese stories, they read the Chinese textbooks they brought from China. Yang was also keen on retelling stories his mother told him. He was interested in space and big animals such as dinosaurs, and he was able to retell information about several planets, and make up stories about them. One evening, he told me a story about a spaceship and a UFO in Chinese, which he also illustrated later. The story went (translated from Chinese):

> In the space, the stars crashed. One UFO did not fly away. The UFO shined with light. The light was so hot that it melted all the other stars around it and they exploded.

Yang initiated some of the mother-son shared activities such as their routine "mother and son" talk, where Yang took out a piece of paper and a pencil and requested his mother to have a little conversation with him and take notes on their talk if necessary. Yang reported what he did and learned at school that day. This talk was how Nie-dong learned what Yang's school was all about since the work Yang did at school was seldom sent home. Yang often used "Sandwich English," that is, English words preceded and followed by Chinese words. A typical talk went like this:

Nie-dong: 你们没有做 (Did you do) Pink Book?
Yang: 没有 (No, we didn't). 我们做了 (We did) snowglow, two snow man, 一个 (one) Christmas tree. 本来一个 (we only needed to do one) snowman, 我做了两个 (I did two).
Nie-dong: What is snowglow?
Yang: 我还画了一个 (I also drew) snowman picture! [Indicating to his mom that this is important] 写下来 (Write this down)!
Nie-dong: 你写 (you write).
Yang (writing on a piece of paper): Snow pict ... 怎么拼 (how to spell)?
Nie-dong: P-I-C-T-U-R-E
Yang: Picnic! ...

Yang appeared to enjoy these kinds of literacy plays with his parents, especially with his mother. Through these activities, he established a strong bond with his parents. He appeared to be a cheerful, outgoing, and talkative child. However, his life in Canada was far from burden free. As indicated in his home literacy practices, he not only had daytime school, but also nighttime school at home. This double burden had a great impact on his socioemotional quality at home and at school. In the next section, I explain how his life had been influenced by the cultural and educational differences between his home and school practices.

### Socioemotional Quality in Home Literacy

Several factors had influenced Yang's socioemotional well-being inside and outside home. Initially when he started school in Canada, his main barrier was his limited English language ability. As he progressed in English and his school performance, other factors such as his family's social integration, the relationship between Chinese and English, and more significantly, the cultural differences between home and school became more prominent indicators of his socioemotional quality in his literacy learning.

Yang's mother considered Yang a lonely boy who had no siblings or friends to play with. Yang was used to playing with toys such as a plane or a motorcycle or other things in sight such as a dictionary to aid him in imagining his journey of encountering aliens through outer space. He made continuous "wuuuuu" sounds and totally immersed himself in his imaginative worlds. Yang did not have much contact with other classmates after school. His only occasional playmate was a Chinese girl, Amy, daughter of the downstairs Chinese cafe owners.

Yang lived predominantly in a Chinese world. He went to his family friends' homes to visit them on weekends or to borrow Chinese books and videos. Sometimes, he went to the Chinese festival parties sponsored by the Chinese Students' and Scholars' Association at the University. These activities helped Yang adapt to a new life in a new country although he still missed his Chinese classmates, his grandparents, and the things they used to do together. He even tried to write to his grandma and grandpa in Chinese. He told his mom what he wanted to say to them and his mom wrote it in Chinese. He then copied it down and sent it to China. It was hard for him to write this way; he said, "I forgot most of my Chinese!"

Losing his Chinese began to affect Yang's ability to express himself. His parents noted that he was very eloquent in Chinese, but as his English rapidly progressed, his ability in Chinese rapidly receded. Nie-dong told me during one of our telephone conversations, "He [Yang] could not express himself as well as before. He got very frustrated sometimes because he could not remember some Chinese words. Now he uses some English words to replace them. But sometimes he does not have English words either."

Yang became more confident in his ability to succeed in school as his English progressed. His father, who came from a harsh childhood in China, set a high standard for his son. He deliberately guided Yang to have high ambition for the future. "Harvard medical school is the best!" he told Yang. To meet this goal, Li-yong expected Yang to be independent, successful, and strong because he was going to be a man, carrying the family name. To achieve that, Yang should be able to discipline himself to do homework or some housework assigned him; he should be able to get dressed and get ready for school without further reminding; he should follow a routine, doing his homework, and going to bed at 9:00 P.M. Therefore, at the age of 6, Yang was already under a lot of pressure to excel.

Because his parents came from a very traditional Chinese background, Yang was often caught in between the different cultural practices of the school and his home as he became more and more involved in school life in Canada. The Western approach of schooling, as Li-yong understood it, was that students finished all their exercises in class, and the teachers corrected them right away in class; after school, they emphasized play and did not assign homework. Not only was there no homework, there were no textbooks, or examinations, unlike in China where students are tested regularly in every subject. In order to help Yang, Li-yong and Nie-dong asked the teacher to send Yang's work home. The teacher sent Yang's work home the day they asked, but did not send any work home again. No textbooks, no homework, and no exams made the Lis feel uncertain of the best way to help Yang. So they continued every day to teach Yang math and supervise his reading and copying. In Yang's parents' opinion, the no textbook, no homework, no exam kind of schooling did not seem to be challenging enough for Yang's academic development:

> They [the Canadian schools] do not have much training in basics. School is too light and relaxed for them [students]. They do not have strict require-ments for the academics.... Here is the kind of relaxed style of teaching. Of course you do not learn as much as you do in China.

Li-yong and Nie-dong discovered that the differences they experi-enced between Chinese and Canadian schooling lay not only in subject matters but also in extracurricular activities. For example, a school-spon-sored activity, "Readathon," called for parents and friends to encourage their children to set aside time for recreational reading and to raise funds for the school. It was a contest among all students, and those who pledged the most money for their reading won. Li-yong and Nie-dong thought this was unorthodox. They believed it was a student's obligation to read books and to improve their literacy development. If parents or friends were to pay children to read books or study, they would create a bad influ-ence on children's morality and sense of responsibility. Yang did not want to feel left out and wanted to participate in the activity, so Nie-yong and Li-dong filled in the forms, and sent in some money. But at home, the rule remained the Chinese way: Yang did not get any money for reading books—he read the books as an obligation as a student.

Yang also experienced cultural discontinuity during other school activ-ities that were different from Chinese cultural practices. Yang was always enthusiastic about school's activities, and Nie-dong and Li-yong tried their best to support those activities. When they did not agree with what the school did, they had to work out ways to compromise. These moments put both parents and child in a difficult situation. Li-yong explained how he felt and how it was more demanding for Yang to assimilate than for him:

> Those activities, for example Halloween, do not accord with our own cul-tural values and traditions. But if they hold these kinds of activities and Yang does not participate, it is not good. I am too old to melt into their cul-ture. I am who I am and how I am. For Yang, it is different. He needs to mingle with the children here. So sometimes I explain to Yang that we need to keep our own traditions, although they [the school] emphasize that you have to speak English and adapt to their traditions.

Although Li-yong and Nie-dong realized that Yang was experiencing these cultural differences, they never went to the school to express their feelings. In fact, they had little communication with the teachers except for parent-teacher conferences. They regarded the teachers as the authority and would not challenge them; therefore, they did not initiate communication about the activities with which they disagreed. Rather, they made compromises based on their own understanding of the school activities and educated their child in their own ways.

## CONCLUSIONS: LEARNING FROM THE LI FAMILY

I have described Yang's home-related educational experiences in light of Leseman and de Jong's (1998) four facets of home literacy practices: (a) literacy opportunities, (b) instructions, (c) cooperation, and (d) socioemotional qualities. Yang's home experiences demonstrate that he had a bilingual, literate home environment where he was engaged in a wide range of literacy activities. His parents were highly supportive of his learning of English in order to successfully adapt to Canadian schools. They heavily drew upon the instructional and learning techniques of their native country and utilized resources that were available in their new country to help Yang master English language literacy. In many ways, Yang had a Chinese style school at home after his regular Canadian school experiences during the day. His parents were his teachers of reading, writing, math, and science at his home school (Rasinski & Fredericks, 1988). They used a variety of methods of instruction—flash cards, bilingual word lists, copying, independent and joint reading, and use of visual aids. Li-yong and Nie-dong's teaching could also be characterized as direct teaching of literacy skills and attitudes that reflected their traditional Chinese perceptions of literacy learning (Anderson, 1995; Chao, 1996).

Li-yong and Nie-dong placed high expectations and values on Yang's education and academic success. Their influence on Yang's learning is highly *cultural*, embedded in their Chinese ways of learning and living (Zhang & Carrasquillo, 1995). Education has been historically regarded as the only path toward upward social mobility in China, and pressures to succeed in education are exerted on children early in life, and this continues throughout their school years until they enter higher education institutes (Lin & Chen, 1995). For Yang, living in a new country, his journey to success in education added another new layer of complexity. That is, he had to succeed in a new language and culture with a whole array of adjustment needs such as life style, economic change, social adaptation, and separation from his grandparents (Yao, 1985). These pressures, as Lin and Chen (1995) point out, may inevitably have a negative impact on students' intellectual, psychological, and physical development.

Coming from this very traditional Chinese background, Yang's learning was therefore shadowed by the apparent incongruencies between the school and home. He was often in the middle of cultural conflicts reflected in the different activities and practices in the two learning contexts. The characteristics of western schooling such as emphasis on play, flexibility, creativity, and autonomy (e.g., overemphasis on drawing, no homework, no standardized textbooks) (Zhang, Ollila, & Harvey, 1998) were considered drawbacks to students' learning by Yang's parents. This was one of the reasons that Li-yong and Nie-dong "operated" a Chinese school at home to ensure that Yang learned something in depth to lay a good foundation for his future. Their concerns and cultural values, however, were not communicated to the school because there was a lack of communication between the teacher and the parents. This lack of communication also made it difficult for them to align with the teachers to further support Yang's academic learning.

Despite the high pressures from his parents, and the cultural incongruencies between school and home, Yang actively participated in the family's learning activities such as shared reading, and "mother-son" talks. He was, under the influence of his parents, determined to learn English well and succeed in school. His success in English was unfortunately at the cost of his native language—Chinese. When he first started school in Canada, he developed negative attitudes towards the Chinese language and the concept of being Chinese because he could not speak English within six months of school. As he was becoming more proficient in English and more involved in schoolwork, he was losing his Chinese language ability. Yang's story of "losing one language while acquiring another" is representative of many immigrant children documented in research (Jiang, 1997; Thomas & Chao, 1999; Townsend & Fu, 1998).

Learning about Yang's home literacy practices provides us with valuable insights for teachers. Since cultural values played a central role in Yang's home literacy practices, I advocate for a culturally relevant pedagogy when teaching children like Yang. Ladson-Billings (1992, 1994) suggests that the notion of cultural relevance needs to move beyond just knowing students' culture to transcend the negative effects of the dominant cultural practices in the classroom. Teachers of children like Yang can use students' cultural background as a strength to help students construct positive school experiences. This way, this pedagogy becomes one that "empowers students intellectually, socially, emotionally, and politically by using cultural referents to impart knowledge, skills, and attitudes" (Ladson-Billings, 1994, p. 17). For example, teachers can use children's knowledge in their first language as strength in the classroom by creating situations in which Chinese language can become uniquely meaningful and valuable (Jiang, 1997). Yang's pride in Chinese culture and ability in

Chinese language could have been maintained if he had more support from the teacher in the early stage of his Canadian schooling.

Teaching from a culturally relevant approach, teachers need to become adept at collecting information about students' sociocultural backgrounds, and interpreting and making instructional decisions based on the data to maximize the individual student's learning (Au, 1993; Davidman & Davidman, 1997). That is, teachers need to get to know whom the students are and how they live in order to build cultural continuity between students' home and school learning experiences. One of the most effective ways to collect information is a home visit (McCarthey, 1997). Though teachers may have practical challenges in entering students' homes, looking at students' life outside the classroom will yield valuable insight in their literacy learning in different settings, which in turn will inform teaching in the classroom. In Yang's case, he did not need to have two discrepant schools—a Canadian school during the day and a Chinese one at night. His home and school learning could have been complementary to each other according to his learning needs, rather than two dichotomous operations that conflicted with each other. Therefore, learning about students' home literacy practices such as Yang's can help teachers constantly adapt and adjust instructional approaches that match with students' cultural features and individual development needs (Au, 1993). Teachers who work with students like Yang, for example, can find information about Chinese culture and its traditional practices through reading research on existing literacy practices; they might call upon parents to learn more about Chinese literacy practice in their home practices. Through understanding minority students' (such as Yang's) literacy opportunities, instructions, cooperation, and socioemotional qualities at home, teachers can adjust to their instructional approaches and work with the parents to meet these students' academic, social, as well as socioemotional needs.

In conclusion, I want to note that although Yang's story demonstrated the distinct cultural practices in his home, generalization of Chinese or Asian immigrant children's home literacy experiences should be avoided. Research shows that the nature of immigrant children's home literacy practices is complex and diverse; different factors such as parents' educational background, socioeconomic status, parenting styles, and English language proficiency may yield qualitatively different home experiences (Li, 2002; Xu, 1999). Therefore, each child needs to be recognized as a unique individual from a unique home environment with different levels of proficiency in English and their native language, and different funds of knowledge (Moll, 1994; Xu, 1999).

## ACKNOWLEDGMENT

This chapter has been reprinted with permission from F. Boyd, C. Brock, & M. Rozendal (Eds.), *Multicultural and multilingual literacy and language practices* (pp. 304-322). New York: Guilford Publication.

## REFERENCES

Anderson, J. (1995). Listening to parents' voices: Cross cultural perceptions of learning to read and to write. *Reading Horizons, 35*(5), 394-413.

Au, K. (1993). *Literacy instruction in multicultural settings*. New York: Harcourt Brace Jovanovich.

Barton, B. (1988). *I want to be an astronaut*. New York: Crowell.

Beijing Children's Press. (1993). *The collections of children's fables* (Chinese). Beijing, China: Author.

Bryant, D. (1988). *One day at the supermarket*. Nashville: Ideals Publications.

Chao, R. (1996). Chinese and European American mothers' beliefs about the role of parenting in childrens' school success. *Journal of Cross-cultural Psychology, 27*(4), 403-423.

Davidman, L., & Davidman, P. T. (1997). *Teaching with multicultural perspective: A practical guide*. New York: Longman.

Eastman, P. D. (1967). *Are you my mother?* New York: Beginner Books.

Garcia, E. (1999). *Student cultural diversity: Understanding and meeting the challenge*. Boston: Houston Mifflin.

Goodall, J. (1991). *Elephant family*. Toronto: Madison Marketing.

Ingoglia, G. (1998). *Disney's Mulan*. New York: Disney Press.

Jiang, N. (1997). Early biliteracy: Ty's story. In D. Taylor, D. Coughhin, & J. Masasco (Eds.), *Teaching and advocacy* (pp.143-159). Yorke, ME: Stenhouse.

Ladson-Buildings, G. (1992). Reading between the lines and beyond the pages: A culturally relevant approach to literacy teaching. *Theory Into Practice, 31*(4), 312-320

Ladson-Buildings, G. (1994). *The dreamkeepers: Successful teachers of African American Children*. San Francisco: Jossy-Bass.

Leseman, P. P. M., & de Jong, P. F. (1998). Home literacy: Opportunity, instruction, cooperation and social-emotional quality predicting early reading achievement. *Reading Research Quarterly, 33*(3), 294-318.

Lin, J., & Chen, Q. (1995). Academic pressure and impact on students' development in China. *McGill Journal of Education, 30*(2), 149-167.

Li, G. (2002). *"East is east, west is west"? Home literacy, culture, and schooling*. New York: Peter Lang.

McCarthey, S. J. (1997). Connecting home and school literacy practices in classrooms with diverse populations. *Journal of Literacy Research, 29*(2), 145-182.

Moll, L. C. (1994). Literacy research in community and classroom: A sociocultural approach. In R. B. Ruddell, M. R. Ruddell, & H. Singer (Eds.), *Theoretical models and processes of reading* (pp. 179-207). Newark, DE: International Reading Association.

Moll, L., & González, N. (1994). Lessons from research with language minority children. *Journal of Reading Behavior, 26*, 439-456.

Rasinski, T. V., & Fredericks, A. (1988). Sharing literacy: Guiding principals and practices for parental involvement. *Reading Teacher, 41*, 508-513.

Supraner, R. (1999). *I can read about seasons*. Mahwah, NJ: Troll.

Thomas, L., & Chao, L. (1999). Language use in family and society. *English Journal, 89*(1), 107-113.

Townsend, J., & Fu, D. (1998). A Chinese boy's joyful initiation into American literacy. *Language Art, 75*(3), 193-201.

Valdés, G. (1998). The world outside and inside schools: Language and immigrant children. *Educational Researcher, 27*(6), 4-18.

Xu, H. (1999). Young Chinese ESL children's home literacy experiences. *Reading Horizons, 40*(1), 47-64.

Yao, E. L. (1985). Adjustment needs of Asian immigrant children. *Elementary School Guidance and Counseling, 19*(3), 222-227.

Young Naturalist Foundation. *Owl*. Toronto, Ontario, Canada: Author.

Zhang, S. Y., & Carrasquillo, A. L. (1995). Chinese parents' influence on academic performance. *New State Association for Bilingual Education Journal, 10*, 46-53.

Zhang, C., Ollila, L. O., & Harvey, C. B. (1998). Chinese parents' perceptions of their children's literacy and schooling in Canada. *Canadian Journal of Education, 23*(2), 182-190.

# AFRICAN AND AFRICAN AMERICAN FAMILIES

CHAPTER 6

# "SOLAMENTE LIBROS IMPORTANTES"

## Literacy Practices and Ideologies of Migrant Farmworking Families in North Central Florida

**Maria R. Coady**

*Ignacio, a 13-year-old migrant boy, fidgets at the kitchen table while his mother, Señora Álvarez, describes her schooling in the rural mountainous state of Hidalgo, Mexico. The kitchen smells of tortillas, which Señora Álvarez prepares each evening for the family meals. In Mexico, books, she describes, were limited to school and church, the former conducted in Spanish and the latter in her native tongue of Otomí. She motions to her husband, Jorge, who is listening in from the doorway. He opens a nearby cabinet, revealing the family's coveted hymnal. Opening the book to the first page, Sra. Álvarez and her husband begin to read, pointing out the word Hmü (Lord). Jorge tells me that he cannot really read the text. The couple maintains that they were never taught to read or write in Otomí, but their ability to connect with the text, identify words, decode and interpret diacritics, and derive meaning from the symbols demonstrate otherwise.*

Sr. and Sra. Álvarez are migrant farm workers in north central Florida, who left Hidalgo, Mexico, in 1995 in search of work. Their commitment

*Multicultural Families, Home Literacies, and Mainstream Schooling*
pp. 113–128
Copyright © 2008 by Information Age Publishing

to their five children's education drives many of the family decisions, including the recent decision to discontinue the migrant lifestyle of following seasonal harvests for work. They believe that their children will have more educational opportunities than they had, both having completed *primaria* (sixth grade education) in Mexico. Despite their ability to decode the religious hymnal in Otomí, they deny knowing how to read or write in the language and question their ability to facilitate their children's literacy development, which, they believe, should occur in English.

In this chapter, I present two migrant farmworking families and show the ways in which the families negotiated literacy ideologies, as well as how those played out in the home. Using qualitative methods, I collected data over a 6-month period. Data from this study revealed that the families' literacy ideologies were socioculturally situated. All of the families faced the challenge of negotiating their home country literacy experiences in the United States. At times, these ideologies conflicted with US mainstream ideologies of literacy and what constituted literate practices. Findings from the study suggest religious artifacts and icons played a prominent role in the literacy practices of the family, but families discredited those practices as literacy events. In addition, mothers' educational level appeared to influence how school literacy expectations were negotiated. In this chapter, I present these families as a collective case study and draw implications from the data.

## MIGRANT FARM WORKERS IN THE UNITED STATES

Migrant workers face numerous social, economic, and political challenges and are often characterized as poor, mobile, and having low educational attainment. In the United States, there are approximately 3 million migrant workers, and about half (47%) are documented (National Agricultural Workers Survey [NAWS], 2005). Migrant workers follow seasonal fruit and vegetable harvests, 84% of which must be hand picked, and also work in dairy and fishing industries (NAWS, 2005). The average farm worker earns less than $10,000 per year, and in 2005 agricultural work was considered the second most dangerous occupation in the United States (U.S. Department of Labor, 2006), following only coal mining. More than three quarters of these farm workers are Spanish speakers who have a median educational level of sixth grade (NAWS, 2005).

The children of migrant workers face similar challenges of poverty and mobility, but also encounter obstacles related to education. Their highly mobile lifestyle can negatively impact their academic achievement and school experiences. For example, frequent mobility due to seasonal work causes academic disruption and difficulty maintaining peer and social networks (López, 1999). This disruption makes meeting standards and passing standardized tests difficult, as various states have different academic demands, deadlines, and graduation requirements.

Under Title I of the Federal Elementary and Secondary Education Act (ESEA), migrant children can qualify for assistance under the Migrant Education Program (MEP) (Branz-Spall & Wright, 2004; Pappamihiel, 2004). However, migrant families must move across district lines more frequently than every 36 months in order to qualify for academic support services (Pappamihiel, 2004). It is not surprising, then, that the dropout rate of migrant children is over 50%. This number jumps to about 70% with just one academic retention (León, 1996).

## MIGRANT FARMWORKING FAMILIES IN NORTH FLORIDA

In Florida, there are approximately 300,000 migrant farm workers who harvest citrus and other crops before moving north along the eastern migrant stream (Riley, 2002). In the north central region of the state, migrant workers harvest blueberries and peanuts, bale hay, and work on plant nurseries and dairy farms. While the trend is that these workers will move north following harvest seasons, some families in the region opt to round out their work with employment in construction and restaurant industries. This makes their qualifying as agricultural worker less categorical or limited to crop industries, fishing, and dairy as outlined in federal definitions (Pappamihiel, 2004).

Most of the seasonal workers in the north Florida region are from Guatemala and Mexico. In 2005, there were about 1,600 migrant farmworking children who qualified for assistance under the Migrant Education Program in the thirteen counties of the region (N. Norris, personal communication, November 10, 2005). The region is rural, and, as a result, farmworking families have limited access to services such as health care and dental facilities, libraries, and community centers, which might otherwise be provided in centralized locales such as Immokalee, Florida, a large migrant farmworking community. These were issues and concerns faced by the participants in the study.

## THE SOCIOCULTURAL CONTEXT OF LITERACY

Unfortunately, we know little about the educational experiences and literacy development of migrant children. This may partly be due to the difficulty of investigating children and families with a mobile lifestyle. Moreover, we know little about families' beliefs regarding literacy and how these beliefs interact with literacy demands that children face in school. While school success in the twenty-first century demands high degrees of literacy, including the ability to read, write, and interact with text that consists of lexically dense and low frequency, academic words (Cummins, 2001), it is not clear how these practices are negotiated by migrant families. That is, how do two migrant farmworking families negotiate mainstream literacies ideologies and practices?

Over the past 20 years, scholars have begun to investigate and understand the ways in which literacy is culturally and socially situated (Heath, 1983; Pérez, 1998; Purcell-Gates, 1995; Taylor & Dorsey-Gaines, 1988). That is, literacy events cannot be separated from their social and cultural contexts. Heath's seminal 10 year ethnographic study of two working class communities, Trackton and Roadville, for example, documented the ways in which children are socialized into language and literacy uses. Expectations, beliefs, and parents' or caregivers' ideologies influenced the ways in which language development occurred. Neither of the two communities was "better" than the other; rather, they differed in language development processes. The difference was especially notable in educational settings when language expectations of children were incongruous with mainstream school language and literacy practices.

Other scholars note similar findings with respect to the socio-cultural context of literacy development. Purcell-Gates (1995) investigated the literacy development and practices of a low income urban Appalachian family. While working with Donny, the son, and Jenny, his mother, Purcell-Gates showed how literacy was situated in social and cultural contexts, including the stereotypes of the family as deficient. She notes the mismatch between mainstream literacy practices and those used by poor White families, suggesting that among the former group, "children born into a rich and varied literate world in the sense that important others in their lives use print often for many reasons, find learning to read and write in school relatively easy" (p. 182). Nonmainstream, diverse, and marginalized groups face the more difficult task of reconciling different literacy ideologies.

More recent ethnographic work begins to shed light on the relationship between home and school contexts of migrant farm working families. In her ethnographic study of three migrant fifth grade boys, López (1999) found that the boys' interactive discourses (that is, "interactions of a socially organized group whose members share the same language and identity" [p. 9]) shaped their personal identities. The boys struggled with negotiating their identities in schools, which was difficult given the schools' inability to connect with the home context of the boys. López (1999) found that the home and school contexts were culturally incongruous, thereby positioning the migrant boys as deficient and largely invisible in school, with little opportunity to negotiate personal identities in school.

López' findings underscore the work of Shen (2006), who investigated two Spanish-speaking, migrant second grade boys in an English as a second language classroom during a 6-month period. Through interviews, observations, and document analysis, Shen noted teacher interactions and expectations of the boys, as well as the quality of the work they engaged in. She found that the boys were often given menial tasks, such as coloring, and were excluded from interactions with others in the classroom. Similar to Shannon and Escamilla's (1999) findings, Shen noted further that the teacher's infrequent interactions with the boys, who worked almost exclusively with a classroom tutor, demonstrated a form of "symbolic violence" (Bourdieu, 1991). That is, the boys appeared to be positioned as inferior in the classroom.

Finally, Guerra (1998) found that transnational migrant farm working families did engage in literacy events in the home. Using data from a 10-year longitudinal study, Guerra noted language and literacy practices that occurred both in the "home front" where families resided, and in the "contact zone" where families negotiated these practices as they came into contact with other groups. Much like the findings of Heath (1983) and other literacy scholars, Guerra noted that home literacy practices diverged from those in mainstream settings, showing how letter writing, for example, played an important, communicative role in the lives many of the Latinas. Guerra showed how the sociocultural context of literacy functions and uses determined the literacy events.

Ultimately, these qualitative, ethnographic studies reveal the incongruity between home language and literacy practices among culturally and linguistically diverse groups and those promoted and prized in public school settings. These studies further suggest that culturally and linguistically diverse groups do not lack literacy; rather the types of literacy practices are divergent from mainstream practices that occur in public school settings. As each of these scholars demonstrate, without knowledge of the home context and a genuine attempt to make these congruent with school practices, culturally and linguistically diverse students continue to face academic and social obstacles in school.

## METHODOLOGY

This was a collective case study (Stake, 1995) of two migrant farmworking families in North Central Florida. The data here are part of a larger study that investigated five families. I collected data from November, 2004, until July, 2005; follow up with the families occurred through September,

**Table 5.1.    Demographics of Two Migrant Families**

|                                       | *García*      | *Álvarez*            |
| ------------------------------------- | ------------- | -------------------- |
| Number of family members              | 5             | 7                    |
| Parents' country of origin            | Mexico        | Mexico               |
| Primary agricultural area             | Blueberry     | Tree nursery/farming |
| Time in U.S. (as of March 2005)       | 3 months      | 10 years             |
| Home language use (oral)              | Spanish       | Otomí                |
| Religious denomination                | Catholic      | Pentecostal          |

2005. The families, though all qualifying for migrant services and meeting federal definitions of "migrant," diverged along a number of criteria (see Table 6.1). The families consisted of five to seven members, and both families were from Mexico. The families followed different religious practices, including Catholic and Pentecostal. The primary language of communication in the home was Spanish for one family and Otomí for the other.

I was introduced to each family by the migrant education advocate, who was responsible for the services provided to each of the participating families under the Migrant Education Program. The advocate initially accompanied me to the family home and presented the project to the family. After my initial visit, I arranged to meet each family one night per week, during which time I observed the family, interviewed parents and children, and collected documents. The primary data collection method was detailed field notes. I also used an observation protocol of material culture referents, adapted from Johnson (1980). In that protocol I noted print and other materials in the home environment that reflected language and literacy uses. I also noted the language in which those items were found. Some of the items included academic products, artwork, books, bibles/religious materials, bills, comics, cookbooks, computers, labels, message taking (phone) and note taking, and world maps, I did not limit my observations to those items on the list, but rather expanded the list based on what I observed in the home.

In addition, I audiotaped formal interviews with each family approximately three times. I also videotaped in the homes of the families on one occasion each, and took photographs in both homes. During the study, I formally interviewed all four parents. I also interviewed the migrant education advocate, migrant education director and associate director, and two teachers in the district's English to Speakers of Other Languages (ESOL) center school. The interviews were semistructured in format and allowed for open-ended responses. All of the interviews with parents were conducted in Spanish. Interviews with the children were generally bilingual (English-Spanish), largely based on the child's preference and language ability. Other interviews with participants were conducted in English.

One of the additional functions I performed in the context of this study was taking on the role of advocate for the families. This occurred with all three families for different purposes. For example, two of the García family children had extensive dental problems, which inhibited their ability to participate in school. When the school nurse sent home a note to the mother in English, she asked me to translate it. The parents subsequently granted permission for me to interact with the school nurse in order to obtain emergency dental services (funded through the district) for the children. I assisted the family by bringing the boys to a reduced-cost dental clinic, about 20 miles from the university, and interpreted for the family at that site. In order to obtain funding for the emergency services, I had to interact with various dentists, district administrators, nurses, and advocates.

Other events occurred in a similar fashion. For example, when the oldest child in the Álvarez family was found to be in possession of a nip of alcohol at school, the parents were required by the district to enroll him in an alcohol rehabilitation program that lasted for about eight weeks. I brought Ignacio directly to the rehabilitation program, which was located about 12 miles from the family home. I observed and participated in six of the eight weekly meetings. The parents also required interpretation services in order to understand their son's offense and the academic work to be completed by Ignacio over a two week school suspension period. The parents asked me to interact with the school counselor and administrators and interpret those conversations, which largely occurred by telephone. Ignacio was also required to participate in a school-based peer review process and "jury trial" at school. In those events, I was able to assist the parents to negotiate their son's penalty.

Those interactions allowed me to interact with the family in times outside of the evening visits and to get to know them in a different context. For me, these interactions built *confianza*, or trust, between us. Participating in these alternative settings (e.g., dental clinic, alcohol rehabilitation program, and schools) allowed me to learn more about family interactions, beliefs, and ideologies, especially as they related to literacy.

Field notes were written immediately after each of my visits, while the data was fresh in mind. I used a method of constant comparison of data both within subjects (families) and across subjects. Data were coded and analyzed thematically (LeCompte & Schensul, 1999). I noted emerging themes in the data and checked them both in and across subjects. When themes emerged in the data, I checked my findings with the participants and obtained more in-depth data and details in order to better understand their practices and views. I frequently wrote personal notes and formed hypotheses in the margins of my field notes, both before and after they were transcribed. For example, the oldest son in the Álvarez family was the same age as my son and in the same grade (different schools but in the same school district). By virtue of understanding the academic pressures and expectations required of my son, I was able to note similarities and differences between the two boys' ability to access media and other print materials to support their academic work at home.

About 1 year after the study ended neither of the families qualified for local migrant education services: the García family relocated out of the area in May of 2006 and the Álvarez family, though continuing to work in agriculture, "settled out" by not moving across district lines for work. Below I describe each of the families and present findings.

## ÁLVAREZ FAMILY

The Álvarez family consisted of five children (three boys and two girls) and two working parents. The parents and eldest child, 12 years old at the start of the study, arrived in the United States 9 years prior. The family originated from the mountainous Hidalgo region of Mexico where the language of communication was Otomí, an indigenous language spoken in that region. The remaining four children, between the ages of 4 and 10, were born in the United States.

Four of the Álvarez children attended the local elementary school. They walked or hitched a ride down a two mile dirt road to the bus stop in the morning and returned along the same route in the afternoon. The eldest son attended middle school, located about eight miles from the home, and took a different bus than his siblings. Education was very important to the family, and their children's educational continuity was the main reason that the family chose not to qualify for migrant services and remained in the district's school system. Both parents attended school through sixth grade, *primaria*, in Mexico, where the language of instruction, reading, and writing was Spanish. In Mexico, the parents participated in church services in Otomí and acquired literacy in the context of church. They felt comfortable in their ability to read and write in Spanish, but uncomfortable assisting their children with their homework in English.

The Álvarez home consisted of a single-wide trailer situated on a private farm in the rural countryside. A bright display of children's artwork, masks, an outdated Chinese calendar, and Christmas decorations, remained on the walls throughout the year. The refrigerator displayed a similarly large amount of children's schoolwork and papers. Sra. Álvarez smiled proudly when asked about the children's work in school, but she conceded that the children were the ones who displayed their work on the walls. The print environment of the home also included items such as notepads, a telephone book, various bills and school communications, a bilingual dictionary (English-Spanish), and some reading materials (miscellaneous school papers and short stack of eight donated books) located on a shelf between the two bedrooms. A computer in the hallway was used by the boys to play games but lacked word processing software, a printer and internet access.

The family had little access to other forms of print materials, such as newspapers, encyclopedias, and magazines. These were sometimes required by the children for school work. Their limited access became problematic when Ignacio faced a ten day out-of-school suspension. The suspension included a "suspension packet" of work that was to be completed by him at home. In order to adequately complete the various assignments, Ignacio required access to print materials and library services, neither of which were readily available. One example of the work was to investigate a famous scientist and write about his or her contributions to modern science. Another example was to choose a current event from a local newspaper and discuss the event, in writing. The family's rural setting, long work hours, and limited communication with the school of what was expected made it difficult for Ignacio to complete this work, and he received little guidance from the school.

As noted in the opening vignette, the Álvarez family took pride in their home language, Otomí, as well as the well-guarded hymnal. The book, kept safely in the corner cabinet in the kitchen-living room, represented the family's religious beliefs, as well as a link to their heritage and culture. The family has followed Pentecostal faith since arriving in the US, and they traveled about an hour each way on Sundays to attend a church that provided services in Spanish. Like their parents' experiences gaining literacy in Otomí, the children learned to recognize words and decode symbols in Spanish through its use in church, but discredited their ability to read or write in Spanish.

The Álvarez children were multilingual and spoke Otomí, Spanish, and English. The eldest son, Ignacio, had a particular affinity for Otomí and regularly initiated conversations in the language with his siblings and parents. Sra. Álvarez reminisced fondly of the language, noting that "*eso es lo que más hablamos. En el pueblo de nosotros no hablamos español, no hablamos de otro, sino ese idioma, no más.*" [That is what we speak the most. In our village we don't speak Spanish or anything else, only this language, that's all".] Despite their pride in the language and connection to it, the children were cautioned against speaking it in public. Sra. Álvarez noted, "*siempre le he dicho a mis niños no lo hablen porque la gente va a pensar que estamos diciendo algo malo y o algo … y mejor evitar eso."* [I have always said to my children not to speak it (Otomí) because people are going to think that we are saying something bad or something … and it's better to avoid this.] Thus, despite the pride they showed for the language they spoke, the family was also fearful of using the language and discredited their ability to read it.

Three of children in the Álvarez family stated that they enjoyed reading story books, though this was not necessarily part of the family's night-time routine. The two eldest boys, who shared a bunk bed in the back bedroom, would occasionally read books before falling asleep. They preferred to play games on the computer and watch movies. The children read story books and novels when required by the school to do so. For example, the eldest daughter in fourth grade, María, was instructed by her teacher to read to her younger second grade sister, Lisbeth, at night. Sitting on a bed in one of the bedrooms, María dutifully read aloud, with her sister listening on.

The parents were comfortable with these instructions about homework and reading when they came from the teachers. The parents felt that the school knew what was best in terms of education for their children, and they emphasized the importance of English. They noted,

> *Ellos tienen que aprender el inglés. Ese es el idioma de aquí. Trato de ayudarle en lo que yo puedo y lo que yo no lo puedo hacer o ellos no lo pueden hacer, pués, lo llevan así, con tal de que lo intentan hacerlo.* [They have to learn in English. This is the language here. I try to help them however I can, and what I cannot do or they cannot do, well, the rest is left to fate.]

The parents' home country experiences appeared to influence their use of books in the United States. Sra. Álvarez stated that books were not used in her home in Mexico for pleasure reading; schoolbooks were used in school settings, and religious materials were used in church. One of five children, Sra Álvarez' parents were *comerciantes* or merchants, who bought and sold household items such as *mantelas bordadas*, or embroidered tablecloths. As a child growing up in Mexico, she had little time to do schoolwork outside of school or to read and was required to help support the family at home.

Sra. Álvarez believed that certain types of print materials and books were not beneficial, academically, for her children. For example, when Ignacio stated that he mostly enjoyed reading *cómicos*, or comics, she interjected that these books were not useful for him to read—*solamente libros importantes*, or important books such as text books and school-related academic books, were better choices. Other materials were simply not necessary for educational purposes.

The Álvarez parents' literacy experiences in Mexico appeared to contrast with mainstream discourses in the United States regarding what literacy practices should occur in the home and the kinds of materials that are expected for students to complete their work. These different literacy expectations were constantly negotiated by the parents and made even more difficult due to the limited communication that the school had with parents in Spanish.

## GARCÍA FAMILY

The García children and their mother arrived in the United States two months before this study. Their home was a trailer located on one field of a large, private blueberry farm. Because the owner of the farm did not maintain the trailer, it was in a highly dilapidated state and largely unsafe for habitation, with exposed electrical wires and propane gas piped in to the kitchen stove from a barbeque grill-style tank outside. Sra. García kept the space clean and functional, and was committed to making the trailer their home.

Sr. García had been living in the United States for ten years prior to the arrival of his wife and three children from Jalisco, Mexico. The García children consisted of two boys, in fourth and second grades, and a 3-year-old daughter, who attended a local preschool program. Because the boys required English to Speakers of Other Languages services in the district, they were bussed about 15 miles at 5:55 each morning to the district's ESOL-center school. On several occasions, the bus did not arrive, and the children were unable to attend school because the parents were unable to communicate with the transportation office regarding changes to the bus schedule and route.

This was just one example of the language issues the family faced. When the children required dental care, there were few facilities or services available to them and none readily available in the area that had interpreters. Other communication was limited with the school. For example, emergency medical forms and other school documents, such as school climate surveys, newsletters, calendars, and so on, arrived in only English.

Sra. García felt strongly that her children should acquire English and made many attempts to understand school documents, homework assignments, and classroom newsletters from teachers. She used a bilingual (English-Spanish) dictionary to translate school forms and information, but requested help from bilingual friends when she could. When her 4-year-old daughter's daycare teacher sent home information on reading strategies, Sra. García responded to the information by requesting books from the migrant education advocate. She subsequently read to her daughter, two or three evenings per week.

Sra. García continued to negotiate these language and literacy expectations even as they contrasted with her experiences in Mexico. As a child, Sra. García did not engage in free reading, as books were largely not accessible to her. As a secondary student, she worked cleaning houses in the morning so that she could attend school in the afternoon. There, the library and nearest bookstore were reserved for *gente rica,* or rich (wealthy) people. She stated, "*se leen libros en casa, para tarea lo usía, pero este es todo. Gente más pobre no usa libros en casa pero gente más rica sí tiene, tiene librerías.*" [Books are read at home for homework but that is all. Poor people don't use books at home but rich people have them, they have bookcases.]

Over the course of the study, the García family acquired technology and media to use in the home, including a television, video cassette recorder, and computer. They attempted to acquire internet access with the computer so that they could communicate less expensively with family members living in Michigan; however, setting up lines on the farmowner's property complicated this, and the family abandoned the effort.

Some of the significant print materials in the home reflected the religious beliefs of the family and, like the Álvarez family, a connection to the home country. For example, on one wall of the kitchen, the family displayed a poster of the Festival of Santa María, an event that occurred annually in the home village of the García family. The poster depicted the church, mountainous backdrop of the state of Jalisco, and several symbols representing the Virgin Santa María, positioned over the church as a protector of the faith. The reverse side of the poster was a detailed schedule of the religious events that took place, times, and locations, written in Spanish.

I often encountered Sra. García at home in the evening attempting to translate school documents in order to understand the children's homework assignments, school information (schedules and medical), and literacy practices in the form of charts and reading logs. These expectations were of the children as well as the parents, and the difficulty of negotiating these was frustrating for Sra. García.

## DISCUSSION

The parents that participated in the study held high expectations of their children and supported their education in various ways. Two trends were discernible in the data: first, the parents' (principally the mothers') home country experiences with literacy and books contrasted with schools' (mainstream) literacy ideologies and expectations, and secondly, that the use of religious materials and texts was an important literacy tool.

The families in this study used Spanish and Otomí in the home, and both sets of parents were able to read and write in Spanish; however, the schools did not communicate, either in writing or orally, with the families in a language that they understood. They also did not explicate their literacy expectations. Thus, parents were left to decipher the schools' expectations in a language they did not understand. They were then left to negotiate differences between literacy experiences in the home country with dominant and mainstream literacy expectations the United States. One example of this was the display of children's work in the home, which Sra. Álvarez noted did not occur in her home in Mexico. Another example of this was her support of the girls' reading events at night; rather than engage in reading with her children in Spanish, she let María read to Lisbeth in English, which reinforced beliefs about acquiring literacy in English.

Another finding was that the families engaged in religious literacy events, including reading bibles, singing religious songs, and reciting prayers. Despite the different religious denominations represented by the families in this study, religious literacy was an important event they engaged in. Both families displayed religious materials, bibles and pictures or icons that reflected their religious beliefs. These practices and the ability to decode meaning from symbols were integral to the household functioning and well being (Moll, Amanti, Neff, & González, 1992). However, while the families recognized these practices as important to their lives, they did not view themselves as "literate" in them. This was true even in the case of the Álvarez parents, who were able to decode and interpret words and meaning from an Otomí hymnal but had not formally been "instructed" in it.

For families in this study, other materials, such as newspapers and magazines, were not used on a regular basis. This was likely due to several reasons, including cost, frequent mobility of the family, and language. The migrant lifestyle and income level precluded families from purchasing these materials directly. The rural setting of the homes made access to libraries very difficult. Transporting books and materials was also difficult, and the materials required by schools for children to complete their work were also difficult to obtain in Spanish. While parents stated that they would read a newspaper in Spanish, this was difficult because only one was available several counties away.

The parents' literacy ideologies, including their beliefs about types of books in the home, nighttime reading, and displays of children's work in the home, reflected their sociocultural perspective. However, the families engaged in literacy practices that reflected their sociocultural views.

These practices were different, not deficient, and responded to their particular social context and cultural background, migrant status and home country practices and experiences. This finding reinforces findings from Heath (1983) and Purcell-Gates (1995) that families' literacy ideologies were situated in a social and cultural context. The families in this study had to negotiate their home country literacy ideologies, the demands of the migrant lifestyle, and mainstream literacy practices. This study suggests that literacy ideologies are not static; rather, migrant parents must negotiate between these to support their children's educational advancement.

Moreover, the children in the study were all becoming bi- or multilinguals. However, their diverse language abilities and literacy practices did not appear to be tapped into as resources for schooling (Moll et al., 1992). Their linguistic resources appeared invisible to schools, which did not communicate with parents in a language that they understood, send notices and information to parents in a language that they could read, and learn about the children's first language abilities that could support their language and literacy in English (Cummins, 2001). As Guerra (1998) has observed, "[immigrants] come to this country equipped with a range of social, linguistic, and rhetorical abilities that human beings born into any language and culture inevitably develop, not only to function and survive in everyday life, but to progress and thrive under typical and unexpected circumstances" (p. 153). This holds true for migrant children and families who bring rich cultural and linguistic resources to schools and communities throughout the United States.

## CONCLUSION

Migrant children face numerous obstacles including poverty, mobility, and lack of health- and dental care, in addition to the challenges of public education that require access and socialization into mainstream literacy events. Findings from this study revealed that migrant families in north central Florida were required to negotiate mainstream literacy ideologies and practices that would allow their children to successfully complete academic assignments and participate in school events and activities. These different ideologies, combined with the rural nature of family's homes, a mobile lifestyle, and few materials in Spanish all contributed to their limited access to a wide variety of print, including storybooks for pleasure reading and materials to complete school work.

In addition, the families engaged in literacy practices and had access to certain genres or types of print, namely religious texts. These played a prominent role in their homes and served as reminders of their home country and cultural practices. Essentially, the language uses and the literacy practices of the families were different rather than deficient; these differences add to the cultural and linguistic fabric of the United States.

## REFERENCES

Branz-Spall, A., & Wright, A. (2004). A history of advocacy for migrant children and their families: More than 30 years in the fields. In C. Salinas & M. Fránquiz (Eds.), *Scholars in the field: The challenges of migrant education* (pp. 2-10). Charleston, WV: ERIC Clearinghouse on Rural Education and Small Schools.

Bourdieu, P. (1991). *Ce que parler veut dire* [language and symbolic power]. Cambridge, MA: Harvard University Press.

Cummins, J. (2001). *Negotiating identities: Education for empowerment in a diverse society* (2nd ed). Sacramento: California Association for Bilingual Education Press.

Guerra, J. (1998). *Close to home: Oral and literate practices in a transnational Mexicano community.* New York: Teachers College Press.

Heath, S. B. (1983). *Ways with words: Language, life, and work in communities and classrooms.* New York: Cambridge University Press.

Johnson, N. B. (1980). The material culture of public school classrooms: The symbolic integration of local schools and national culture. *Anthropology & Education Quarterly 11*(3), 173-190.

LeCompte, M., & Schensul, J. (1999). Designing and conducting ethnographic research. Book 1. *The ethnographer's toolkit.* Walnut Creek, CA: Altamira.

León, E. (1996). *Challenges and solutions for educating migrant students* (JSRI Working Paper #28. East Lansing, MI: Julian Samora Research Institute. Retrieved November 18, 2008, from http://www.jsri.msu.edu/RandS/research/wps/wp28.pdf

López, M. E. (1999). *When discourses collide: An ethnography of migrant children at home and in school.* New York: Peter Lang.

Moll, L. C., Amanti, C., Neff, D., & González, N. (1992). Funds of knowledge for teaching: Using a qualitative approach to connect homes and classrooms. *Theory Into Practice, 31*(2), 132-141.

National Agricultural Workers Survey. (2005). *A demographic and employment profile of United States farm workers.* Retrieved November 18, 2008, from http://www.doleta.gov/agworker/report9/toc.cfm

Pappamihiel, N. E. (2004). The legislation of migrancy: Migrant education in our courts and government. In C. Salinas & M. Fránquiz (Eds.), *Scholars in the field: The challenges of migrant education* (pp. 13-27). Charleston, WV: ERIC Clearinghouse on Rural Education and Small Schools.

Pérez, B. (1998). *Sociocultural contexts of language and literacy.* Mahwah, NJ: Erlbaum.

Purcell-Gates, V. (1995). *Other people's words: The cycle of low literacy.* Cambridge, MA: Harvard University Press.

Riley, N. (2002). *Florida's farmworkers in the twenty-first century.* Gainesville: University Press of Florida.

Shannon, S., & Escamilla, K. (1999). Mexican immigrants in US schools: Targets of symbolic violence. *Educational Policy, 13*(3), 347-370.

Shen, T. (2006). Invisible children in the classroom. Paper presented at the *Centennial conference: Closing the achievement gap through partnerships.* St. Petersburg, FL.

Stake, R. (1995). *The art of case study research.* Thousand Oaks, CA: SAGE.

Taylor, D., & Dorsey-Gaines, C. (1988). *Growing up literate: Learning from inner-city families.* Portsmouth, NH: Heinemann.

U.S. Department of Labor. (2005). *Bureau of Labor Statistics.* Retrieved October 23, 2006, from http://www.bls.gov/news.release/pdf/cfoi.pdf

CHAPTER 7

# LITERACY PRACTICES AMONG IMMIGRANT LATINO FAMILIES

**Leslie Reese**

> Imagine sitting your baby in your lap and reading a book to him for the first time. How different from just talking! Now you're showing him pictures. You point to them. In a lively way, you explain what the pictures are. You've just helped your child take the next step beyond talking. You've shown him that words and pictures connect. And you've started him on his way to understanding and enjoying books. (U.S. Department of Education, 2005)

The above paragraph, from a U.S. government publication available in English and Spanish, describes for parents how to carry out the activity of joint reading with young children. The elements are familiar—reading aloud, engaging in conversation about text and pictures, sitting in close proximity to one another, one-on-one interaction with the young child, and a warm affective environment. In general, research has shown that more literacy and language in the home are associated with higher levels of children's language and literacy development (Booth & Dunn, 1996; Hart & Risley, 1998). Based on findings such as these, recommendations for parent support of children's learning typically include the recommendation to read to their child at home (Hernandez, 2001), with the assumption that the reading will or should occur in the manner described above. Conversely, when students are not achieving at expected levels in

*Multicultural Families, Home Literacies, and Mainstream Schooling*
pp. 129–149

reading, the assumption is often made that home reading is not occurring.

As part of what has been termed the "new Latino diaspora," Latino immigrants are moving into and beginning to transform areas of the United States which until relatively recently had low levels of Latino immigration (Wortham, Murrillo, & Hamann, 2002). Effective instruction of the Latino student population, including immigrants and nonimmigrants alike, continues to pose serious challenges for the country's schools. Overall, evidence indicates that Hispanic students are less than half as likely as white, non-Hispanic students to be at proficient levels in their literacy and academic skills (see, e.g., nces.ed.gov/nationsreportcard/reading/results). To address underachievement by Latino students, schools are encouraged to implement home reading programs and/or to train parents in helping their children at home. But these programs often operate without information about what actually goes on at home and thus fail to build on literacy practices that may already be in place in the home but which may not exhibit the same characteristics as the reading together description above. The purpose of this chapter is to describe literacy practices occurring in the homes of working class, immigrant Latino families involving their young, second-generation children.

## SOCIOCULTURAL PERSPECTIVE ON LITERACY PRACTICES

Home literacy practices include observable literacy activities involving use of text. Activities are varied and may include copying a recipe, searching for a job in the want ads, interpreting Bible verses, and reading a flier from school. However, the concept of literacy practices is not limited to observable tasks or activities in which text is used, but includes the cultural values, attitudes, feelings and relationships as well which shape and give meaning to those activities (Barton & Hamilton, 2000; Street, 1993, 2000). Family members engage in literacy use for a variety of purposes, partly in response to demands in the social settings in which they live.

Sociohistorical activity theory (Leont'ev, 1981; Vygotksy, 1978) and extensions of this work (Rogoff, 1990, 2003; Tharp & Gallimore, 1988; Wertsch, 1981, 1985) provide a helpful framework for looking at the role of cultural values and assumptions in shaping activities involving use of text. Everyday family activity settings (e.g., dinner time, after-school activities, Bible study) are a key unit of analysis for understanding the lived culture of each family. Home activity settings are partly determined by the surrounding environment, partly constructed by the families in accordance with personal and cultural schemas (Gallimore, Goldenberg, & Weisner, 1993; Reese, Kroesen, & Gallimore, 2000; Reese, Goldenberg,

Loucky, & Gallimore, 1995). Activity settings can be described and analyzed using the following dimensions: the personnel present and available for participation; the cultural goals and beliefs that participants bring to the activity; the motives and intentions guiding the action; the nature of the tasks that are accomplished; and the scripts, or patterns of appropriate conduct, used during the activity. "Scripts" refer to the way in which activities, such as reading aloud to a child or assisting a child with homework, are carried out. Implicit in this dimension is the notion that scripts are culturally appropriate, and often unconscious, ways that participants engage in a task. As we will see, home language and literacy activities can take on very different characteristics and follow quite different scripts depending on participants' goals and motives in engaging in the activity.

Cross-cultural research has found that children develop competencies, sometimes at very early ages, in tasks that they are expected and have the opportunities to perform, such as caring for infants (Rogoff, 2003). Similarly, children develop competencies in reading and writing through participation in tasks requiring their use. For bilingual children learning to read and write in one or more languages, research suggests that the more children have the opportunity to draw from all continua of biliteracy—to interact with decontextualized as well as contexualized text, to engage in vernacular as well as academic uses of literacy, to make use of L1 as well as L2—the greater their chances of full biliterate development (Hornberger 1989, Hornberger & Skilton-Sylvester, 2000).

In this chapter, I examine the home environments of young children (ages 5 through 7) who are learning to read and write (in Spanish, English or both languages), while documenting the types of literacy practices in a variety of domains that form part of the children's home experiences. In the present analysis I investigate the common domains of literacy use in the homes of immigrant Latino children, and how literacy practices within these domains may differ. In particular, I am interested in documenting the ways in which children observe and participate in the literacy practices of their families.

## METHODS

The UCLA Latino Home-School Project was a federally funded longitudinal study of the academic trajectories of a group of second-generation Latino immigrant children in the metropolitan Los Angeles area. This chapter presents findings from the first 3 years of the longitudinal study, when children were in kindergarten through Grade 2, drawing primarily from ethnographic interviews with a subgroup of 29 randomly selected case study families. (For information on the sample and data collection from the full study see Reese, Garnier, Gallimore, & Goldenberg, 2000.)

The case study families were interviewed at home using semistructured, open-ended interview protocols that took the form of guided conversations, inviting parents to converse in greater depth about their children's learning and upbringing. Interviewers were three bilingual graduate students, one Latina and two non-Latinas, including the author. Each interview began with a discussion of homework and school issues, followed by questions delving into other aspects of home literacy such as workplace, church, and household uses of literacy. Parents were asked to reflect on their own experiences in their home country settings, especially as these related to childrearing, learning, and educational aspirations. Parents completed a Home Reading Inventory in which they reported the number and types of reading materials in the home, the language in which the material was found, and sample titles. Each interview transcription was supplemented with an observational field note describing the setting in which the interview occurred and the activity of the target child during the interview. During the 3-year period, 12 two-hour home interviews were conducted with each of the case study families.

## Analysis

Narrative interview transcriptions were analyzed following the sequence outlined by Miles and Huberman (1994), in which field notes and transcriptions of open-ended interview responses as well as observational notes were reviewed and coded according to themes of interest. Coding themes for this study included the domains of literacy practices (school, religion, work, household, other), scripts for reading aloud with children, descriptions of learning/reading strategies, etc. The coding process was flexible enough to allow for themes to emerge from the data as well. Data displays (matrices) aided in the identification of trends, patterns and preliminary hypotheses, which were then tested with a return to the field data.

## Population Description and Setting

The children in the sample were mainly American-born children of immigrant Spanish-speaking parents. The great majority of the parents (84%) came to the United States from Mexico; most of the rest were from Central America. The average number of years of formal schooling for both mothers and fathers was 7 (range = 0-16). With few exceptions, parents were employed in blue-collar jobs or lower paying jobs in the service sector. In contrast to their parents, all of whom were immigrants, the majority (75%) of the children were born in the United States (94% of these in California), and 22% were born in Mexico.

The community in which three of the schools were located was a low-income predominantly Latino community located near a large airport. Families resided in apartment buildings, or small homes and duplexes in various states of repair. Spanish was the language heard most often in the street, and many of the small local businesses and churches catered to their Spanish-speaking clientele. In the participating schools, students were initially placed in a transitional bilingual program of instruction, although some students found themselves in English programs when they moved out of district. The second community, where one school was located, was located approximately 15 miles away in a diverse port city. The community was also low income, but more diverse ethnically and linguistically than the first community. In this neighborhood, Spanish was often heard in the streets and in some of the businesses, along with English, Tagalog, and occasionally Vietnamese. Although this school offered a transitional bilingual program as well, implementation of the program was less systematic, and some children were placed in English instruction by teachers operating from their individual criteria or understandings of the program.

## FINDINGS

Farr (1994) has identified five literacy "domains," which I have adapted to comprise a useful framework to catalogue family literacy practices. These domains include (1) education (homework, parent classes, notices from school), (2) religion (Bible or Bible stories, religious tracts), (3) commerce/work (job related materials, ads, job applications), (4) family/home (news, entertainment, communicating with relatives, household tasks, information), and (5) politics/law (political flyers, application for drivers license, naturalization papers). Use of these domains helps us map how family practices are shaped by the demands, constraints, and resources in community and family settings.

### The Role of School in Home Literacy Practices

Although all of the case study parents were native speakers of Spanish who reported having little fluency in English, and most were employed in low-wage jobs in factories or in the service sector, there was considerable variation across families with respect to parents' level of education. Regardless of parents' educational level, however, results from the Home Literacy Inventory indicated that all households reported use of literacy materials in the home for school-related purposes. School-promoted activities included help with homework, reading aloud to children, reading notes and fliers from the school or teacher, and creating study materials such as flash cards to assist the child with learning.

The Medina household illustrates some of the activities associated with school tasks. The family lived in a one-room duplex where few books and printed materials were in evidence. A Bible and a book of prayers rested on a shelf, along with two coloring books and a plastic bag with some of kindergartner Delia's school papers. Because of her concerns about the safety of the neighborhood, Mrs. Medina allowed her three girls to play in front of the house only under her watchful eye and encouraged them to play indoors. Delia often played school, taking the role of teacher to her 3-year-old sister and incorporating her school papers in their play. Mrs. Medina observed, *"Las pocas palabras que sabe Delia en inglés, las sabe Yadira también"* ("The few words that Delia knows in English, Yadira knows too.")

Mrs. Medina was scrupulous in ensuring that Delia, a below average achiever, completed her homework assignments. Although initially placed in a bilingual classroom, Delia was placed in an English-only classroom after the family moved during her kindergarten year. Mrs. Medina was often unable to understand the English papers and reported pressing her daughter to remember the instructions, *"¿Qué te dijo la maestra?"* ("What did the teacher tell you?") She concluded, *"Siempre lleva la tarea auque sea equivocada"* ("She always takes her homework [to school] even if it is incorrect.") By Grade 2, Mrs. Medina reported taking Delia to the library and reading to her on a regular basis *"porque me exigen en la escuela que les lean. Me mandan un papel que tengo que firmar"* ("because the school requires that I read to them. They send me a paper that I have to sign").

In the spring of Delia's kindergarten year, a new element appeared in the home. Mrs. Medina had taped a paper onto the wall above the girls' bed with the handwritten words *"ey bi si di i ef …"* She explained that Delia needed to learn the alphabet in English. Since her mother did not speak English, they had enlisted the help of Delia's father, who had written out in Spanish the names of the English letters. Mrs. Medina looked at the handwriting and commented, *"Mi viejo casi no escribe bien"* ("My husband doesn't write very well.") She explained that he had been brought to the U.S. at age 8 and put to work in the fields with his parents, so he did not have much formal schooling, but he is the one in the household who speaks English. On several occasions, when letters came from school in English, Mrs. Medina sought out a neighbor with a boy in the same school to read and translate the letter for her. The translation was done with the help of the boy, who interjected what he remembered the teacher telling the class that the letter was about. The school-related activities in the Medina household illustrate the collaborative nature of many of the negotiations around print, particularly when the child is in an English language school setting. Families and neighbors pool skills in order to make sense of materials in an unfamiliar language.

In the Lara household, where parents had higher levels of education and were employed in the white-collar job sector as accounts clerks in Mexico prior to immigrating, there were more books in the home— approximately 10 children's books, an encyclopedia set, a couple of adult novels, and three English text books that the father had used in an English class. Mrs. Lara explained that when they went to the grocery store, Teresa would often ask for paper doll books, but her mother would tell her that the activity books she buys are *"lo que más te conviene a ti, lo que te va a enseñar algo"* ("what is best for you, what is going to teach you something"). Mrs. Lara reported checking daily to see if her daughter had homework and asking Teresa what her completed school papers were about. During kindergarten, Mrs. Lara recounted that when Teresa came home from school *"lo primero que hace es empezar a contarme el cuento. Le llaman mucho la atención los cuentos"* ("the first thing she does is start to tell me the story [that they read in school]. Stories really capture her attention").

Teresa, a serious child and higher achiever, had also been placed in an English-language program of reading instruction. Although in a designated bilingual classroom, Teresa's teacher felt that the "more mature" children would benefit from instruction in English rather than Spanish. When the teacher suggested that children should be read to at home, Mrs. Lara complied by choosing the easiest of the books that were sent home and reading through the book first. If she did not understand a sentence, she would try to understand the story from the pictures and then invent that part when she read aloud to her daughter. When Teresa's family moved toward the end of the kindergarten year, her new teacher sent a letter asking the parents to help Teresa learn the letters of the alphabet that she did not know. Mrs. Lara laughed breathlessly and said that she and Teresa had subsequently practiced the letters *"día y noche"* ("day and night"), even while they walked to school. Like the Medina family, the Lara family responded to requests and suggestions from the teachers by utilizing strategies and resources available to them, often expending greater effort than might be necessary for a native speaker of English.

As the Lara and Medina family cases illustrate, parents draw on a range of personnel, including spouses, neighbors, fellow parents, and even a university project fieldworker, to support them in responding to school demands. All parents interviewed reported supervising their children's homework in some way. For some this supervision consisted of asking, ¿*Traes tarea?*" ("Do you have homework?"). In some families older siblings were recruited to help with their younger brothers and sisters. For example, Maricela's mother worked outside of the home and occasionally asked her older son to check his sister's homework. Thus, the stack of Maricela's papers that had been sent home from school showed that someone had always signed that her homework was checked; sometimes the signature was her mother's, sometimes the father checked and signed it, and sometimes it was the brother. Other parents reported sitting with their children and making sure the homework was done correctly. For example, Tomás was one of the lower achievers in his first grade class. At home, he would sometimes race through his homework in order to play outside. His mother reported making him do his work over again, erasing the letters that were incorrect or too big and writing them over again. She concluded, "*Y tanto que le hago que borra y borra ya las hace bien. Igual con las letras*" ("And since I have him erase and erase so much, now he is doing it right. The same with the letters").

In Spanish, "*tarea*" is a task or obligation and the term may be used to refer to tasks around the home as well as at school. For the families, homework and schoolwork are serious enterprises, and parents tried to encourage children to do all of their work and to do their best. These *consejos*, or advice, were viewed by parents as one of the ways in which they helped their children succeed and were motivated by their desires that their children continue in school and "become someone" in life. One mother's advice to her daughter consisted of telling her, "*Tú tienes que ser mejor, le digo, por eso estás estudiando. Para llegar a ser alguien, una doctora, una maestra, lo que tú quieres ser, tienes que estudiar*" ("You have to be better, I tell her, that's why you're studying. To get to be someone, a doctor, a teacher, whatever you want, you have to study"). Another boy's father echoed the same sentiments, "*Les digo que tienen que estudiar, para que no vayan a ser lo que soy yo. No pude estudiar—no tuve esa oportunidad*" (I tell them that they have to study, so they don't end up like me. I couldn't study—I didn't have that opportunity"). At the beginning of kindergarten, over 90% of the parents in the sample aspired to their children's attending the university. Their aspirations declined somewhat over the years; however, by the end of second grade, over 80% still expressed the hope that their children would attend college.

### Literacy as Source of Critique and Resistance

While parents generally held high aspirations for their children's eventual educational attainment and encouraged their children's literacy development through support of school tasks, parents were not uniformly accepting of school practices. For example, Mrs. Alvarez, who came to the United States after completing 2 years of university in her native El Salvador, complained energetically about the quality of the Spanish language instruction in her son's classroom. She said of the teacher: *"Debe de usar el diccionario si no sabe la palabra. Es importante enseñarles un buen español"* ("She should use the dictionary if she doesn't know the word. It's important to teach the children good Spanish"). In this case, a parent carefully read the materials sent home from school and found them lacking. Mrs. Alvarez had both the educational background and the confidence to approach school personnel; however, her actions only gained her the reputation of being a difficult parent. A similar situation occurred with Mrs. Laosa, a parent at a different school, who recounted an incident in which a school assignment had come home with the word *"cucede"* used. She wrote back to the teacher asking if this was a new word, or if she meant to write *"sucede."* Her husband added that if this is the level of Spanish being taught, *"mejor les enseñan en inglés"* ("it would be better to teach them in English").

In these instances, print materials from the school were not simply the generators of activity by children and assistance by parents, as was the teacher's intent. Rather the texts became focal points of critique, both of the level of academic Spanish used by teachers as well as the status implications of use of informal language in instructional settings. By extension, the parents were calling into question the quality of instructional program their children were receiving.

School-related literacy can take forms that are embedded in and serve to reinforce unequal social relations between schools and immigrant families. Mrs. Lara's experiences illustrate the ways in which language and literacy can serve as both gate-keeping mechanisms and as resources for addressing discriminatory practices. When the Lara family moved, Mrs. Lara hoped to enroll her daughter in the school closest to her new home, which had the added advantage of having a bilingual program. Her new home was located in another school's service area, however, she was told that she would need to obtain and fill out transfer forms from that school. When she went to the school, she was ignored by the office staff after trying unsuccessfully to communicate what she needed. She left without obtaining the needed forms and was unable to enroll her daughter. In tears during our next interview, Mrs. Lara asked me to accompany her to school to see if she could get the forms. When the forms were handed to me without question, Mrs. Lara commented to me softly, *"Mira tan rápido que te atendieron a ti"* ("Look how quickly they attended to you").

This experience prompted Mrs. Lara to recount another that had happened the year before, which she also described in terms of *"racismo."* Teresa's Head Start preschool class was the only one that did not go on fieldtrips to the library and the fire station. A mother who spoke English told the others that she had overheard the children's teacher tell another teacher that she would not take "these little animals" anywhere, and if their parents wanted them to go, they could take them themselves. Mrs. Lara brought up the issue at a parent meeting and was told that the parents should organize and file a complaint. Mrs. Lara then drafted a letter of complaint to the director that all of the parents signed. She said that subsequently the teacher was taken off the job and the aide took over the class.

A native of Mexico City and who, having completed *secundaria comercial* (commercial secondary equivalent to Grade 9 in the United States), had a higher level of education than the majority of parents in the study, Mrs. Lara had the cultural capital—both the literacy skills and the confidence—to use her letter writing ability to help redress a wrong on behalf of the group of parents. However, even possessing these skills in her native language, she was unable to put them to use when English was the sole medium of communication, as in the incident in the school office.

## Reading Aloud to Children

As described above, parents responded to school demands to monitor and help with homework. One of the school demands was reading aloud to children, typically as part of homework. For the total sample ($n = 121$), the percentage of parents who reported reading to their children at the beginning of kindergarten was 26.7%. Many more parents (61.7%) reported assisting their children to learn the alphabet and to write their name, and 37.5% of the parents reported helping with homework only. However, once children entered formal schooling, the reports of reading to children rose by a substantial figure. By the middle of kindergarten, 62% of the case study families ($n = 29$) reported reading to children; and by the middle of first grade, 90% reported reading to children. Thus, although the practice of reading aloud to children was not reported as a regular activity in the majority of the homes prior to the child's entering kindergarten, it became over the course of a year or two a common practice in most of the homes. For example, Mrs. Duarte, who had reported only having seven children's books in the home during Maricela's kindergarten year, said two years later that she had *"un alto así de libros"* ("a stack this high of books"), gesturing about 2 feet high.

In one of the kindergarten interviews, parents were asked to describe how they learned to read and how they observed that their children were learning to read. Mrs. Luján described learning to read *"deletreando, conociendo las vocales primero y luego las sílabas, luego las frases"* ("spelling, learning the vowels first, then the syllables, then the sentences"). She added, *"en el pueblo no había mucho material didáctico. Se escribía más—la s con la a, sa, la s con la e, se, y así por sílabas'* ("in the town there were not many learning materials. One wrote more—s with a, sa, s with e, se, and so on by syllables"). With few exceptions parents described the reading process in a similar fashion, as putting letters together to make syllables and putting syllables together to make words. In helping their children with homework, parents attended to the form of the letters and to correct identification of sounds and letters. When helping their children by reading aloud, parents tended to focus on these same elements. For example, when the teacher sent home a note saying that she needed to read with her daughter, one mother described her response: *"Le digo que tiene que estudiar. Me siento a leer con ella. Le leo yo despacio pa' que sepa las letras"* ("I tell her she has to study. I sit down with her to read. I read to her slowly so that she learns the letters"). In the Mejía home, Emilio's mother described her role in her son's homework: *"No lo ayudo con la tarea sino que le corrijo lo que hace mal. Quiero que aprenda las cosas como son y no como él quiere"* ("I don't help him with homework, but rather I correct what he does wrong. I want him to learn things the way they are and not how he wants").

When parents read aloud in response to teacher demands, they activated the cultural model of *"tarea"* and carried out the reading as they would any other homework assignment designed to help the child learn to read. Parents' descriptions of their children's homework and how they assisted with homework provide indicators of how parents perceive the task of learning to read and the cultural model (D'Andrade, 1995; Strauss, 1992) they activated to inform their participation in the activity. They assumed that literacy learning followed a bottom-up sequence of learning letters first, then syllables, followed by words and sentences. Because parents expected homework in kindergarten and first grade to focus on learning letters and words, they did not readily see the instructional value of other types of materials. For example, Mrs. Medina described the papers that Delia brought home as *"solo monillos y cosillas"* ("only little figures and little things"), and Mrs. Duarte pushed one of Maricela's papers aside with the deprecatory comment, *"es solo dibujo"* ("it's only drawing"). Even when the *dibujos* represented story sequencing or vocabulary development exercises, the mothers did not report doing anything when their children brought home papers like these because they did not recognize the learning value or pedagogical intent of the papers.

Thus, in reading aloud to children in response to school demands, parents' goals in carrying out the activity included helping the child learn to read and to succeed in school, while the more immediate motive was completing the homework. These goals and motives shaped the parents' scripts for carrying out the activities, scripts that focused on the accurate identification of letters and words and on repeated practice until the letters and words were learned.

## Literacy Practices in the Domain of Religion

Data from both the reading inventory and the home visits indicated that school-related literacy materials were present in all homes. At the same time, school is not the only domain in which family literacy practices take place. As described by Coady (this volume) as well, religion is an important aspect of many families' lives and can serve as a powerful motivator for a variety of literacy practices involving both children and adults.

Religious literacy was not observed in all families, but it did play a role in the majority of homes. Although only 66% of the case study families reported attending church regularly, 79% owned Bibles and 55% reported reading the Bible or religious material on a regular basis. Reading for religious purposes, therefore, was often associated with church but was not necessarily limited to church activities and attendance. Parents reported using the Bible in different ways—as support for difficult aspects of their lives or as a source of guidance. For example, in a discussion about laws regarding use of corporal punishment in this country, Mrs. Alvarez reinforced her arguments against this law by citing the Bible, *"En la Biblia está que se castiga al niño con una barra de dos centímetros de ancho, que uno no debe castigarle con la mano porque es sagrada. La mano es para mostrar amor. No sé en que se basan las leyes"* ("In the Bible it says that a child is punished with a rod two centimeters wide, that one should not use one's hand to punish because the hand is sacred. The hand is for showing love. I don't know what they are basing the laws on").

Some families engaged in regular Bible reading, sharing of Bible stories, and reading associated with catechism classes. For example, in the Ramos home, the family said the rosary together each evening and attended services at the Catholic church about 10 blocks from their home. Mother and grandmother both read the Bible in the evenings, trading off because there was only one Bible. Mrs. Ramos also liked to attend a Bible study group at church on Friday evenings.

During his first grade year, Tomás Ramos went to classes for *la doctrina*, or catechism classes, to prepare him for his first communion. Although he had been a struggling student who was almost retained in kindergarten, his mother was enthusiastic about his participation in the *doctrina* classes: *"Va muy adelantado. Sabe persignarse, contestar preguntas, como por ejemplo*

*¿donde está Dios? El sabe decir 'Dios está en todas partes' y no 'está en el cielo' como otros niños."* ("He is very advanced. He knows how to cross himself, how to answer questions, like for example 'Where is God?' He knows how to say 'God is everywhere' instead of 'God is up in heaven' like most children.'") She added that the only thing that he could not do was read, but that this was not necessary in his class; it was only necessary to memorize the prayers.

The religion-focused literacy activity in the Ramos household described above was typical of the Catholic families in the sample in the sense that, while adults engaged in reading the Bible or religious texts, church-sponsored practices centering on use of text for children was relatively rare. The one exception to this was in the Ayala family. The Ayalas preferred to attend church on Saturday night rather than on Sunday because there was a special children's moment. *"Les leen y luego les hacen preguntas como 'Tú, ¿qué piensas de eso?'"* ("They read to them and then they ask them questions like 'What do you think of that?'") However, in the rest of the Catholic families, children were expected to memorize prayers and responses and recite these with the congregation or family.

However, in the six families in the case study sample who attended evangelical churches, literacy practices played a more prominent role, both in church activities as well as home activities. For example, the Dominguez family attended the Asamblea de Dios Betania church, participating in services all day long on Sunday, on Tuesday evenings, and sometimes on Monday evenings. Kindergarten-aged Gualberto had a special folder in which he kept his materials from church. In one interview, Mrs. Dominguez recounted that the previous Sunday her son *"nos mostró lo que había hecho y le leí el librito engrampado que le dieron"* ("he showed us what he had done and I read him the little illustrated book that they had given him"). Mother reported that both she and her husband read the Bible several times a week, and she read aloud to her son from a book of children's Bible stories. In the Baldano family, everyone attended church services on Sunday, Daniel attended Sunday school on the days that his older sister taught, and his mother and sister sold religious texts in the church store. The importance of text-based activity was observed as well in the Chávez family where Mother reported: *"También les leemos la Biblia. Es para que ellos vayan sabiendo lo que es bueno y lo que es malo, lo que a ellos les conviene hacer y lo que no les conviene hacer"* ("We also read them the Bible. It's so that they know what is right and what is wrong, what it is good for them to do and what isn't good for them to do"). She added that when the Bible verses are read in church, Emilia finds the verse in her Bible and underlines it just like her parents do. *"Marca el versículo que leen. Ya tiene todo marcado"* ("She marks the verse that is read. Now she has everything marked").

An observational study carried out with 10 families during the pilot year for the longitudinal study provides another example of how children acquire the literacy practices of their community of believers, in this case within a family of Jehovah's Witnesses (Reese & Gallimore, 2000). In the afternoon after school, Mrs. Delgado encouraged her daughter and niece to *"jugar al culto"* ("to play church") much in the same way that many children play school. One afternoon she joined in their play, covering her head with a scarf before opening her Bible and saying, *"Ahora voy a presedir. A ver hermanos, ¿Qué dice Génesis 1:1?"* ("Now I'll preside. Let's see, brothers and sisters, what does Genesis 1:1 say?") Each girl held her own Bible and, as if reading the words, recited the text with their mother monitoring.

On the other hand, both Catholic and evangelical families described discussing stories with children that had a moral to be learned. For example, Manuel's mother said that he enjoyed the story of Jonas and the whale, which she used to teach him about correct behavior. She reported telling her 5-year-old son *"si no se porta bien se va quedar en la panza de la ballena."* ("If you don't behave well you're going to end up in the belly of the whale.")

These examples illustrate how the parents' goals and purposes for engaging in activities involving religious texts resulted in different scripts for carrying out the activities than had been observed when the purpose was help with *tarea*. When the goal was helping children understand the moral of the text and its meaning in their own lives, parents asked children to recount what happened in the story or to evaluate the behavior of the protagonist in the story. In these instances, the content was the key component, and reading was how one accessed that content. In the Delgado family's church, recognizing, memorizing, and citing *"la palabra de Dios"* or word of God were important activities of the faithful, and children were encouraged to participate in these at an early age. By way of contrast, in the school activities that parents considered to be part of teaching young children to read, parents focused on the form of the text and the process of breaking text into decodable segments.

## Job-Related Literacy Experiences at Home

Much less common than either school or religion-related literacy practices were practices associated with the parents' jobs. This is not surprising considering the kinds of jobs that parents held. At the time the study began, 97% of the fathers and 43% percent of the mothers were employed. The majority of the fathers worked in the census categories of Service (30.4%), Repair (23.2%) and Laborer (34.4%). Parents with jobs in the service industries worked as cooks, waiters, maids and housekeepers, janitors, gardeners, bartenders, bus boys, parking attendants, childcare workers, cafeteria workers, and two teacher's assistants. There were also skilled workers such as mechanics, electricians, carpenters, welders, construction workers, as well as a dressmaker. The largest percentage of both men and women, however, were employed as laborers in construction and factory work such as assembly, packing, machine operation, and loading.

Slightly over half of the working parents (52% of the mothers and 54% of the fathers) reported using reading or writing, in either English or Spanish or both, on the job. Some of the parents did not report that they used literacy on the job *per se*, but reported that knowledge of reading and writing was related in some way to their job. For example, Mr. Gallo remarked that on his job as a bartender the orders are given to him verbally; however, he had to attend "American School Bartender" in order to obtain a certificate as a bartender. Mr. Sandoval, who worked cleaning buildings not far from his home, was another parent who reported that no reading or writing was done on his job. He did, however, assist the owner of the buildings by reading and translating insurance documents when these arrived for her.

Although job-related literacy was not reported to occur on a daily basis, parents described various ways in which the demands of their jobs motivated literacy activity at home. For example, Valeria's mother sold silk flower arrangements out of her home, organizing parties in which she demonstrated how to create the arrangements. She kept a written account of her appointments and sales. Tomás' mother also worked at home, using her bilingual skills to answer the telephone for her brother-in-law's gardening business and to schedule appointments for him. Teresa's mother worked cleaning houses. Although she initially laughed, saying that this job did not have any reading or writing involved, she later described how she regularly took an English-Spanish dictionary to work in case her employer left her a note or in case she needed to check product labels or instructions.

One of only seven parents (24% of the sample) who reported having job-related literacy materials at home, Mrs. Ayala operated a beauty parlor in the front of her home. She had about 10 books related to cosmetology and reported reading product instructions on the job. She described how difficult her beauty school training was; although she had been told the class would be in Spanish, it turned out to be in English. She got through *"usando la cabeza y la inteligencia para darme cuenta de lo que estaba hablando. Pero hay que usar la cabeza demasiado para tomar un curso en inglés"* ("using my head and my intelligence to figure out what she was saying. But you have to use your head too much in order to take classes in English").

Several of the parents were taking classes or participating in training as part of their jobs, sometimes studying at home. For example, during one of the interviews in the Duarte home, Maricela and her younger sister were playing school at a small table in the corner of the living room while their father spread his books on the dining room table to study. Mr. Linares, who obtained a job as a shuttle driver at the nearby airport, brought his training materials home and enlisted his family's assistance in memorizing the script that he had to repeat as he directed passengers to the different airlines and terminals.

Although children occasionally observed their parents studying, taking messages, or completing reports, the majority of the parents who used reading and writing on the job reported that they did not bring any of this reading home. The one exception to this generalization was Mrs. Franco. Her work as a paraprofessional in the elementary school classroom and the computer lab gave Mrs. Franco a familiarity with the school curriculum and instructional strategies that was uncommon among the mothers in the sample. On numerous occasions during the first three years of interviews, she described how she was helping Josué with his homework or how she devised games for additional practice. For example, when Josué brought home word cards to practice, his mother used them to play a Concentration-like game with him. She also picked up materials from school that the teachers gave to her or were throwing away. On one visit Josué was observed working on a stack of these discarded worksheets that had been stapled together like a book. Mrs. Franco reported having 187 adult books and 97 children's books in her home, far more than any other family in the sample.

## Literacy Practices for Other Purposes

Results from the Home Literacy Inventory indicated that all households reported use of literacy materials in the home for "instrumental reading" (Taylor & Dorsey-Gaines, 1988). Instrumental uses of literacy included reading directions on products, instructional manuals for appliances, forms for insurance or medical visits, legal documents such as immigration papers or birth certificates. Literacy use for medical purposes was reported in 90% of the homes and for legal purposes in 96%. Slightly under half of the families (48%) reported writing lists for shopping or other household tasks. During the early 1990s when the interviews were carried out, none of the families owned a computer, although this would probably be different if the study had been carried out a decade later. Letter writing to relatives was a commonly reported activity, with 90% of the families exchanging letters with relatives in Mexico, Central America, or other parts of the United States.

Reading for enjoyment was less common in the homes of the families than was reading for religious purposes or in response to school requirements. Mrs. Duarte was not alone in referring to reading novels as a *"pérdida de tiempo"* ("a waste of time"), preferring to read informational magazines such as *Buen Hogar* [*Good Housekeeping*] and *Padres e Hijos* [*Parents and Children*] instead. Although storybooks for children were present in many homes, fiction books for adults were very rare. In 11 of the homes (or 38% of the families) there were 10 or fewer books of any type for adults and children, and in 4 homes there were fewer than 5 books. (The average number of books was 37, with numbers ranging from 0 in one home to 294 books in the home of a family in which the mother worked as a teacher's aide). Therefore, if one were to look exclusively at the number of books or the frequency of reading for enjoyment in the homes of the immigrant families in the sample, one would greatly underestimate both the frequency that literacy practices occur as well as the range of domains in which these practices occur.

## DISCUSSION

In the present analysis, I have used the dimensions of activity settings (personnel, tasks, goals, motives, scripts) as a frame for examining families' literacy practices. With respect to school-related literacy, we have seen that the personnel involved in homework activities and home school connections are not limited to parent-child dyads. Older siblings, aunts and uncles, and occasionally grandparents may be present and drawn into helping the child or helping to understand the school task. The script, or way in which an activity or task is carried out, varies depending on the perceived goal of the activity. When parents perceive the task as reading *"tarea"* or homework, they draw on their understandings of how children learn to read and write, focusing on correct sounding out of words and syllables, on correct formation of letters, and on repeated practice until the task is learned. However, when reading is done for moral purposes, there is a greater focus on comprehension of the content. Thus, families' cultural models, including understandings of what a task entails and how it should be carried out, shape children's literacy practices at home.

In addition, the findings suggest that certain characteristics of literacy practices are more amenable to change and are more easily manipulated than others. For example, when schools require reading aloud to children as part of homework, parents who did not previously engage in this practice begin to do so, and in a relatively short time frame. Changes in "deeper meanings" and cultural values seem to be more impervious to change. Likewise, the scripts for carrying out tasks which derive from the deeper meanings held by the participants are changed only after repeated exposure to and participation in new activities. Thus, even though parents began to engage in what was for them a new activity, reading aloud to children as part of reading homework, they continued to imbue the activity with their understandings of how one teaches a child to read.

These findings have important implications for schools engaged in parent education efforts. Often an after-school workshop is offered for parents where they are taught how to read with their child, followed by teachers' laments at what they see as little follow through on the part of parents. Our findings suggest that when schools establish home reading clubs and encourage children's participation, or when they regularly send home books and require parents' signatures to confirm that children have been read to at home, the immigrant parents find ways to comply with these demands. However, the ways in which they comply might not conform to the expectations of story reading described at the onset of the chapter. For changes in scripts to occur, longer term participation in activity settings that demand these new scripts is necessary. Among our families this occurred for Mrs. Franco, as she worked as a teacher's aide in the classroom. Participation in on-going parent education sessions as well as observation and participation in the classroom are other ways in which parents gain familiarity with the ways in which literacy tasks are approached at school (Degado-Gaitan, 1990).

A dynamic view of culture, such as the one employed here, as changing in response to changing demands in the environment and with sustained participation in new activities challenges the applicability of some aspects of work in the "cultural differences" tradition. In a cultural differences perspective, the home language and literacy practices of immigrant families have been theorized as different from, and sometimes in opposition to, those of the school (Valdés, 1996). Children's underachievement is seen as associated with the disconnect between the school and home practices derived from the family's home culture (Carger, 1996; Ioga, 1995).

In our interviews with parents, we certainly found many examples of differences and discontinuities between home and school. Many of these centered around language, as parents struggled to make sense of English texts. Other differences, as we have seen above, were rooted in parents' cultural understandings of learning to read and how children should be assisted in their literacy development. It would be possible, therefore, to focus on these discontinuities and conclude that these account for problems that immigrant Spanish-speaking children experience in school and for their disproportionate underachievement in American schools. However, an exclusive focus on cultural and linguistic discontinuities is to ignore the many other areas in which the values and experiences of Latino homes are not at odds with those of the school.

A more helpful concept for teachers in working with Latino parents may be that of "complementarities" or practices that may not be identical to mainstream homes but nonetheless serve to support schooling and academic performance. Similarities or continuities between the Latino immigrant families in our study and mainstream middle class families include the readiness to assist children with homework, the value placed on schooling as an avenue for success in life, and the belief that parents should monitor and guide children's activities. Follow-through on homework included reading to children when this was requested by teachers. However, the notion of complementarities includes the assumption that home activities, while similar, may differ in some important ways from school activities. Thus, reading aloud to children may not take on characteristics of "storytime," in which parents and children engage in conversations about the text and pictures in addition to reading the story. "Help with homework" may not include the kind of scaffolding that teachers might provide to assist children in completing the activities, for example prompting them to retell a story using picture cues. Yet, parental encouragement and advice (their *consejos*) are consistent with the kinds of dispositions that teachers hope that children will develop with respect to learning. Recognition of the complementarities between home and school that exist in immigrant Latino homes also opens door to greater levels of home-school collaboration than does emphasis on cultural discontinuities only.

Immigrant Latino students face considerable challenges in American schools, not the least of which is entering school with less than full proficiency in English. Although they may come to school with experiences and understandings that are different from those of mainstream families and teachers, there is insufficient evidence to indicate that these differences account for children's underachievement relative to their mainstream peers. It is also true that, as residents in low income neighborhoods, many Latino children attend schools that differ greatly from schools in more affluent areas on a variety of measures such as resource allocation, availability of experienced teachers, and instructional norms (Mehan, Villanueva, Hubbard L., & Lintz, 1996; National Research Council, 1993). Evidence presented in this chapter indicates that at least some of the immigrant families are aware of these inequities in the educational system and take steps to try to address them. As educators, therefore, we have a dual task of seeking to improve schooling for immigrant children from within, while reaching out to include families who share many of our values with respect to their children's education.

## REFERENCES

Barton, D., & Hamilton. M. (2000). Literacy practices. In D. Barton, M., Hamilton, & R. Ivanic (Eds.). *Situated literacies: Reading and writing in context* (pp. 7-15). London: Routledge.

Booth, A., & Dunn, J. (Eds.). (1996). *Family and school links: How do they affect educational outcomes?* Mahwah, NJ: Erlbaum.

Carger, C. (1996). *Of borders and dreams: A Mexican-American experience of urban education.* New York: Teachers College Press.

D'Andrade, R. (1995). *The development of cognitive anthropology.* Cambridge, England: Cambridge University Press.

Delgado-Gaitan, C. (1990). *Literacy for empowerment: The role of parents in children's education.* New York: The Falmer Press.

Farr, M. (1994). *En los dos idiomas*: Literacy practices among Chicago Mexicanos. In B. Moss (Ed.), *Literacy across communities* (pp. 9-47). Cresskill, NJ: Hampton Press.

Gallimore, R., Goldenberg, C., & Weisner, T. (1993). The social construction and subjective reality of activity settings: Implications for community psychology. *American Journal of Community Psychology, 21*(44), 537-559.

Hart, B., & Risley, T. R. (1998). *Meaningful differences in everyday experiences of young American children.* Baltimore: Paul H. Brookes.

Hernandez, H. (2001). *Multicultural education: A teacher's guide to linking context, process, and content.* Columbus, OH: Merrill Prentice Hall.

Hornberger, N. H. (1989). Continua of biliteracy. *Review of Educational Research, 59*(3), 271-296.

Hornberger, N. H., & Skilton-Sylvester, E. (2000). Revisting the continua of biliteracy: International and critical Perspectives. *Language and Education, 14*(2), 96-122.

Ioga, C. (1995). *The inner world of the immigrant child.* Mahwah, NJ: Erlbaum.

Leont'ev, A. N. (1981). The problem of activity in psychology. In J. V. Wertsch (Ed.), *The concept of activity in Soviet psychology* (pp. 37-71). Armonk, NY: Sharpe.

Mehan, H., Villanueva, I., Hubbard L., & Lintz, A (1996). *Constructing school success: The consequences of untracking low-achieving students.* Cambridge, England: Cambridge University Press.

Miles, M., & Huberman, A. M. (1994). *Qualitative data analysis* (2nd ed.). Thousand Oaks, CA: SAGE.

National Research Council. (1993). *Losing generations: Adolescents in high-risk settings.* Washington, DC: National Academy Press.

Reese, L., & Gallimore, R. (2000). Immigrant Latinos' cultural model of literacy development: An evolving perspective on home-school discontinuities. *American Journal of Education, 108*(2), 103-134.

Reese, L., Garnier, H., Gallimore, R., & Goldenberg, C. (2000). A longitudinal analysis of the ecocultural antecedents of emergent Spanish literacy and subsequent English reading achievement of Spanish-speaking students. *American Educational Research Journal, 37*(3), 633-662.

Reese, L., Goldenberg, C., Loucky, J., & Gallimore, R. (1995). Ecocultural context, cultural activity, and emergent literacy of Spanish-speaking children. In S. W. Rothstein (Ed.), *Class, culture and race in American schools: A handbook*. Westport, CT: Greenwood Press.

Reese, L., Kroesen, K., & Gallimore, R. (2000). Agency and school performance among urban Latino youth. In R. Taylor & M. Wang (Eds.), *Resilience across contexts: Family, work, culture and community* (pp. 295-332). Mahwah, NJ: Erlbaum.

Rogoff, B. (1990). *Apprenticeship in thinking: Cognitive development in social context*. New York: Oxford University Press.

Rogoff, B. (2003). *The cultural nature of human development*. Oxford, England: Oxford University Press.

Strauss, C. (1992). Models and motives. In R. D'Andrade & C. Strauss (Eds.), *Human motives and cultural models* (pp. 1-20). Cambridge, England: Cambridge University Press.

Street, B. (1993). *Cross-cultural approaches to literacy*. Cambridge, England: Cambridge University Press.

Street, B. (2000). Literacy events and literacy practices: theory and practice in the New Literacy Studies. In M. Martin-Jones & K. Jones (Eds.), *Multilingual literacies: Reading and writing different worlds* (pp. 17-29). Philadelphia: John Benjamins.

Taylor, D., & Dorsey-Gaines, C. (1988). *Growing up literate: Learning from inner-city families*. Portsmouth, NH: Heinemann.

Tharp, R., & Gallimore, R. (1989). *Rousing minds to life*. Cambridge, England: Cambridge University Press.

U.S. Department of Education. (2005). *Helping your child become a reader.* Washington, DC: U.S. Department of Education, Office of Communications and Outreach.

Valdés. G. (1996). *Con respeto: Bridging the distances between culturally diverse families and schools*. New York: Teachers College Press.

Vygotsky, L. S. (1978). *Mind in society: The development of higher psychological processes* (M. Cole, V. John-Steiner, S. Scribner, & E. Souberman, Eds. and Trans.). Cambridge, MA: Harvard University Press.

Wertsch, J. V. (1981). *The concept of activity in Soviet psychology*. Armonk, NY: M. E. Sharpe.

Wertsch, J. V. (1985). *Vygotsky and the social formation of mind*. Cambridge, MA: Harvard University Press.

Wortham, S., Murrillo, E., & Hamann, E. (Eds.). (2002). *Education in the new Latino diaspora: Policy and the politics of identity*. London: Ablex.

# EUROPEAN AMERICAN FAMILIES

CHAPTER 8

# SHARING A LANGUAGE AND LITERACY LEGACY

## A White Middle Class Family's Experience

**Billie J. Enz and Dawn A. Foley**

*"Annie, Annie, look at mommy!" A few moments old and still wet from birth, Annie opened her eyes. An almost startling expression of recognition of her mom's voice crossed her face as she looked into her mom's eyes for the first time. Her cries quickly stopped as she listened to her mom's voice cooing to her. Within moments Annie turned her head rapidly to the direction of her dad as he said, "Oh Annie! We love you!" Even with all the sounds and distracting activity in the delivery room, Annie had focused her full attention on the two people whose voices she had heard consistently in the womb.* (August 10, 2001)

Annie was born into a family of educators. Her mother, Dawn, is a fourth generation teacher and has a bachelor's degree in early childhood education, a master's degree in literacy, and is pursuing a doctorate in early childhood education. Annie's father, Rob, has a bachelor's degree in special education and specializes in working with high school students. He earned a master's degree in educational administration before Annie reached her first birthday. Annie's maternal grandparents (who spend significant time each week with Annie so her mother can go to work and

*Multicultural Families, Home Literacies, and Mainstream Schooling*
pp. 153–174
Copyright © 2009 by Information Age Publishing
All rights of reproduction in any form reserved.                    153

school) both have doctoral degrees. Billie is a professor and faculty member in early childhood at a state university and Don was a school principal and superintendent. Now semiretired, he serves as the state director for a national school accreditation organization.

Annie's world, like most middle-class children born in the United States, is full of language and print that is pouring into her environment through multiple sources—radio, videos/DVDs, television programming, books, environmental print, games, and especially family talk. From infancy Annie has seen her parents talk, read, write, and use the computer daily—to accomplish specific tasks, to seek information, and just for the joy of learning.

Annie's parents and grandparents view literacy broadly, defining it as the pursuit of information and knowledge, not simply decoding symbols. Her family view themselves as Annie's first teachers and, though Annie is a novice in the world, her family sees her as an able and motivated learner. This view of learning and the behaviors this perspective promotes gives Annie an academic advantage in many ways. Research suggests that Annie's family background will play heavily into her development as a communicator, reader and writer, therefore impacting her future success in school (Christian, Morrison & Bryant, 1998; Hart & Risley, 1995; Heath, 1982).

We will describe Annie's 5-year journey to becoming an accomplished communicator and fairly sophisticated interpreter and consumer of print (though not yet a conventional reader). Her development is like that of most healthy middle-class children in the United States, except that it is being studied and intensely documented by her family.

## METHODOLOGY

### Data Collection

To document Annie's development over 5 years, her family collected several types of data including:

- Observation and documentation of the literacy/language event while it occurred;
- A simple calendar-notation. When Annie's mom reviewed the calendar each morning, new words were briefly recorded for elaboration later;
- Anecdotal notes written in the evening recounting an event that transpired during the day;

- Interviews with Annie's parents and grandparents recorded and transcribed;
- As Annie began to attend school, her teachers were also interviewed about her progress;
- Occasionally during family celebrations, a video camera was used to record the events of Annie's use of language and print in greater detail. Videotapes also documented a few storytime sessions;
- As Annie began to draw and write, pieces of her work were collected and dated, along with a brief description of the activity she was engaged in; and
- When Annie went to preschool and prekindergarten her work was collected from the school system.

Thus, Annie's growth was comprehensively documented over time. Her mother and grandmother systematically organized this information in chronological order (twice a month) then discussed their data to analyze her language and literacy achievements. Data analysis was ongoing throughout the data collection procedures in an integrated manner which allowed us to triangulate our data and findings.

## Data Analysis

Since data analysis was ongoing throughout data collection, it quickly became clear that Annie was not the only person who needed to be documented. Her actions were in response to her families interactions with her —from imitating their words, facial expressions and nonverbal gestures, to later developing and using her literacy skills in ways she had observed her family use them to accomplish specific goals. So as we collected data we were careful to provide more context of the situation and it's consequent and interactive effect on Annie's ability to take literacy meaning from her home context (Heath, 1982; Gee, 1991, 2004).

## THEORETICAL FRAMEWORK

Research in language acquisition and early literacy development has increasingly identified the family as a critical factor in school success or failure (Rogers, Marshall & Tyson, 2006). Or as James Gee (2004, p. 13) suggests:

> Children who learn to read successfully do so because, for them learning to read is a cultural and not primarily an instructed process. Furthermore, this

cultural process has long roots at home which have grown strong and firm before the child has walked in to a school.

The purpose of our work is not to tell the virtues of Annie's home literacy environment, rather to more deeply understand the ways in which the culture in the middle-class home provides a child with a legacy of language and literacy abilities and skills, particularly in an age where literacy is more than reading storybooks. We will interpret Annie's development through a sociocultural perspective. Sociocultural approaches emphasize the interdependence of social and individual processes in the coconstruction of knowledge. This paper uses three central tenets of a Vygotskian framework to examine the relationship between learning and development:

- genetic (developmental) analysis,
- social sources of individual development, and
- semiotic (signs, symbols, and language) mediation in human development.

## Genetic

The role played by culture in human development is an essential aspect of the Vygotskian framework and provides an overarching theme for this work. His tenets are based on the concept that all human activities (and subsequent learning) take place in cultural contexts and both the activity and the learning can be best understood when investigated in their original context, in this case the home environment.

Human development starts with dependence on caregivers. Vygotsky's "genetic law of development" emphasizes the critical importance of social interaction in human development. Fortunately, for humanity, most adults (and children) find infants irresistible and instinctively want to nurture and protect them. It is certainly no accident that the actions most parents offer their babies (e.g. touching, holding, comforting, rocking, singing and talking) provide precisely the type of stimulation that lays the ground work for a child to become a member of the social community called family.

## Social Sources of Development

As children observe the activities in their homes they begin the process of learning to do whatever activity they are watching—ranging from eating with a spoon, reading a storybook, writing a list, to using a computer to conduct a web search. Initially young learners depend solely on others with more experience; but over time they take on increasingly more responsibility for their own learning and participation in joint activity. Familiar routines and novel experiences between children and their care-givers provide children with thousands of opportunities to observe and participate in the skilled cognitive activities of their culture (Gee, 1991, 2004; Lave & Wenger, 1991). One particular form of social stimulation that makes a significant difference in children's cognition abilities is lan-guage (Hart & Ristly, 1999). Children who are conversed with, read to, and engaged in a great deal of verbal interaction with adults and older siblings usually show more advanced linguistic skills than children who are not as verbally engaged by their caregivers. Language is fundamental to cognitive development, and this relatively simple action, talking and listening to children, may provide an academic advantage in certain types of home environments. Or, in other words, a family's verbal interaction legacy appears to significantly impact academic achievement. Though words cost nothing, family patterns of interaction, or what Heath (1982) calls "ways with words", varies. These differences in family language inter-actions often reflect socioeconomic status (SES), with lower SES families talking less and higher SES families (often but not always) talking to chil-dren more (Christian et al., 1998; Hart & Risley, 1995). The acquisition of language provides another example of a social source of development. Zukow-Goldring and Ferko (1994) and other researchers have shown the close relationship between promoting shared attention between young children and their caregivers and the emergence of the specialized home culture vocabulary.

## Semiotic Mediation

A child's environment is inclusive of the family's history, culture and organization. This background plays the major role in patterning experi-ence and the creation of knowledge (John-Steiner, Panofsky, & Smith, 1994). For example, the activities children must learn, such as talking, walking, and attaching meaning to their experiences are derived from the cultural environment into which they are born. Their thoughts are shaped by their ecological environment (urban apartment life, suburban homes, rural farm, or a hogan on the reservation), by the traditions of parenting within this environment, and by the language and visual symbols used by their family. John-Steiner (1985) suggests even the earliest days of a child's life influence their perceptions of culture and ultimately how the child thinks, for instance:

Children who are born into tribal or agricultural communities spend many hours strapped to the back of their mothers and other caregivers. In this position, they observe and represent the life of their community in a way that is not possible to children who are placed in cribs and playpens. (p. 130)

Vygotsky (1981) listed a number of examples of semiotic means: "language; various systems of counting; mnemonic techniques; algebraic symbol systems; works of art; writing; schemes, diagrams, maps and mechanical drawings; all sorts of conventional signs and so on" (p. 137). Other tools, used in modern societies such as the paint brush, the computer, calendars, and symbol systems—are also central to the appropriation of knowledge (integration of new information for personal use). Children build their knowledge through first-hand manipulation of the tools in their immediate culture. Thus they develop cultural access and knowledge of their culture by being actively engaged in the practices of their communities.

Hence, the development of the mind of the child is both individual and social (Vygotsky, 1981). A focus of sociocultural research is the study of the way children coconstruct knowledge. We will try to demonstrate how Annie internalizes, appropriates, transmits, and transforms cultural knowledge in formal and informal settings. To help with organization and directionality of her development, we will present this information chronologically. Illustrative examples of Annie's new language and/or literacy development will be described in italics, and then the interpretation of the event will be offered immediately before or after the vignette has been presented. As we analyzed the data, themes emerged that typified how this middle-class family viewed Annie's growth. The themes lead the major sections of the discussion.

## ANNIE'S HERITAGE

### Children Should Be Seen and Heard

Annie's development is typical of children who grow up in homes where storybooks, environmental print, electronic media and writing materials are readily available. She had the opportunity to observe the functional and recreational uses of language and literacy occur on an hourly basis. Annie's literacy development is a reflection of middle-class ways with words and print (Heath, 1982). Annie's family view her as an important member of their home. Even as an infant they treated her

Figure 8.1.    Annie (4 months) and Daddy reading. By 6 months Annie was turning the pages.

cries, coos and babbles as important attempts to communicate and they listened intently as she "conversed."

Annie's family also viewed her as an active and intentional learner. Her parents were aware she was already beginning to recognize consistent objects in her environment. They deliberately gave her time to look at and handle books, rattles, and other objects that interested her. They talked about and labeled both the familiar and unique objects in her world. By 6 months Annie delighted in turning the pages of her baby books. At this time she began to take the initiative to "label" the objects in her books with coos and babbles. She then looked at her parents waiting for them to respond to her "words." Turning pages appeared to lead her to the new ability to anticipate what happens next, not only within the text of storybooks but with the content of children's videos as the following vignette illustrates.

> Grandma sits beside 6-month-old Annie, who is sitting in her bouncer watching a Baby Einstein video. The videos include beautiful music, animal puppets doing interesting things such as painting or throwing confetti, and features many types of brightly colored mechanical toys moving repeatedly through a cycle of action. In one of the videos, a cow puppet "farts." Annie

Figure 8.2.   Five-year-old Annie engages in formal writing instruction.

seemed to be able to anticipate this scene and would get predictably excited (smiling and bouncing harder) just prior to its occurrence and then laugh loudly when it occurred. (January 2002)

## A ROSE HAS MANY NAMES AND PARTS

By the time Annie was 8 months old, her parents instinctively increased the cognitive requirements of the labeling game. As they read story books they first narrowed the focus by asking Annie to find the objects they mentioned, for example, *"Where is the butterfly, Annie? Can you find it?" Annie hunts for the butterfly on the page.* But as soon as Annie found the object, they begin to elaborate the many aspects of the item. For instance: *"Look at the pretty bright colors Annie. See the antenna? These are the butterfly's wings. Annie points and laughs when she finds the many objects on the page"* (April 2002).

Middle-class families tend to have and use extensive vocabularies (Hart & Risley, 1995; Jusczyk, 1997). These families often utilize story book interactions as time to provide their child with dozens of new vocabulary words at each reading. These types of parental interactions also help children to view reading as a layered experience, in other words the page offers more each time you visit. When her parents drew her attention beyond the main object to describe more subtle features it helped Annie become more sensitive to the unique parts of objects. Annie also appeared to learn that an object can have many names.

## Words are Powerful

By 11 months Annie began using words to accomplish goals. This initially imitative process was quite powerful and eye-opening as her parents realized just how well Annie was observing her environment. For example:

> Holding her arms up, and sounding just like her mom, Annie would shout for RRRRRoooOBBBBB to come and rescue her from her crib. Quickly everyone started to call Rob "Daddy" to help Annie adjust her label for her father. Soon, dadadada, became an extremely popular word. (July 2002)

Annie didn't rely on imitation alone as she began to construct her own ideas about words and their meanings, as the following example illustrates.

> Annie had also been listening to her parents call her grandma "Gee" since she was born. By 9 months, Annie began using the label "Gee." Interestingly, Annie had also been listening to her parents call her grandpa, "Papa," yet Annie refused to use this name and poor grandpa went nameless until her first birthday, when she began to call him Da-Gee. (August 2002)

As we examine this vignette more closely we see that Annie was integrating information from her understanding of the relationships between the people in her world. Somehow Gee and this man were connected. The label Dada was somehow connected to a loving man in your environment. Hence she created a unique name for her grandfather—DaGee. If we consider again Vygotsky's transformation cycle we see how Annie may have created this unique label for her grandfather.

- Transmission (communication of a message or information); *Gee the label for the older female—Dada the name for the younger male in my environment*;
- Construction of new meaning by putting together the separate parts of a message to make new meaning; *Gee (older) + dada (male) = DaGee*;
- Transaction of communication where two or more people in the conversation are influenced, *Annie and DaGee are pleased that he has a label*; to finally,

- Transformation where the message causes a change in thought or action. *DaGee is so christened and all family members now refer to him by this new and unique name.*

## Words are Priceless

Between age 1 and 2, Annie would point to objects and request labels virtually dozens of times daily. This action of pointing is one half of the vocabulary equation. The next essential step is for an adult (or older sibling) to share the child's gaze and label the object (Woodward & Guajardo, 2002), as the following scene illustrates:

> Pointing and looking intensely Annie shouts, "Whaa dat?" Annie's mom, now also gazing to the big man in the red suit, responds, "Santa Claus, that man is Santa. Do you remember we saw him on the TV yesterday?" (December 2002)

This scene, though quite common, is extraordinary. Annie's parents willingly share these moments with their child and often extend the moment by elaborating, talking about details of the object and usually connecting them to other events, past, present and future. By interconnecting these events across times and places middle-class parents continually reinforce new vocabulary and help to build stronger memories and related cognitive concepts (Flom, Deak, Phill, & Pick, 2003; Namy & Waxman, 2000).

## The World Lives in Storybooks

Annie's middle-class family had dozens of children's storybooks for Annie's enjoyment. They also use storytime as a time for labeling and describing events to Annie. When parent and child sit together and share a storybook, virtually anything may appear on the pages. It may be at this point where the language and literacy opportunities often associated with a middle-class environment begin to emerge. Children who have frequent access to storybooks and shared reading opportunities typically are exposed to thousands more words than children who do not have similar contact (Dickinson, & Snow, 1987; Hart & Risley, 1995). The frequent readings and rereading of storybooks also allow young children to develop a sense of story and early comprehension, as the following scene portrays.

> Eighteen-month-old Annie is sitting on the bedroom floor reading *The Itsy-Bitsy Spider.* The book has a detachable spider, which can travel up and down the waterspout. As she "reads" she bounces the spider from page to page,

and talks to herself, "ider up, ider ou. Ider in the spppouttt!" (January 2003).

This vignette also illustrates that the hundreds of social interactions and demonstrations with books have already taught Annie tacit lessons about the conventions of print and the joy of story time (Griffin & Morrison, 1997). Because Annie has storybooks available to her, she enjoys reading several times a day. While the time spent in reading is only a few minutes per session, it still adds up to hundreds of engagements with stories, new and familiar words and concepts. Annie's family actively engaged her in reading by asking Annie prediction questions about the story as they read (Bus, van Ijzendoorn, & Pelligrini, 1995) and questions that relate the story to her personal experiences. Observe a typical storybook session with Annie as her mom reads her *The Very Hungry Caterpillar*.

M:  "What do you think will happen next Annie?"
A:  "Eat pizza and pie."
M:  "You're right! Look at his face! How do you think he feels?"
A:  "Tummy hurts."
M:  [laughs] "Yes, his tummy hurts! How does your face look when you have a tummy ache?"
A:  [Schrunches her face] (March 2003).

These open-ended questions encourage curiosity about the story with each page. Though her responses were limited to only a few words, Annie's mind was actively engaged in the story and she was learning that the reader can bring personal experiences to the story (Enz, 2003).

## To Teach Is to Learn Twice

On April 15, 2003, Annie's brother Robbie was born and many things in Annie's life changed dramatically for a while. Annie had to learn to share her mother's lap with a nursing baby, and she had to wait her turn for attention. Sometimes her mom or dad would have to say, "Annie, let's wait to read this story until the baby is asleep." Annie would become so irritated sometimes she would produce a low growl in her throat (like her cat, Jessica) when she had to wait for something. Yet, she was also fascinated by this little guy. She spent hours talking to him, mimicing the voice she heard her family use to talk to Robbie, the exaggerated tones of parenteese. Annie, like all older siblings, became a de facto teacher for her baby brother. All the ways her parents used to teach her were now being used to teach Robbie. Though not quite two, Annie was also sharing the legacy of her family's ways with words with her brother. When her parents would hold them both to read a story, Annie began the process of pointing to objects and labeling and describing them to her baby brother, as this scene portrays.

> "Robbie, see baby? Pretty baby. Good. Ok, see toy? Look Robbie!" The wiggling baby seemed content to follow his sister's suggestions, while a tired mom was simply happy to have both children content for a few minutes.

## Toddlers Have Popular Culture

At this time, Annie also developed a new interest—television and the world of children's popular culture! Though only two, Annie was also a member of U.S. toddler culture and, like most U.S. toddlers; Annie was immersed in practices relating to popular culture through television, video and DVD technologies since birth (Tobin, 2000). Like others of her age group, Annie had developed a wide range of skills, knowledge and understanding of this electronic world; for example, she could insert and turn on the videos (a feat which sometimes her Gee had difficulty with). She had learned (by watching her family operate the technology) to fast-forward and reverse the tape in order to watch favorite parts again and again. In many ways, Elmo videos were electronic texts, and her parents treated them as such by asking questions about what would happen next, or commenting on Elmo's kindness to babies or puppies, or asking Annie to describe her favorite part (Marsh et al., 2005). The following scene offers a common experience in the Foley household.

> Each morning Annie's routine was to eat her breakfast with her mother and to watch Sesame Street. Whenever her parents asked Annie what she would like to watch, she would always say, "Elmo on See-me Street." Annie would smile, laugh and hum along to the entire show but she was always particularly delighted when her favorite character, Elmo, was on. Each morning Sesame Street ended with a segment called "Elmo's World," where Elmo, with his crayons in hand, would write and draw about what he was learning. After watching Elmo write and draw, Annie would immediately run to get her crayons and paper and get to work "writing." When asked about what she had written, she would sing at the top of her lungs "Elmo!"

## Symbolic Substitution Begins Early

From 12 to 36 months young children begin to develop the ability to substitute the real object for a picture of an object. Shortly hereafter, they are able to further substitute the picture of an object for symbols—letters/words (Marcus, 2003). Psychologists call this ability representational thinking (Black, 2003) and Vygotsky would label this as a human's way to use semiotic mediation. Between ages two and three, most children who live in a print rich environment have learned:

- A photograph of a cat is not the same thing as a real cat, but is a representation of a real cat.
- The sound of /c/a/t/ stands for the picture of the cat or the real cat.
- A string of symbols is not just a bunch of squiggly lines, but stands for a word—cat, which in turn stands for a picture of a cat or the real cat.

Often children begin to make this connection while becoming aware of environmental print. Environmental print (EP) refers to print that occurs in real-life contexts (e.g., the word "Pepsi" on a soda can or "McDonald's" on a sign in front of a restaurant). Children begin to recognize EP at a very early age, and research has shown that many preschoolers recognize and know the meanings of common product labels, restaurant signs, and street signs (Prior & Gerard, 2004). The following vignette demonstrates Annie's new ability.

Going through an envelope of store coupons, 2½-year-old Annie recognized the picture of pizza on a plate as an advertisement for Peter Piper Pizza. "Mom, I want to eat this Peter pizza" (January 2004).

## Print Is Powerful

In addition to learning that print is informational by observing her parents' use of print; Annie also realized that print is functional—it serves a purpose and can accomplish desired goals. Annie realized print actually governs the actions of adults; for example, notes on refrigerators can inform you when daddy is coming home, grocery lists tell you what to buy at the store, and catalogs show you what you can order to be delivered to your door. The following vignette illustrates this point:

Annie's dad would bring home science videos to preview for his students. Annie was fascinated with a video called *Insect World*. She was especially intrigued by the segment which talked about lady bugs. After she watched this video, she found her book called *Lady Bug, Lady Bug Fly Away Home*. She would ask her daddy to rewind this part over and over so she could listen about these bugs again. A few days later a science teaching catalog came in the mail. One day as she was flipping though the pages of this catalog,

Annie saw a kit for "growing" lady bugs. Approaching her mom, she requested, "Order ady bugs, peazze." The arrival of the longed-for lady bugs was exciting! Along with the rather ugly premature caterpillar-bugs, came a brilliantly colored information brochure. Annie carefully studied the developmental stages described and demanded to know "the words" which labeled each stage (we didn't know lady bugs had a metamorphosis). Each day Annie would sit, magnifying glass in hand, examining her bugs! A few weeks later in the Target store, Annie saw a DVD with several butterflies and lady bugs gracing the cover. The science documentary became another part of her ongoing quest to learn more about these tiny creatures. (April 2004)

While Annie is not yet a "real" reader, she is, however, a literate consumer of information. Her own interests are driving a strong motivation to learn more, and she is using all forms of media to inform herself even before she can formally read (Bus et al., 1995). Through participation in activities that require cognitive and communicative functions, Annie, like all children, is drawn into the use of literacy in ways that continue to nurture and support even greater uses. Literacy learning is embedded within social events and occurs as a child interacts with people, objects, and events in the environment (Vygotsky, 1986).

## Preschool Rules

When Annie turned 3 she was enrolled in a multiage preschool that also served as the psychology and child development lab in her father's high school. In addition to the adult teaching staff, the instructional faculty also included teenage students (mostly 16-18 year old girls). These students also kept notes about the children and Annie's researcher family collected copies of these notes for data collection. This new environment had new rules and social expectations that challenged Annie.

Initially, preschool was not a happy adventure for Annie. She seemed to temporarily regress in her use of language to accomplish her goals and instead resorted to crying for long periods of time. One day, a few weeks after the school year started, Annie was wailing at the drop-off door; just then Megan, a four-year-old, approached and said, "Hey, you, new girl! Don't cry. They always come back (pointing to the parental sign in-out sheet)." Annie promptly stopped, and from that day forward she never cried again when her parents dropped her off. (September 2004)

During that year Annie became a member of the preschool class—and a member of a community of practice (Lave & Wenger, 1991). Annie's status as a member of the group grew as she learned the ways of preschool; for instance, "We don't cry when our parents leave—they come back," or

"We must stay seated until everyone has finished lunch," or "We take turns, even when we don't want to." As a member of this preschool community of practice, Annie really began to assert herself in a verbal manner. At home she accomplished most of her goals through actually doing; for instance, instead of asking her parents for a snack, she would go to the refrigerator and get it. Instead of asking for a toy, she would simply get it. But in preschool, the ways to accomplish goals were different—she had to explicitly communicate her wishes (Wenger, 1998). For example, if Annie wanted a snack, she had to ask for one or wait until snack time. Likewise, certain behaviors, like shouting or shoving, were not tolerated by the teachers or peers. In preschool, Annie learned that asserting her will required more than asking or just saying please. Annie needed to know the rules and how to play the game, or at least figure out how the rules were made.

> At preschool there were several activities Annie deeply enjoyed, but the dramatic play center was her favorite. However, there was a rule that only four children at a time could play in each center (there were at least three play periods during the day, so most children were able to get to the center they liked at least once a day). However, one day, Annie wanted more than one turn in the center, but the four little girls ahead of Annie proclaimed loudly, "No, you can't play here." Annie thought about it for a while and apparently realized that rules were written, so she went to the writing center and drew a picture and scribble-wrote a new rule. She took her rule to the girls and said, "this sign has a new rule, it says, Annie can play here.'" The girls then allowed Annie to play. (December 2004)

Annie became a member of this community of practice through the process of learning the implicit and explicit rules. Because learning is intertwined with community membership, it is what lets us belong to and adjust our status in the group. As Annie learned more about being a preschooler, her identity and her relationship to the group changed. It is interesting that Annie's position in the group would continue to evolve and become more secure as she began to become interested in the interests of the group, like knowing what other preschoolers did and liked. The vignette below offers an example of this need to be a part of the preschool in crowd.

> By 3½, Annie had become a full-fledged member of the *Dora the Explorer* fan club. Annie, like millions of other preschoolers, admired Dora, the spunky Latina explorer. *The Dora the Explorer* show aired daily, but there were dozens of Dora the Explorer adventures available on video and DVD. Annie wanted all things Dora! She wanted to dress like Dora, talk like Dora, and carry a Dora backpack to school "just like the other girls." Bilingual Dora solved problems with her can-do attitude, with the help of her friends and by read-

ing a map. It was Dora's ability to read the map to solve problems that greatly intrigued and inspired Annie and the other preschool girls who formed a Dora Club to solve many play-ground mysteries. The admiration and emulation of Dora's map reading skills would also emerge during weekly grocery store trips when her mom would wonder where something was located in the store. Annie, would cheerfully sing, "Check the map, Check the map, Check the MAP!" (April 2004)

## Video Literacy

While television has been a staple in the American household since the early 1950s, the advent of owning personal copies of Dora, Ruby and Max, Wiggles, and Teletubbies is only a decade old. Likewise, more complex stories like Disney's *Snow White*, *Cinderella*, *The Little Mermaid* and dozens of other children's classics have become a standard part of middle class families' film libraries (Marsh et al., 2005). Children watch these shows repeatedly, know the story lines and have even memorized character dialogue. Rapid changes in our media environment has not been accompanied by a similar growth in knowledge of how new media and repeated viewing of stories may impact children's cognitive, social, emotional or physical development. Many experts have argued that it is especially critical to understand media use by the youngest children, noting that since social and intellectual development are more malleable in these early years, media use at this age could have an especially significant impact (Rideout, Vandewater, & Wartella, 2003). However, initial studies of nearly 2000 families in England suggest that parents view their children's engagement with media in an extremely positive manner (Marsh, et al., 2005). These parents (representing experiences with over 4,000 infants, toddlers, and preschoolers) felt that film media promoted play, language and listening skills, and motivated the children to want to read stories with these familiar characters. In addition, engagement with media appeared to be a social, not individual, activity, taking place most often with other family members and in shared parts of living spaces. Preliminary research also suggests that middle-class parents also use this medium much the same way they use printed text, to prompt conversation and encourage comprehension (Walker, 2004), as this vignette with Annie and Grandma illustrates.

A:  "Gee, why doesn't Ariel listen to her daddy?"
G:  "Do you follow your mom's rules all the time, Annie?"
A:  "I always listen and follow rules."
G:  [smiles and says nothing]

A:  [minutes later] "Well, sometimes I want to do something and Mom doesn't listen."

G:  "I wonder why King Triton doesn't want Ariel to go to the surface?"

A:  [thinking] "Well, he doesn't want her to get hurt."

G:  "Do you suppose that is why Mom has rules?"

A:  [No answer, just a sly smile and hug]. (August 2005)

Annie's family also has found film to be extremely positive, and like the British families in the Marsh et al. (2005) study, they feel that age-appropriate films can actually increase conversation about children's emotions and offer children opportunities to develop more complex comprehension. The only negative feature of these videos appears to be the heavy marketing of related products that accompanies these preschool movie stars.

> Grocery shopping with Annie and Robbie had always been interesting, but now it was an exercise in commercial dodging! Most cereal manufacturers have discovered that children want to purchase cereal based on the celebrity that graces the front of the box. Annie's favorite cereal(s) are the Disney Princesses—no matter what is in the box. Likewise, Robbie is crazy for Life cereal—ever since Curious George (the books and movie) appeared. (January 2006)

## The Computer: A Cultural Power Tool

Children from middle class backgrounds are most likely come to school with knowledge of computers and an awareness of their function and use. Many middle class preschoolers have also learned to use this technology and a growing number of games are being developed for this specific audience. One of the concerns about computer use for preschoolers has been that computers may isolate children from one another, thus negatively impacting their social development. However, recent research suggests that computer activities in preschools are extremely social experiences with children working fairly cooperatively with one another to demonstrate new strategies or share information. In fact, children's interactions while working at a computer may include a wide range of social skills, including conflict-resolution, problem-solving, and cooperative learning strategies (Clements, 1999). When children are working together, they are more likely to ask their peers than the teacher for help (Stanton, 2006). Like videos and DVDs, computers and computer games can be an amazing literacy tool. The power and flexibility of this technology can cognitively challenge children to solve problems, seek information, and create new works of art and literature (Gee, 2003). Annie, like most middle-class children, had ready access to a home computer and had developed an understanding of its usefulness, as the following vignette demonstrates.

> The household computer had always been fascinating to Annie. When she was 2, it was a slide show of favorite pictures that would scroll through family pictures. By 3, she used it (with her mom's help) as a way to shop for Halloween costumes or bid for interesting toys on eBay. By nearly 5, it had become the household encyclopedia to hunt down information on hatching chicks, killer whales, desert tortoise, ringworm on kittens, hamsters, parakeets, sign language and Koko the gorilla. Just about anything Annie studied in class or saw on TV and science DVDs she began to demand to learn more about on the Internet. By 5, Annie realized that she (working with her mom) could produce interesting products on the computer. Annie made this discovery as she watched her mother put together PowerPoint presentations for her classes, and create birthday cards and postage stamps. Annie decided she wanted to use this format to tell her story when she was Student of the Week. The PowerPoint presentation quickly translated itself into an Annie storybook. (Notes from June 2003; December 2005; May 2006)

## Print Extends Your Voice

Though still not a conventional writer, Annie has become extremely sophisticated about the uses of print. She had just recently watched and actually helped her mom construct a letter to the puppet theater asking for some type of atonement for a cancelled performance (for Annie's 5th birthday party). When the theater agreed that this action was unfortunate and they would make up the performance at the theater by putting on a play at Annie's school, Annie had learned an extremely valuable lesson of using print to voice your concerns. Within days after this event she had reason to write her own letter of concern/complaint.

> While shopping at Wal-Mart Annie always enjoyed visiting the pet center. While she was shopping, she noticed a dead fish that was left in the tank. Incensed at the disregard for the fish's life and the conditions in the tank for the other fish, Annie came home to write a letter to the manager about how this was not acceptable and that they needed to do a better job of taking care of the fish that they sell. This note came complete with a picture of each point she wanted to stress as well as a picture of herself with her finger pointing to the fish tank with a sad face! August 2006

## CONCLUSION

Annie has learned the ways of interacting with print and words that reflects her family's use of language and print (Heath, 1982; Rothstein, 2004; Snow, 1993). This fall, as Annie begins kindergarten, she is an accomplished communicator, able to negotiate nearly anything she wants (except a later bedtime). She is able to recall and share the complex story lines of a dozen classic stories (the movie version), and compare and contrast characters from one story to another (e.g., likening Sebastian the Crab from *Little Mermaid* to MuShu the Dragon in *Mulan*). She understands the purpose and functions of print and uses the power of print to regulate others in her environment and to accomplish her goals. She can recognize, without effort, over 300 environmental print logo-graphics, yet Annie cannot formally read. If we, as Annie's first teachers, defined reading simply as mastering the alphabetic code, we would have missed an amazing opportunity to acknowledge the real foundation of Annie's literacy development. The teachable moments she has experienced on a daily basis surrounded by authentic and meaningful print have provided a solid base for her literacy development to flourish. We believe her daily experiences with print have helped to shape her desire and motivation to learn about letters and sounds. Annie's talented and gracious kindergarten teacher has inspired her students to become alphabet hunters and sound sleuths. At this moment the most important game in Annie's world is to find letters and share, with all who will listen, the sound the letter makes. Already she is beginning to blend three letter words and play with word families. Annie is ready for this next step because of the level of language and literacy knowledge she already brings to school.

One advantage of a sociocultural approach is that in studying human beings dynamically, within their social circumstances, in their full complexity, we gain a much more complete and a much more valid understanding of their growth and development. Though social class is an overly broad label for an intricate set of inter-related variables it is, never the less, a highly predictive variable of a child's school achievement (Snow, 1993). Regardless of family background, children are born ready to learn language. Their biological development in the first year of life provides nearly identical potential for becoming literate. But how children learn to interact and use print is directly related to what they observe in their family setting. Clearly, we are not arguing that middle-class interactions with print are inherently better than other families interactions with print. All families support literacy development via modeling uses and knowledge about print. Rather, most middle class parents engage their children in many main stream and school-type uses of print (Heath, 1982; Rothstein, 2004; Snow, 1993). The constant access to the many uses and functions of print offers children from this environment with many cultural opportunities that enable them to manipulate language and print successfully. The question now becomes one of how educators can share this rich legacy with children from other environments or how the literacy legacy children from other home environments can be similarly privileged?

## REFERENCES

Black, J. E. (2003). Environment and development of the nervous system. In M. Gallagher & R. G. Nelson (Eds.), *Handbook of psychology: Vol. 3. Biological psychology* (pp. 655-668). Hoboken, NJ: Wiley.

Bus, A., van Ijzendoorn, M., & Pellegrini, A. (1995). Joint book reading makes for success in learning to read: A meta-analysis on intergenerational transmission of literacy. *Review of Educational Research, 65,* 1-21.

Christian, K., Morrison, F., & Bryant, F. (1998). Predicting kindergarten academic skills: Interaction among child-care, maternal education, and family literacy environments. *Early Childhood Research Quarterly, 13,* 501-521.

Clements, D. H. (1999) Effective use of computers with young children. In J. V. Copley (Ed.), *Mathematics in the early years* (pp. 119-128). Reston, VA: National Council of Teachers of Mathematics.

Dickinson, D. K., & Snow, C. E. (1987). Interrelationships among prereading and oral language skills in kindergarten from two social classes. *Early Childhood Research Quarterly, 2,* 1-25.

Enz, B. J. (2003). The A B C's of family literacy. In A. DeBruin-Pareki & B. Krol-Sinclair (Eds.), *Family literacy: From theory to practice* (pp. 49-69). Newark, DE: International Reading Association.

Flom, R., Deák, G. O., Phill, C., & Pick, A. D. (2003). Nine-month-olds' shared visual attention as a function of gesture and object location. *Infant Behavior and Development, 27,* 181-194.

Gee, J. (1991). *Social languages and literacies* (pp. 137-149). London: Falmer Press.

Gee, J. (2003). *What video games have to teach us about language and literacy.* New York: Pelgrave MacMillan.

Gee, J. (2004). *Situated language and learning.* New York: Routledge.

Griffin, E., & Morrison, F. (1997). The unique contribution of home literacy environment to differences in early literacy skills. *Early Child Development and Care, 127*(128), 233-243.

Hart, B., & Risley, T. (1995). *Meaningful differences in the everyday experience of young American children.* Baltimore: Paul H. Brookes.

Hart, B., & Risley, T. R. (1999). *The social world of children: Learning to talk.* Baltimore: Brookes.

Heath, S. B. (1982). What no bedtime story means. *Language in Society, 11*(1), 77-104.

Li, X., Atkins, M., & Stanton, B. (2006). Effects of home and school computer use on school readiness and cognitive development among head start children: A randomized controlled pilot trial. *Merrill-Palmer Quarterly, 52*(2), 239-263.

John-Steiner, V. (1985). *Notebooks of the mind: Explorations in thinking*. New York: Harper & Row.

John-Steiner, V., Panofsky, C. P., & Smith, L. W. (1994). *Sociocultural approaches to language and literacy: An interactionist perspective*. New York: Cambridge University Press.

Jusczyk, P. W. (1997). *The discovery of spoken language*. Cambridge, MA: MIT Press.

Lave, J., & Wenger, E. (1991). *Situated learning: Legitimate peripheral participation*. Cambridge, England: University of Cambridge Press.

Marcus, G. (2003). *The birth of the mind: How a tiny number of genes creates the complexities of human thought*. New York: Basic Books.

Marsh, J., Brooks, G., Hughes, J., Ritchie, L., Roberts, S., & Wright, K. (2005). *Digital beginnings: Young children's use of popular culture, media and new technologies*. Sheffield, United Kingdom: University of Sheffield, Literacy Research Centre.

Namy, L., & Waxman, S. (2000). Naming and exclaiming: Infants' sensitivity to naming contexts. *Journal of Cognition and Development, 1*, 405-428.

Prior, J., & Gerard, M. (2004). *Environmental print in the classroom: Meaningful connections for learning to read*. Newark, DE: International Reading Association.

Rideout, V. J., Vandewater, E. A., & Wartella, E. A. (2003). *Electronic media in the lives of infants, toddlers, and preschoolers* (Report of the Study of Entertainment Media and Health). Menlo Park, CA: Henry J. Kaiser Family Foundation.

Rogers, T., Marshall, E., & Tyson, C. A. (2006). Dialogic narratives of literacy, teaching, and schooling: Preparing literacy teachers for diverse settings. *Reading Research Quarterly, 41*(2), 202-250.

Rothstein, R. (2004). *Class and schools: Using social, economic, and educational reform to close the Black-White achievement gap*. New York: Teachers College Press.

Snow, C. (1993). Families as social context for literacy development. In C. Daiute (Ed.), *The development of literacy through social interaction* (pp. 11-24). San Francisco: Jossey-Bass.

Tobin, J. (2000). *"Good guys don't wear hats": Children's talk about the media*. New York: Teachers College Press.

Vygotsky, L. S. (1981). The instrumental method in psychology. In J. V. Wertsch (Ed.), *The concept of activity in Soviet psychology* (pp. 134-144). Armonk, NY: M.E. Sharpe.

Vygotsky, L. (1986). *Thought and language*. Cambridge, MA: The MIT Press.

Walker, S. L. (2004). Emergent literacy in family day care: Perceptions of three providers. *Journal of Research in Childhood Education, 19*(1), 18-31.

Wenger, E. (1998). *Communities of practice. Learning, meaning and identity*, Cambridge, England: Cambridge University Press.

Woodward, A. L. & Guajardo, J. J. (2002). Infants' understanding of the point gesture as an object-directed action. *Cognitive Development, 17*, 1061-1084.

Zukow-Goldring, P., & Ferko, K. R. (1994). An ecological approach to the emergence of the lexicon: Socializing attention. In V. John-Steiner, C. P. Panofsky,

& L. W. Smith (Eds.), *Sociocultural approaches to language and literacy: An interactionist perspective* (pp. 170-190). New York: Cambridge University Press.

CHAPTER 9

# THE "MAJORITY IN THE MINORITY"

## Literacy Practices of Low-SES White Families in an Inner City Neighborhood

**Guofang Li**

It is a consensus in research that home environment exerts an important influence on children's literacy development and their school learning. Research on the relationship between home environment and literacy learning, however, has been focused on culturally diverse families from minority ethnic backgrounds such as those of African American, Hispanic, and Asian American families. While we have gained much knowledge about home literacy practices among these culturally diverse families, we know very little about those practiced in mainstream White families, especially in White working class and poor families who have been invisible in academic research. In contrast to the popular belief that there is a complete eclipse of the White working class, researchers such as Weis (1990, 2004) and Hicks (2004) argue that White working class (and poor) is very much alive and has rearticulated itself as a new distinct class fraction in urban America. Though White poverty rates are significantly

*Multicultural Families, Home Literacies, and Mainstream Schooling*
pp. 175–194
Copyright © 2009 by Information Age Publishing
175

lower than those of African Americans and Hispanics, data from the National Survey of America's Families (NSAF) show that in 2002, 7.9% of Whites are poor[1] and 21.4% of Whites are low-income.[2] In addition, 17.1% of Whites are reported to experience food hardship and 10% experience housing hardship (Finegold & Wherry, 2004). This new class fraction, however, is often misunderstood, ignored, and marginalized in social science research—their voices are often not heard and their experiences remain foreign to their middle class counterparts and to the general public (Fine & Weis, 1998; Hicks, 2004; Weis, 1990, 2004).

The purpose this chapter is to bring the voices of this group from the margin to the center by highlighting the experiences of two low-SES White families, the Sassanos and the Claytons, who are part of this new class fraction. I examine the purposes and uses of literacy in their everyday living in an urban neighborhood as these home experiences intersect with their schooling experiences. In addition, since these two families, being White, but poor and low-income and a racial minority in the neighborhood, are at a particular class and racial location, I will also explore how these race and class elements shape their daily literacy practices as they cross borders between home and school.

## LITERACY, CLASS, AND RACE

Research has long associated family literacy with class and race. Communities and families of different ethnic and social class backgrounds are believed to have different cultural models of literacy practices (Gee, 1989; Li, 2006). Heath (1983) in her seminal work on the literacy and living in three communities of different ethnic and social class standings (one Black working-class, one White working class, and one middle-class mixed race community) reveals that each community has its own "ways with words." In the Black working class community, for example, literacy was a social activity always surrounded by oral communications (e.g., discussion, storytelling) and was often used to accomplish practical goals of daily life. In this community, adults did not create reading and writing tasks or model reading behaviors, and the children were often left to find their own reading and writing tasks. In the White working class community, literacy was also viewed as a tool to help them remember events and to buy and sell items. Though parents in this community collected reading and writing materials so that children were surrounded by print, the parents rarely read themselves, and used literacy for mostly functional purposes. The ways with words in these two communities, however, are different from the mixed race middle class communities whose practices are very similar to those endorsed in schools and whose children were therefore more successful in schools. Similar findings were also found in Baker, Sonnenschein, and Serpell's (1994) study that middle-income parents (both Black and White) tend to endorse literacy as a source of entertainment in their lives while low-income parents tend to treat literacy as a skill to be cultivated.

Social class also influences how parents socialize their children into different kinds of literacy practices through different parental involvement patterns at home. For example, middle-class European-Americans parents are reported to be more responsive to their children's needs, more communicative to their children at home, and are more likely to use inductive reasoning and authoritative parenting (clear setting of standards and firm enforcement of rules, and encouragement of independence and individuality, etc.) than their working-class and poor counterparts (Lareau, 2000). They often engage in a process of *concerted cultivation* in which children's talents are cultivated early on in life through organized activities such as music lessons and sports; this concerted, deliberate cultivation usually fosters a sense of entitlement that helps negotiate more class advantages when interacting with schools (Lareau, 2003). In addition, middle-class parents are also reported to be more involved in their children's education in school and at home. They are more likely to be more directly involved in school than low SES parents. Lareau (2000) finds that upper-middle-class parents influence their children's school programs through requests for teachers and for placement in specialized programs, and through direct intervention of classroom instructional practices in subjects such as spelling and math. They also take a more assertive role than working-class parents in shaping the promotion and retention decisions. These childrearing and parental involvement practices are reported to inculcate more positive attitudes in children toward school and help form better study habits, reduce absenteeism and dropping out, and therefore promote more positive academic outcomes.

In contrast, working-class or poor parents, on the other hand, are reported to rely more on commands and directives in parenting rather than reasoning and are more authoritarian (i.e., obedience- and status-oriented, and expecting their orders to be obeyed without explanation) (Baumrind, 1991). They tend to undertake a child rearing process that is characterized as the *accomplishment of natural growth* in which parents see a clear boundary between adults and children, and children are often left to have control over their own free time and leisure activities. These kinds of child-rearing practices are often found to result in a sense of constraint in their interactions in institutional settings (Lareau, 2003). In terms of parental involvement, working-class (and poor) parents are said to hold the idea of separate responsibilities between school and home, whereas middle-class parents see themselves as having shared responsibilities with school in the education process of their children (Lareau, 2000). They tend to view the academic development of the student as a function of the school, and the role of home and school should not interfere with each other (Chavkin & Gonzalez, 1995; Heath, 1983). These parenting practices are believed to be less inductive to positive attitudes toward school and often correlate with lower school achievement.

These research findings are problematic to the two families in this study who are at a contradictory class and racial location. As White, but working-class and poor, they are not in the official poor Black and White middle-class dichotomy. Furthermore, as remaining Whites in the inner city, they are a racial minority, not a majority. Their identity is therefore that of "being not-Black, not-Asian, not-Latino ... not-'ethnic' as well as not-rich-White" (Perry, 2002, p. 182). This unique identity will no doubt shape their home literacy practices and their interaction with inner city schools. In the following, I examine the two families' home literacy practices and their school experiences and I pay particular attention to how their unique racial and class identities shape these experiences.

## METHODS

Data for this study were collected using ethnographic methods including semi-structured interviews and participant observations (Creswell, 2005). The families were selected through a local international elementary school, Rainbow Elementary, where each family had one child attending the school. They were part of a larger study on school and home literacy connections of fourth grade students (Li, 2008). During May 2004 and July 2006, my research assistant and I visited the families and carried out observations and interviews. Since each family had different schedules and different rapport with us, the number of visits to the families varied. Depending on our rapport with the families, the number of our telephone conversations with the two families also varied.

However, the two families including parents and children were formally interviewed twice at their houses during the research process. The two interviews were conducted to understand the families' beliefs and values about their children's education and to gain more specific information about the literacy practices in terms of their access to literacy materials and their uses. In addition to these interviews, observations and casual conversations with the participants were also recorded in fieldnotes. Each interview was audiotaped and subsequently transcribed.

Data analysis in this study was on going throughout the data collection period. Content and thematic analysis was used to examine field notes and transcripts whereby themes relating to the research questions were identified and illustrated by using verbatim comments from formal and informal interviews (Creswell, 2005). A coding system was created to identify patterns from the participant responses. Based on the identified patterns, a table of contents that contain bigger themes was created to visualize the data in a categorical organization. To better demonstrate the "true value of the original multiple realities" (Lincoln & Guba, 1985, p. 296), direct quotes from the formal and informal interviews were used to give voice to the participants.

## The Two Families

The two families highlighted in this study are the Sassano and the Clayton family who resided in an inner city neighborhood in Buffalo, New York. The Sassano family was local to the city and was among the few Whites remaining in the neighborhood. At the time of the study, Loraine Sassano worked as a part-time clerk in the meat department in a local grocery store and was studying in a community college to become a nurse. Her husband Stanley worked for a local jeweler. For a period of time, they also applied for social welfare but were denied. They had two sons: Scott was 13 and in seventh grade; and Rod was 10 and in fourth grade. Scott and Rod both attended Rainbow Elementary where they were among the few American-born White students in the school. Scott had been on the merit roll in the school and was admitted to Madison Tech, a good high school, in 2005, but was having a hard time coping academically in the high school; his first report card showed only a 72% grade average. Rod had been on the honor roll in Rainbow Elementary school with a 90% grade average, but according to Loraine, he started to "regress" like his brother between 2004 and 2006.

The other White family was headed by a single mother, Pauline Clayton, a high school dropout, who survived on welfare and did not own a vehicle. She had three children: two from a previous relationship, Kate, 10 and Joshua, 3, who suffered from asthma, and a baby boy with her current boyfriend who was also on a disability allowance. During the second year of the study, she was pregnant with her fourth child. Kate's report cards showed she was constantly absent from school and was struggling with reading and writing such as comprehension, using reading strategies, and constructing connected sentences but was strong in math. Due to their own financial situations and Kate's varied experiences in school, the family moved constantly from apartment to apartment.

## HOME LITERACY PRACTICES IN THE TWO FAMILIES

### The Sassano Family's Home and School Experiences

*Home (and school) literacy practices in the Sassano family: "We read all the time."* In the Sassano household, Stanley was the "hands-on" person who was in charge of fixing and building things. He did not read or write much at home except for reading newspapers and writing some notes to Loraine or grocery lists. Loraine, on the other hand, was an avid reader and read a lot of medical mysteries. There were books and materials everywhere in their house. Besides writing e-mails and letters to family and friends, when she was a full time student, Loraine had to read her class textbooks and do homework, writing reports and research papers in the evenings, and thus "was on the computer all the time." When she had some free time, she did planning and writing for the Boy Scouts group with which her family had been heavily involved throughout the years.

Loraine hoped that her love of reading and writing would "rub off" on the children. She always bought them new books or took them to the public library to borrow books. Loraine emphasized in our interviews that "whenever they ask for a book, I never say no," no matter how tight their budget was. Both of the kids had book shelves in their rooms, full of books. When the kids were little, she used to read with them. They took turns to read and if the kids seemed to be confused about meaning, they would go back and read it again. When they ran into a new word, they sounded it out first, and if they could not figure out the meaning, they would look it up in the dictionary. Loraine always tried to have the kids read independently as much as possible as she believed it was the only way the kids could learn.

Rod, a fourth grader when the project began, was also an avid reader. Like his mother, he enjoyed reading mystery books. He loved to read for fun but hated to read for duty. He loved chapter books such as *Fudge*, a popular book in the Judy Blume series, all of which he had read. When he went to the public library close to their house and saw some new books he was interested in (e.g., an animal book that he had never seen before), Loraine always encouraged him to take it home. She told him, "If you don't like it, you don't have to read it." This unfortunately changed in 2006 when the library closed due to a lack of funding from the city. Now they did not have free access to books and had to rely mostly on their own purchases.

Sometimes when Loraine was reading a good book, Rod would also want to read it. She joked that sometimes they competed for good books. One of their favorite times was sitting out on the front porch and reading together. Rod sometimes liked to read for school. He had to write reports based on reading and answer text-based questions. Rod, however, equated writing with printing. He stated that he "[liked] to write essays because it helped his handwriting [get] better." He sometimes made greeting cards for holiday occasions. But mostly, he did not write much except for homework.

Scott, in contrast, did not like to read. Loraine described that "he hates to read, hates with a passion." Understanding this, Loraine constantly made an effort to push him to read and she managed to make him finish the Goosebumps series. When they used to go to the library, Scott took some books home, but he did not really read them. Every month he had to complete a book report for school, and Loraine had to force him to read. The day before a book report was due, there was always a big fight to get Scott to finish the book so he would write the report. Loraine reasoned that two factors probably had affected Scott's attitude toward reading. One was the motivational factor, as "Scott doesn't have a choice on what he reads for book reports. There's a list of books that he has to read, and he hates it. He hates the fact that he has to read these certain books." The other factor was his problem with vocabulary, as he had problems with verbs and his vocabulary was limited. Scott himself admitted that too many new words were the reason why he did not like to read or write. He explained, "Because you have to try to figure out what this word is and stuff, but you don't know what word it is." He also admitted that sometimes he did not know how to spell the words "because you kind of sometimes mess up." He realized that school was getting increasingly tough because there were more exams.

Besides reading, the boys' other home literacy activities included listening to music, watching TV, and playing computer games. For music, both Scott and Rod were into new rock, such as Nicole Becham, Linkin Park, and Trapped. In addition to new pop rock, the family pretty much listened to the same music, especially rock songs from the late 1960s and early 1970s. While they rode in the car, they all listened to the oldies station and sang along because they knew most of the lyrics. With TV, Rod was a cartoon addict. Everyday when he came home from school, he did his homework first and then watched cartoons for about half an hour. Scott liked to watch programs such as *American Choppers* and *Myth Busters* on the Discovery channel. Both of them also enjoyed watching MTV and some of the comedy shows such as *Pimp My Ride*. At night, Scott and Rod sometimes joined Loraine and Stanley to watch some of the regular TV series that they all loved, such as *House, Law & Order, Close to Home*, and *Without a Trace*. Rod loved *CSI*, but had to miss it because it was on at 10:00 P.M. which was his bedtime. As a family, they also rented a lot of movies from Blockbuster Video. They enjoyed family movies such as *Four*

*Brothers*; *Yours, Mine, and Ours*; and *The Wild*. Though Scott and Rod loved computer games, they did not play often. Scott had a TV and a computer in his room to play video games, but his parents took these away in 2006 because of his declining grade point average.

The family engaged in a wide array of outdoor activities together, especially in the summer such as bike riding, fishing, and playing ball. In the evenings, they sometimes tried to play family games. On Sunday evenings, they often went bowling for a couple of games. On weekends, they were active in Boy Scouts activities such as water skiing, camping, fund raising, silent auctions, or community service. Scott was only 9 months away from becoming an Eagle Scout in 2006. Loraine and Stanley highly valued these Boy Scouts activities. They believed these activities could teach them to respect others as Boy Scouts was very different from the school where "everybody kind of hangs in their own group, and they don't mix with other people." Loraine explained, "In Boy Scouts when the kids are there, everybody acts the same. Everybody is the same. It doesn't matter what color, ethnicity, none of it. It doesn't matter. It's so weird. It's so different than school. They're all working towards a certain goal … So it doesn't matter what color you are or anything, it's just you're all there, you're all scouts. You are all together." Besides Boy Scout activities, sometimes they got together with Stanley's brother Gary's children in the suburbs. They also took their children to vacations to Florida or Pennsylvania with the financial help of Gary, a wealthy business owner.

*Dealing with a declining neighborhood and dinner table conversations.* Another unique dimension of the Sassano's home literacy practices was their family dinner conversations. Loraine and Stanley made sure that family members all had dinner together and talked about issues which they thought were important. Loraine explained, "We always talk about something at dinner time.… We talk about drugs. We talk about sex. We talk about everything at the dinner table. Everything is flat out open." Loraine and Stanley believed this kind of open conversation was critical to the children's survival in the neighborhood. Loraine further explains, "We are [in the] west side of Buffalo. It is not a good neighborhood. They are gonna be exposed to all of these [things]. I am sure they've been exposed to drugs already.… They won't tell me, but I'm sure they have had cigarettes."

Scott and Rod often talked about things that they saw in school and on the street. Rod, for example, came home one day and told them that somebody was smoking marijuana in the bathroom in the school. Another day when the city had a big drug bust, it happened just around the corner from the Sassano's house. The children watched police pull three Black men out of their car and found what looked like huge bricks of a White drug in their car. As Lorraine said, it was like "watching a movie, except it's happening right outside their house in my neighborhood. My kids are SITING RIGHT THERE!" The children were also aware of sex and the consequences of having sex because they often heard about 9- or 10-year-old girls getting pregnant. This kind of exposure could potentially influence Scott who then had a girlfriend and spent a lot of time with her. Even though Scott and his girlfriend were seldom alone, Loraine and Stanley believed that it was important to educate them and help them make better decisions in this kind of neighborhood. Loraine explained, "Exposing early ... Teach them the right way and the wrong way how the things are done, and you hope to God, when they are all by themselves on the street they make the right choice."

*Parental involvement.* Loraine and Stanley Sassano believed that "education is the most important thing," and that was why Loraine decided to leave a dead-end job at a local grocery store and go back to school to become a nurse. They expected their two sons, Scott and Rod to "get a better education ... do well in school, go to college, get a better job." Loraine told them, "Don't wait like I did ... Get a good job early, and you can earn some money, and you can do the things you want to do in life."

Loraine and Stanley's views on education were well reflected in their involvement in their school and homework. Loraine was a firm believer in parental involvement. In her words, "The more parents are involved, the better the school, the better the schooling is for the children." When Rod and Scott came home from school, Loraine always asked what homework must be completed. She established a very strict homework-first policy, so they understood "after school, it's always homework first. When they walk in the door, homework has to be done, so that they can do anything [afterwards]."

In addition to making sure the children did their homework, Loraine also checked all their homework. Her principle was that she did not change anything they wrote, even if it was wrong. She, however, did point out that there were errors and asked them to locate and correct them. She believed that they needed to learn from their own mistakes, "making them go back and see if they actually figure it out. I don't hand anything to them. No, that makes life too easy and that's not real." She also paid attention to their handwriting and if it was unintelligible, she would ask them to rewrite their work.

Every day, Rod spent about an hour and a half on his homework, writing book reports and other school projects in science, language arts, math, and social studies. Scott's homework, on the other hand, varied, with some days or weeks having very little and others having much more. This situation continued even after he entered high school. Feeling surprised, Loraine asked Scott about this, and was told that he did it in school as they had some free time. Unconvinced, she went to the school to ask his teachers about it. She found that sometimes this was true, and sometimes Scott had "stuff missing that he's never turned in." She realized that Scott, now a teenager, was "playing games" with her. In order to change his attitude toward homework, she sometimes took his TV or computer out of his room as a punishment.

In 2005, Scott's grade point average continued to decline, falling to a C average. Loraine realized that Scott's declining grade point average was a result of his missing homework. She made a point to save his homework on her computer so that she could keep track of what he had completed. Doing this also helped her better communicate with his teachers about what he had or had not finished. In addition to continuing to push him to do more at home, Loraine also pushed the teachers to take more responsibilities. Scott's bio-lab teacher, for example, often lost Scott's (as well as many others') lab reports and Loraine decided to insist that he had completed the assignment because she had those lab reports on her computer and she made sure that Scott turn them in.

In addition to being involved in her children's homework, Loraine was also actively supporting Rod's school's reading programs such as *Parents as Reading Partners*. The program required parents to read with their child for twenty minutes every night for five days a week. Even though Loraine knew many parents just signed off on it without really doing it, she made an effort to complete the program with Rod as required. She did not want to teach her children that it was okay to just sign off on something when they did not do it actually. She sat with Rod, listening to him read for 20 minutes, 5 nights a week for several weeks. Occasionally, she asked some comprehension questions to help him read. After they completed the program, they attended a breakfast party at the school where Rod received a book, a certificate, and a medal for his home reading. Both Loraine and Rod were very proud of the awards.

Loraine and Stanley tried to participate in the children's school activities as much as possible. They attended most of the PTO meetings and were involved in some school activities such as the annual international festival and school plays. If Rod or Scott took part in these activities, Loraine and Stanley always made an attempt to attend. When Rod and Scott were in pre-K and kindergarten, she used to be in the school to help all the time, but now that they were getting older, she wanted them to have their own independence as "they don't need mom sitting there watching them." She now made a point to know what was going on, but she did not "want to be on their shoulder watching what they're doing." She went to the school as often as her schedule allowed and she made it known to the teachers that she was available if they needed her. She stated, "I work my schedule around my kids."

*Rod and Scott's school experiences.* Though Rod was very punctual in handing in his homework assignments and he was earning good grades in school, his school experience became more and more negative as the neighborhood deteriorated over the last several years. In 2005, Rod had a good peer group in his class who wanted to succeed, and they had a friendly competition which enabled them to increase their achievement. However, things started to change as more and more Whites began to leave the school. The academic environment that Rod once enjoyed seemed to have disappeared. According to Rod, in 2006, no more than five people in his class of 37 students wanted to get good grades, and among the five students, he was the only White student. He did not like it, because "if you stand out, you sort of freaking [them] out." Most of the students did not want to be in school and often made excuses not to come to school. Rod noticed that "people like to miss school" to stay home and the school also did not take care of them or want those people to be there, either. Loraine pointed out that, since the parents were out working, "so they [the kids had] the day for themselves to do everything they want to." This "subtractive" school culture had caused a problem for students like Rod who wanted to excel, as the teachers often had to repeat the lessons for those students who had missed the class. Rod often became bored, because "they don't really teach much there. It's all kind of review." Sometimes, it took several days for the class to finish reading one simple book. Since his teachers (such as the social studies teacher) often taught the same content over again, Rod found that school was "kind of easy." As Scott summarized for Rod, "they don't challenge him."

The lack of academic challenge in Rainbow Elementary might have also contributed to Scott's academic difficulty in high school. Scott, now in a better high school, compared his experiences in the new school and Rainbow Elementary. He concurred with Rod that Rainbow was "not very organized" academically and lacked discipline for students. Now facing a much more rigorous curriculum and a stricter school environment, Scott realized that his old school did not prepare him well for high school academically or socially. In his words, "they did not prepare us well at all."

As the only White student in his class, Rod's situation was getting worse in 2006. He was constantly picked on by other students, especially by the Black students. Rod believed that he got picked on because the Black students hated him for his being White and for disagreeing with their behaviors in school. They called him, "a Nigger" or sometimes "Chinese" and hit him. He noted, "A lot of students in my class are racists...They don't really pick on Black people. They pick on White people and Puerto Ricans." When talking about this, Rod expressed a sense of despair and believed that all this was happening because of a general lack of caring and respect in the community. He further explained, "People have just been worse; people just don't care any more ... Fight, scream ... People just punch people ... They don't really care. Teachers are just as bad ... Shout the kids down."

In order to help their children fight this declining school culture, Loraine and Stanley tried to help their children recognize what was going on and make right decisions about their own behaviors. They repeatedly stressed to the children, "You don't change to conform; you don't change to make friends; you stay who you are, and stand by what you believe in." Scott and Rod tried to follow this in school. For example, unlike everyone else, they did not wear baggy pants and huge T-shirts. Scott tried to "do his own thing; [he] doesn't conform to anyone." Even though Scott was trying, he was very pessimistic about the city schools, including his own high school which was one of the better schools. He commented, "All the city schools are going down ... 'coz everyone disrespects everything."

Rod, who loved the school two years earlier, also became very pessimistic. In 2006, during the interview, he stated that he did not like the school any more. He expressed his disappointment at the school, "I have been here since pre-K, 8 years ... It kept going down and down in terms of behavior. The [teachers] are trying their best to teach, but people are bad. They can't teach because people actually have to hear and learn." He described that learning was becoming increasingly hard in the classroom where students were very disruptive, "We have someone who just sits there during teaching, and just sits there, doing nothing, drawing. Someone slapped someone across the face, gave them a bruise like here, and her glasses flew off. People don't care. They just hit people, pick on them."

## The Claytons' Home and School Experiences

*Home literacy practices.* In the Clayton family, home literacy is also highly revolved around the children's school work. Pauline recognized that Kate was struggling with reading and writing. She noticed that Kate read "but was not really interested in reading." Kate was able to talk about (or retell) what she had read, but had difficulties constructing responses to reading. In Pauline's words, "Her weakness was actually writing it down, reading and writing it down." Kate often got very frustrated when she had to write a book report as she was unable to express her thoughts. She also had difficulties in spelling, though she was better in grammar as Pauline noted. That was why Kate preferred to do projects such as posters which required less writing and included more art work. For example, in a project called "My Earth," Kate produced a layered booklet with the shapes of rivers and mountains. Unlike other homework that required a longer writing and a connection with what she had read, all she needed to do was to write a sentence on each layer of her booklet such as "My Earth has oceans" or "My Earth has plains."

In order to help Kate become interested in reading, Pauline made sure that she read with her almost everyday. When Kate encountered some difficult words, Pauline usually asked her to "sound it out." If Pauline herself did not know the word, she would ask her boyfriend or call her mother for help. Pauline also participated in several reading programs that were sent home from school, for example, "Reading Across America" and "Parents as Reading Partners." The goal of these programs was to get children away from TV and do something more educational with their parents. They required parents to read with their children for certain hours per week and submit a brief description of what they read. Pauline and Kate participated in about six of these programs. She described how they read together, "We would read, first I would read a page, she would read a page, or she would read the book to me, and I would read a book to her. Well, if we do a couple of books a day, maybe we do a few hours, but next day, we only do for 10 minutes, 15 minutes." They were very proud of their achievements. The awards and certificates from these programs were hanging on the wall over Kate's bed.

Since Pauline did not have time to take the children to the library, she sometimes allowed Kate to go to the library with her friends where they would just take some books and read there for a while. Sometimes Kate checked out books to bring home to read. Most of the books that the Clayton family owned (e.g., Dr. Seuss series) had been given by others as gifts. Occasionally, Pauline bought books from the schools for Kate and Josh. Most of the time, Pauline read the children bedtime stories at night.

Though Pauline kept trying to help Kate, many times, she also felt helpless about Kate's struggle with reading, "I just don't know what to do. I don't know what to say." She just tried her own way, "I'm sitting there and reading to her, giving her advice to think, it should be said like that, this is what you should say, why do you say that, or what do you think we should say like this? You let me know, and we go over it, and then it becomes very easy. She needs a little push … just say 'let's do it this way. Kate, what do you think?' And she'll tell me."

In addition to assisting with homework, sometimes Pauline used an encyclopedia to help Kate practice writing. As she described, "[We] go through the way, look at the pictures and realize the different names and draw pictures the other day. I go and buy art sets, pencils, and crayons. We'll just sit down and go through a dictionary, or encyclopedia." Pauline also encouraged Kate to keep a diary, but she made a point not to read it unless it was an entry they wrote together. Pauline believed that keeping a diary was very good not only for writing, but also for expressing feelings, "It's very good. She expresses her feeling, who was her friend … if somebody did something to make her mad, she did express her anger." She was very pleased that Kate was "a very open child," who told her everything, and they "share[d] everything."

Besides reading and writing, Pauline was also helping with Kate's math and science homework. Every day when Kate came home, "The first thing she got to do is the homework." Pauline would ask Kate about her day at school so that she could learn about the material covered in class as well as how her day went in general. After her homework was completed, Kate (and Josh) would go down the street to play at her friend's house for a couple of hours before they came home for supper. Even though her class had a lot of math and science homework, Kate loved these subjects, and was very interested in the projects assigned as homework in these subjects. However, at times, the homework in these subjects was very hard for Pauline to assist due to her own limited educational experiences. She often turned to her boyfriend for help. Brian, who had not finished high school either, also found some of the homework was challenging and difficult. Moreover, they found that there was often little instruction given to parents on what they were supposed to do. Pauline complained, "A lot of times Kate came home from school, there was nothing explaining [what to do] … nothing when you look up the book … we just want to know to teach what page and where to find information at." She suspected that either Kate forgot to bring the instructions home or the teachers rushed it at the end of the day and did not tell the students what pages to use to find information. To Pauline, this lack of communication was very frustrating; a few times, she had to call the teacher or whoever they could find in school to get help.

Besides these reading, writing and homework activities, Pauline was also sending Kate to dance lessons twice a week to learn pop and jazz dances which she was interested in. This was why Kate wanted to go the Academy of Arts and Performances when she advanced to the fifth grade or to a middle school. Apart from these activities, Pauline could not afford anything else. The Claytons stayed mostly at home during the week nights; on weekends, Pauline often took the children to see their grandma. Pauline could not afford to go to the zoo, to the museums, or to other sports activities. She took Josh to see a baseball game once, and that was a very nice treat for him. The family did not have a computer, so the children could not play video games. Even though they had a TV and VCR, they rarely used it. The children watched mostly cartoons and some young teen shows. Sometimes, Pauline encouraged them to watch educational programs such as Dora the Explorer, a children's cartoon show that teaches children how to count, how to recognize different shapes, and even how to speak both English and Spanish. Pauline was very pleased that Kate even picked up some Spanish words from the show. However, the children were not allowed to watch TV when they were reading or doing their homework.

Outside the school, Pauline seldom had contact with other parents or other people except for her extended family. She noted that she preferred to "stay on [her] own."

*Changing schools.* Through the interviews, I learned that the family had moved at least four times in the past four years prior to this study, as a result, Kate had changed her school three times. Pauline was also caught in an unfortunate situation—she wanted to move to a better neighborhood but her economic situation would not allow her to do so. When Kate was in preschool, Pauline learned of a good Head Start program, so she moved to a neighborhood which was closer to the program. After the Head Start Program, Pauline enrolled Kate in Rainbow Elementary for the first grade. However, Kate's experience in the school was very negative, similar to Pauline's own story in school. First, the school allowed someone else to take Kate home without Pauline's permission. Pauline did not know the person well; it was just someone to whom she said hello. When she went to the school to pick up Kate, the school had no idea where she was and with whom she left the school. That was a very scary experience for Pauline. Even worse, Kate did not like the school. She felt like the teacher was nasty and mean to her, and every day she came home crying, "I don't like the school. I don't like the teacher!" Realizing that her daughter's attitude was quite different, not what it used to be, Pauline discussed the problem with the principal, but the situation did not change, so she decided to transfer Kate to another school.

Pauline enrolled Kate in a nearby elementary school which was made up of mostly Hispanic children. Pauline described that the school program was more academically focused. She noted, "It was basically just about schooling—math and reading—just about learning." The school was an "awesome" experience for Kate who "loved her teacher and the school." Even though Kate liked the school, the family moved again to another rental place in the inner city. This time it was because Pauline did not like the neighborhood. In our interview, Pauline described how horrible it was to live there because Kate was not able to play outside. Even when she could go out occasionally, she was not allowed to go far out of Pauline's sight. Pauline remembered, "We don't go out at night; we just locked the door. I don't walk to the store which was like a couple of streets. So if she has to go out of the house, she will go with parents or friends."

After being in the elementary school for 2 years, Pauline returned to the Rainbow School community. When Kate found that she had to go back to the school, she cried and refused to go. Through a lunch supervisor in the school whom Pauline befriended, she came to know that the teacher who used to teach Kate had left the school and there would be a new teacher for the fourth graders. She was anxious about the new teacher and wondered whether Kate would have the same bad experiences as 2 years ago. This time, she was ready to go straight to the principal again if Kate had similar problems. To her relief, the new teacher was wonderful, "She gave them a focus point, and Kate stays on, which was very good ... And she calls me to let me know how Kate behaves during the week, [things] you don't know back and forth. I'm very grateful for her help."

Even though Kate was happy attending Rainbow Elementary School, Pauline decided to move again as she and her boyfriend were still not happy about the neighborhood. Pauline explained, "Right in this block, you see there's a high school over there. A lot of adults are aware of after school hours, always fighting." In the spring of 2005, after attending Rainbow Elementary School for one year, Pauline and the children moved to a community outside of the neighborhood where many White, working class families lived. Not long after, they moved again. These constant moves no doubts had a significant impact on Kate's school experiences. I suspect these constant moves had resulted in Kate's absence from school. For example, Kate's report cards from the school showed that in the second and third grade, Kate was constantly absent from school. During the 2001-2002 school year, she was absent for 16 days and was tardy 10 times. In the spring 2003 semester, she was absent for 9 days. In the fourth grade in the Rainbow School, Kate continued to miss a lot of classes. Her spring 2004 report cards showed that she had missed 14 days in the first 7 weeks.

## DISCUSSION AND CONCLUSION

In this chapter, I have described the two low-SES White families' literacy practices in an inner-city environment. Different from previous research findings that White working class families tend not to endorse reading for enjoyment or rarely read or write themselves (e.g., Heath, 1983), the two families not only encouraged their children read for enjoyment, but also used literacy for a variety of purposes—for school work and negotiating unfair school practices, for themselves and for their children. Data analysis reveals that reading and writing for school-related purposes is one of the major domains that literacy was used in the homes of the two families. They took their children's homework seriously and tried their best to respond to school demands and were actively involved in their children's homework with varying degrees of engagement—either supervising or checking their homework.

In addition, different from the working class parents described in earlier studies (e.g., Heath, 1983; Lareau, 2000, 2003), these two low-SES White families did not ascribe to the childrearing practice of "accomplishment of natural growth" and leave their children to find their own reading and writing tasks, nor did they believe that they held separate responsibilities from school in their children's education. Rather, they were actively engaged in shaping their children's reading and writing at home, helping the children read and write and modeling or advising their children what and how to read and write. They also took serious responsibilities not only in influencing their children's school learning but also in helping them navigate the social problems plaguing the declining neighborhood in which they resided. The Sassanos, for example, used dinner table conversations as a means to educate their children with the problems and hoped to inform them to make better decisions if they encountered those problems outside home.

The families' contradictory race and class locations (i.e., being White but poor) had shaped what the families could do to improve their children's learning at home. On the one hand, the families, like those middle-class families described in Lareau's and Heath's studies, actively sought opportunities to cultivate their children's learning outside school. For example, the Sassanos enrolled their children in Boy Scouts activities so that they could go camping, hiking, fishing, and learn about team work. They also relied on their relatives' financial help (e.g., Loraine's brother-in-law) to go on family vacations. These efforts, in Bourdieu's (1977) terms, no doubt had exposed the children to a variety of literacy activities and helped accumulate "cultural capital" that is believed to be conducive to school learning.

On the other hand, their efforts in concerted cultivation of "cultural capital" were heavily constrained by their social class realities in America. Being poor had severely limited what the families could do to accumulate cultural capital. The Sassanos family struggled financially and had to apply for welfare and government subsidy on utility bills. The Clayton family also could not afford much beyond Kate's weekly dance lessons or occasional visits to some sports events. In the Clayton family, the economic pressure had also limited their abilities to move out the neighborhood and the schools even if they desired to do so. As described earlier, in order to live in a better neighborhood and find a better school for her daughter, Pauline Clayton moved six times and changed schools for Kate several times. However, relying on welfare support and not owning a vehicle, Pauline could only move from apartment to apartment within the inner city neighborhoods and sometimes, to even worse neighborhoods. Though she moved with good intentions, the constant moves had adverse impact on Kate's school experiences as she had to constantly adapt to new schools, new teachers and new learning environments.

Their socioeconomic realities were further compounded by their racial realities as a White minority. Though Kate Clayton did not report a similar experience in terms of race (partially due to her constant change of schools), Rod and Scott Sassano's negative experiences as a White minority in the inner city school suggests that race was an another "limit situation" that influenced their learning (Friere, 1970, p. 89). As described earlier, Rod (and Scott) experienced reversed racism in school, which had severely influenced their motivation to learn and their desire to stay in the school. As Loraine Sassano noted that they got to "taste what it's like on the other side."

Therefore, the adversities of social and contextual barriers such as the family and neighborhood socio-economic status, a decaying community and school culture, and reversed racism had become "limit-situations" that constrained their home literacy practices and impeded their school achievement. These barriers suggest that these members of America's "underclass" do not ascribe to the "culture of poverty" or choose inadequate schools or neighborhoods; rather, it is these limit situations and constraints that put them at a social and class disadvantage.

The barriers in the families' home literacy experiences suggest that like other racial minorities in the inner city, the children of low-SES White families are also subjective to a wide array of sociocultural and socioeconomic barriers that impede their learning in and out of school. Therefore, to help low-SES children (Whites and non-Whites alike) achieve school success, it is necessary to move beyond the narrow focus on improving literacy instruction within classrooms and schools to include examinations on the larger sociocultural, socioeconomic, and socioenvironmental issues that are central to the children's everyday lives inside and outside school. Educators must acquire a deep understanding of students' social realities in and out of school—how and for what purpose literacy is used in their sociocultural milieu, and how the different factors such as family, school, neighborhood, race, and socioeconomic status are related to their academic achievement in school. To do so, educators need to broaden the existing minority literacy education to address the "limit situations" in students' lives that constantly thwart our efforts within schools and impede students' learning inside classroom (Li, 2006; Mercado, 2005). They must engage students in literacy activities by which they learn to recognize and rewrite the larger social forces that affect their lives and implement pedagogical practices that link students' learning inside school with their lived realities outside school.

## NOTES

1. Poor families are those with income below 130% of the poverty level.
2. Low income is defined by NSAF as those earning less than twice the minimum wage.

## REFERENCES

Baumrind, D. (1991). The influence of parenting style on adolescent competence and substance use. *Journal of Early Adolescence, 11*(1), 56-95.

Bourdieu, P. (1977). Cultural preproduction and social reproduction. In J. Karabel & A. H. Halsey (Eds.), *Power and ideology in education* (pp. 487-511). New York: Oxford.

Baker, L., Sonnenschein, S., & Serpell, R. (1994). *Children's emergent literacy experiences in the sociocultural contexts of home and school*. Athens, GA: National Reading Research Center.

Chavkin, N., & Gonzalez, D. L. (1995). *Forging partnerships between Mexican American parents and the schools*. Washington, DC: Office of Educational Research and Improvement. (ERIC Document Reproduction Service No. ED 388 489)

Creswell, J. W. (2005). *Educational research: Planning, conducting, and evaluating quantitative and qualitative research* (2nd ed.). Columbus, OH: Pearson.

Fine, M., & Weis, L. (1998). *The unknown city: Lives of poor and working class young adults*. Boston: Beacon Press.

Finegold, K., & Wherry, L. (2004). Race, ethnicity, and economic well-being. *Snapshots of America's Families III, 19*, 1-2.

Freire, P. (1970). *Pedagogy of the oppressed*. New York: The Seabury Press.

Gee, J. P. (1989). Literacy, discourse, and linguistics: Introduction. *Journal of Education, 171*(1), 5-17.

Heath, S. B. (1983). *Ways with words: Language, life, and work in communities and classrooms*. New York: Cambridge University Press.

Hicks, D. (2004). Growing up girl in working-poor America: Textures of language, poverty, and place. *Ethos, 32*(2), 214-232.

Lareau, A. (2000). *Home advantage: Social class and parental intervention in elementary education* (2nd ed.). New York: Rowman & Littlefield.

Lareau, A. (2003). *Unequal childhoods: Class, race, and family life*. Berkeley: University of California Press.

Li, G. (2006). *Culturally contested pedagogy: Battles of literacy and schooling between mainstream teachers and Asian immigrant parents*. Albany: State University of New York Press.

Li, G. (2008). *Culturally contested literacies: America's "rainbow underclass" and urban schools*. New York: Routledge.

Lincoln, Y. S., & Guba, G. E. (1985). *Naturalist inquiry*. Beverly Hills, CA: SAGE.

Mercado, M. (2005). Seeing what's there: Language and literacy funds of knowledge in New York Puerto Rican homes. In A. C. Zentella (Ed.), *Building on strength: Language and literacy in Latino families and communities* (pp. 134-147). New York: Teachers College Press.

Perry, P. (2002). *Shades of White: White kids and racial identities in high school*. Durham: Duke University Press.

Weis, L. (1990). *Working class without work*. New York: Routledge.

Weis, L. (2004). *Class reunion: The remaking of the American White working-class*. New York: Routledge.

# FAMILIES OF MIXED HERITAGES

CHAPTER 10

# SYNCRETIC HOME LITERACIES

## Learning to Read in
## Two Languages and Three Worlds

**Mariana Souto-Manning with Jaime L. Dice**

Oral storytelling or reading from a book? English or Portuguese? These are some of the dilemmas of living in a location informed by two systems of literacy, two linguistic practices. Within such a bicultural and bilingual context, this "kidwatching" study highlights literacy practices (Owocki & Goodman, 2002) in a Latino American household, documenting bilingual and bicultural literacy events over a period of 2 years. It closely examines how a young child negotiates a "third space" (Gutiérrez, Baquedano-López, & Tejeda, 1999), a hybrid between the official and unofficial literacy practices, and how Latino and American models of literacy practices can inform each other syncretically. In this chapter, "syncretic" refers to the attempt to reconcile or unite two apparently different or opposing practices, the merging of two or more literacy practices. Instead of positioning multiple cultural practices as mutually exclusive, we place multiple literacy practices in continuums which become spaces for the child to improvise, create, and imagine.

*Multicultural Families, Home Literacies, and Mainstream Schooling*
pp. 197–217
Copyright © 2009 by Information Age Publishing
All rights of reproduction in any form reserved.

197

## SYNCRETIC HOME LITERACY PRACTICES: WHAT ARE THEY?

Children's language and literacy development starts at home. Researchers agree that the literacy practices of the family play a major role in a child's language and literacy development (Gregory, Long, & Volk, 2004). Despite varied practices and forms, literacy is present in every single household. Narrowly defined, literacy involves book reading and decoding words. Studies of home literacy focus on book reading as the primary indicator of quality in family literacy practices (Roberts, Jurgens, & Burchinal, 2005; Sénéchal & LeFevre, 2002). This narrow view of home literacy practices limits researchers in terms of fully understanding the ways in which sociocultural practices of families affect children's language and literacy development. According to Gregory et al. (2004), a more comprehensive view of home literacy includes syncretic practices, assuming that: (1) young children's language and literacy is not linear or static, (2) children are active members of different groups and learn how to function in them; (3) young children navigate life in simultaneous worlds, so when they are developing language and literacy and experiencing different linguistic and cultural systems at home, they do not remain in separate worlds and code-switch, but they develop a third space (Gutiérrez et al., 1999); and (4) young children who participate in multiple linguistic and cultural systems learn to perform multiple identities and carry out diverse parts that are context-specific, developing deeper metacognitive strategies. Examining syncretic literacy practices offers a broader interpretation of what constitutes literacy and includes what families and communities contribute to children's cultural and linguistic worlds. Within this view, children and adults transform existing knowledge and practices to create new forms (Gregory et al., 2004).

While traditional literacy studies employ a cognitive perspective (Rumelhart, 1977), here we look at the interplay between culture and cognition and how this relationship influences and guides early literacy experiences. This sociocultural dynamic positions children as apprenticed into a culture through interactions with members of that particular culture. According to Gregory et al. (2004), this approach focuses on examining "the inextricable link between culture and cognition through engagement in activities, tasks or events" (p.7).

In this chapter, we expand the definition of home literacy, departing from the narrow definition of literacy as book reading while examining one family's home literacy practices. This family's practices offer a unique view into the integration of multiple literacies as one parent (father) is of Caucasian North American descent and speaks only English while the other (mother) is Latina and speaks Portuguese as a first language. We discuss how there are different conceptualizations of literacy practices that surround each parent's cultural belief systems above and beyond language differences. By exploring the multiple literacies they experience in the home, we highlight the young child's experiences making sense of two literacy systems and syncretically developing a new form of literacy in the home as he navigates a third space.

## CROSS-CULTURAL STUDIES IN HOME LITERACY: WHAT DO THEY SAY?

Most large national studies of home literacy practices focus on book reading activities (McCabe & Brooks-Gunn, 2003). Furthermore, measures of home literacy generally focus solely on book reading activities. The Stony Brook Family Reading Survey (Whitehurst, 1992) and the more recent Home Literacy Environment Questionnaire (Umek, Podlesek, & Fekonja, 2005) both focused on the number of books and reading materials present in the home. In such studies, researchers generally viewed non-white families from a deficit perspective (Volk & Long, 2005) based on their lack of child-focused book reading activities in the home. This conceptualization, in turn, places children at a disadvantage, as researchers fail to recognize the value of home literacy practices in culturally and linguistically complex homes.

In examining home literacy practices, various studies state that Black and Latina mothers read less to their children and have fewer reading materials in the home (Phillips, Brooks-Gunn, Duncan, Klebanov, & Crane, 1998; Raikes et al., 2006). However, it is important to note that the lack of reading materials (i.e., published books, as defined by such studies) is not an indicator of limited literacy practices, but of literacy practices that are not widely acknowledged, recognized, and valued in preschool and school settings including oral storytelling, environmental reading, and rhythmic speech interactions (Gee, 1996; Gregory et al., 2004; Routman, 2003). For example, Heath (1983) documented that children who are socioculturally and racially diverse have multiple opportunities to engage in educational activities in the home and that their family literacy practices are important to consider.

### Literacy Learning in Context

When home literacies are acknowledged and valued in the classroom, there is a respect for cultural and linguistic diversity, and children do not see school and home practices as conflicting (Hull & Schultz, 2002). This stance allows children to negotiate learning multiple literacies and intertextually weave distinct literacy practices across contexts, creating their own third space to explore possibilities. When school and literacy practices conflict, the child is placed in a position where he/she needs to make a choice, valuing literacy practices associated with the school or those associated with the home.

Many studies conducted long ago found a link between children's literacy abilities and parents' own reading habits (Clark, 1976; Durkin, 1966). Researchers suggested other activities that can be considered literacy building, such as parents displaying children's schoolwork in the home, participating in school activities (Morrow, 1995), modeling reading (Heath, 1983), and guided participation (Rogoff, 1990). Other examples include oral storytelling, rapping, shopping, cooking, participating in religious rites, dancing, acting, or drawing the blueprint of a landscape or building. Such alternative literacy practices can be thought of as successful in as much as they are culturally relevant and situated within culturally bound parenting goals.

It is essential to examine language in the context of culture because it is the means by which children learn social and cultural beliefs (Rogoff, 2003). Generally, adults teach children cultural values through their parenting practices and thus teach them how to become competent members of the society in which they are a part (Rogoff, 1990). More specifically, development of literacy occurs in the context of social interactions (Sulzby & Teale, 1991). This conceptualization of literacy is based on Lev Vygotsky's theory that complex mental abilities are a result of activities with a competent mediator within their zone of proximal development (ZPD), "the distance between the actual development level as determined by individual problem solving and the level of potential development as determined through problem solving under adult guidance" (1978, p. 86). Such scaffolding for literacy involves oral language and positive interactions which are supportive of a child's efforts (Sparling, 2004). From this point of view, it is not easy to discriminate emergent literacy skills from other skills such as social and cognitive behaviors (Morrow, 1995).

Studies of Latino families describe the goals of parenting for Latino parents as centering on children's social functioning and making sense of their worlds and experiences (*semantics*). The Spanish term *educación* carries a different meaning from the term education in English in that it includes a "predominant childrearing goal of raising a socially competent child who will become *un persona de bien* (a good person) or *bien educado* (well brought up), [one who is] respectful of adults, behaves properly with others, and therefore is on *el buen camino* (the good path)" (Farver, Xu, Eppe, & Lonigan, 2006, p. 197). A part of this goal is establishing and maintaining warm, nurturing relationships with one's children, specifically, close mother-child relationships and mutual respect for others (García Coll, Cook-Nobles, & Surrey, 1995). In contrast to mainstream European American parent-child interactions, Latino parental teaching interactions do not emphasize asking children questions to which the answer is already known, employing a school-like IRE (initiation-response-evaluation) sequence (Mehan, 1979), such as:

Parent:   What color is the dog? (INITIATION)
Child:    Black. (RESPONSE)
Parent:   Good! (EVALUATION)

Instead, modeling respect and politeness are the focus of Latino parent-child interactions (Roseberry-McKibben, 2002), with the goal of teaching children how to interact with others in a harmonious and respectful manner (Zuniga, 1988).

## Negotiating Multiple Literacies

Being exposed to differing perspectives and practices of parents poses unique opportunities and challenges for children in multicultural families. Children in such families learn in a hybrid culture in which there are diverse ways of participating in learning and diverse modes in which parents mediate literacy practices (Gutiérrez et al., 1999). According to Anderson and Sabatelli (2007), moments of conflict and tension between multiple cultures within the same space may offer an opportunity to reorganize, evaluate, and develop learning activities, thereby creating spaces for morphogenesis. This may also invoke novel forms of participation among family members that require new resources for understanding intrafamily differences and similarities and their relationships with extrafamilial institutions. This development, termed the "third space," represents a child's way of negotiating diversity (Gutiérrez et al., 1999).

Such "third space" negotiations may involve code-switching between languages and within conversations, but may also involve a sort of cultural code-switching in which the child negotiates between literacy practices that are unique to each parent. Researchers ask "what counts" as literacy, a question that speaks to differing perspectives of authority in learning (Volk & De Acosta, 2001). Intrafamily differences of what counts as useful literacy practices may differ, and children negotiate how to become culturally and socially competent in the eyes of each family member without developing mutually exclusive rules for behavior.

## A YOUNG CHILD'S EXPERIENCE OF TWO LINGUISTIC SPACES

This study recounts the language and literacy events of a young bilingual boy named Diego (pseudonym) and his mother (Amara) and father (Ira). The family agreed to be part of a case study and to have a video camera or audio recorder recording their conversations and literacy acts at various times of the day, including meals, bedtime, chores, and play at least one hour per week. They began their recordings when Diego was 18 months old and continued until he was 40 months of age. We selected Diego's family because of the rising prevalence of bilingual Latino families in the United States. By examining a family with one parent from a Latino culture and another from a traditional North American culture we felt we could offer a unique look into how cultural differences are actualized in the home.

The researchers were generally not present in the home during data collection because we wanted to capture so many time points at various times of the day. We asked Diego's parents to record whenever they were comfortable and to review transcripts for clarification and interpretation. In addition, we conducted informal interviews with the parents in which we asked them about the literacy practices that were present in their childhood homes, how they viewed their own literacy practices, and what other events during the study may have influenced their family's literacy practices. We transcribed the recordings and analyzed them using the constant-comparative method, a form of inductive analysis. The constant comparative method involves generating categories that emerge from the data and refining them through the process of coding. This process involves selecting pieces of text termed "incidents" and comparing them to each other and to categories (Dey, 1999). We compared categories that arose as incidents to each other and to categories (Glaser & Strauss, 1967). The constant comparative method of theory generation incorporates coding, writing memos, theoretical sampling, and sorting or delimiting the theory. The following questions guided our inquiry into Diego's literacy experiences: How does a child exposed to multiple literacies manage the conflicts of what is valued as literacy? How might understanding a child's experiences with the third space inform the definition of what is useful in terms of literacy practices?

### The Case of Diego: A Multicultural Child

Diego was the only son of parents from different cultures. His mother, Amara, was from Brazil; his father lived most of his life in the Midwestern United States. Amara spoke Portuguese to Diego while Ira could not speak any Portuguese and spoke only English. From birth, Amara spoke to Diego in Portuguese, and he showed his proficiency in both languages once he began to speak. Diego's parents took turns caring for him because they were both working full time. Therefore, during the week there were very few times when Diego interacted with them both at the same time. Diego stayed home with his parents until he was 22 months old when he started attending school. Diego's family lived in the Southern United States for 11 months per year and in Brazil one month per year on average. This was a deliberate decision Diego's parents made, so that he would see a purpose for speaking Portuguese and value Brazilian literacy practices sponsored by his mother. Diego's father, Ira, was a musician. He held a doctorate and taught at the local university. His mother, Amara, was an elementary school teacher with a masters degree in education. Ira came from a working class family, where his father was the family breadwinner, had completed some high school, and worked as a salesperson, and his mother was a homemaker. Amara came from a middle class family, where both parents worked and held advanced degrees. Ira and Amara were married for six years when Diego was born and strongly agreed that Diego needed to grow up experiencing multiple cultural practices and languages regardless of their place of residence.

During the 11 months per year Diego spent in the United States, he spent an average of 40 days interacting with monolingual Portuguese speakers as Brazilian relatives came to visit. While continuing to attend his English-speaking preschool for part of these 40 days, Diego went home and interacted with his grandmother and/or uncles who were monolingual Portuguese speakers. Such an arrangement, while not as deliberate as their annual visits to Brazil, allowed Diego to see the need to speak Portuguese and the value of engaging in alternative literacy practices even while in the United States.

*Bedtime reading as zones of literacy development.* Diego had an impressive collection of books, both in English and Portuguese, totaling over 400 books. This is an important factor as most of the differences between Diego's literacy events with his parents revolve around the use or nonuse of books. At 18 months, Diego was used to talking in English and Portuguese at home, Portuguese with his mother and English with his father.

There were clear differences in how Ira and Amara carried out literacy events in their household, and Diego's performance varied according to the person with whom he was coconstructing the literacy event. With his father, the bedtime reading routine typically consisted of selecting a certain number of English language books, often containing patterns or rhyming characteristics. Ira sat with Diego on his lap and read the printed words while pointing to the words as he read. When Diego was 24 months of age, Ira started pointing to the letters and speaking about the sounds of specific letters. From then on, Diego would frequently interrupt stories to point out specific letters and sounds. The following is a typical literacy interaction between Diego and Ira.

> Ira: Let me read first and then we can read together.
> Diego: Okay
> Ira: Polar bear, polar bear, what do you **hear**? I hear a flamingo fluting in my ear.
> Diego: [eagerly turning the page] Polar bear, polar bear
> Ira: Diego, wait until I read, okay? Then, we can do it together.

Diego's bedtime literacy experiences with his mother varied more and occurred less often. She would turn off the lights and engage him in stories about distant places using syntactically complex sentences and words that would not commonly be part of the vocabulary of a young child. During this storytelling routine, Diego learned to interrupt his mother by asking questions such as, "And why did Maria have nothing to eat?," "If he doesn't have a place to sleep, could I share my bed?" The focus was on higher order problem-posing, dialogue, and problem solving skills. When using books, Diego and his mother often engaged in a conversation around the book, whether it regarded the pictures or something about which the book reminded one of them. This practice, not traditionally seen as literacy, still fostered the development of concepts about print (Clay, 2002), as Diego learned book handling skills. Diego began to critique the author's choice of words, actions, and pictures. In addition to storytelling, bedtime stories also came to life through embodied literacies. Diego and his mother could coconstruct a story orally, or sing and dance vigorously while representing the lyrics and/or rhythms with their bodies. Graphophonics were not an explicit part of the bedtime routine between Diego and his mother, and books were not commonly part of the equation. It is important to note that this was not a reflection of a lack of Portuguese language books.

Ira and Amara each cited their own childhood experiences with literacy as major influences on how they structured their bedtime literacy events with Diego. Ira said he grew up in a home in which they emphasized graphophonemic skills and believed that one must know letters and sounds before learning how to read. In contrast, bedtime reading and graphophonics were not a common practice in Amara's home. Her parents used semantically engaging and syntactically complicated storytelling more commonly.

At age 22 months, Diego started going to preschool two mornings a week, and for the first time, he saw that his father's literacy practices were more valued than his mother's. Diego started to prefer reading with his father and told his mother that her literacy practices did not comprise reading. This exclusion and condemnation, according to Moll (2001), fosters "disdain for what one knows and who one is ... [and] influences children's attitudes toward their knowledge and personal competence. That is, creates a social distance between themselves and the world of school knowledge" (p. 13). In Diego's case, we found that he did not start doubting his own personal competence and knowledge, but his mother's. From recordings and interviews we learned that Diego started asking his mother not to take him to school or enter his classroom while welcoming his father to take him to school and go into the classroom. He sought to create a distance between his mother and his school, asking that his father take him to school and telling his mother not to speak Portuguese or make up stories at the school. When asked why, Diego answered that his friends spoke English and his teacher said that reading is saying what was written in the book.

Diego and his mother began to experience friction as Diego resisted her literacy practices and linguistic acts that were not common in school. Crying and screaming were some of the most immediate ways that Diego expressed frustration. He questioned his mother and offered her the correct definition of reading, which was different from her literacy practice.

Mother:   Okay, tonight we will travel to Africa and meet Dalmar.
Diego:   I want a book!
Mother:   Really?
Diego:   Uh-huh.
Mother:   Okay, choose one.
Diego:   [gets a book off the shelf]
Mother:   Let's look at the pictures. What story do you want to tell?
Diego:   You need to read the words!
Mother:   Maybe we can come up with a better story, more interesting.
Diego:   This is not how you read! Read the words.
Mother:   Maybe we can just tell a story from our imagination.
Diego:   I want to read just like Daddy.
Mother:   Okay.
Diego:   [pointing to the letter A] This is the letter A.
          [turns the page] This is the letter C.
Mother:   How about the story?
Diego:   I am reading the story, Mommy. My friends read like this.

Why could his friends have practices from home mirrored at school, yet he had such a "messy" mosaic? When not seeing multiple literacy practices represented, valued, and built upon in his school, Diego reorganized his definition of reading, excluding whatever was not common in two or more environments. Since Diego's family lived in the United States and he attended an English-speaking school, more was common between the literacy events he practiced with his father and the literacy events he experienced at school. The literacy events he shared with his mother became something uncomfortable for him, not seen as literacy acts.

## The Cultural Nature of Scaffolding and Guided Participation

In coding for commonalities in literacy events, we found that Ira's practice aligned with the technique of scaffolding, and Amara's practice aligned more with guided participation. Ira's literacy acts taught Diego that he first had to listen and observe, participating on a limited basis. After some exposure to demonstrations, he could engage in responding and participating as best he could. Both of these phases reflect the belief that adults possess the knowledge to be modeled to the child. Routman (2003) proposed this model as the optimal learning model; it is widely acknowledged in the field of literacy education. A downfall of this model is the cultural assumption that children are not yet full participants of society but must first learn how to appropriately participate before being entitled to full participation. Ira offered much support in the beginning of the learning process, placing Diego as a receiver of knowledge. He viewed Diego's position as the learner as slowly fading as he became a more independent learner. According to Ira, this is the model American public schools in the Midwestern United States used with him when he was a child. We see a parallel between this view of literacy and the concept of independence that is so valued in American culture. In order for youth to engage in independent practice as soon as possible, schools expose them to concepts that need to be mastered.

Within Amara's literacy events, Diego learned that he could play an active role in his own learning (Rogoff, 1990). Diego and his mother's interactions reflected shifting roles of guiding and collaborating during literacy events. Together, they coconstructed literacy experiences building upon what Diego already knew and could do. Instead of starting from a modeling stance, their interactions generally started with observations of what Diego knew or had done. These interactions involved components present under guided practice and independent practice (Routman, 2003) but lacked many of the components involved in more dependent components such as demonstration and shared demonstration. The following statement by the mother highlights her perspective, "I need to learn what he knows because he is not a blank slate, you know?", conveying her belief that he was capable of full participation and did not need to listen and observe before he was allowed to participate. Guided participation reflects the concepts of collaboration, coconstruction, and codependence so prominent in Latino cultures and represented by extended families, for example. It is not about complete independence, according to Diego's mother, as she hopes that he continues "learning from other people and never thinking that he can do it all or know it all by himself."

The excerpts presented above shed light on the importance of uncovering the cultural nature of literacy learning. Due to the dire need to reach children from diverse cultural and linguistic backgrounds in the classroom, we propose the development of culturally appropriate practices so that educators consider each and every child ready and valued for what he/she brings to school—so that each and every child can experience the joy of learning at home and at school.

## English or Portuguese? Two Languages, Three Worlds

In terms of language, once he stared attending school Diego showed a clear preference for English, as English was spoken in more contexts. Many tears accompanied the statements "English is better," "Smart people speak English," and "No Portuguese." Starting at 24 months, Diego despised books in Portuguese and could not stand movies in Portuguese, even if they were dubbed versions of his favorite DreamWorks movies, such as *Madagascar.*

Diego's trip to Brazil when he was 33 months old offers further support of the theory that a child experiences friction when faced with multiple linguistic experiences. Before this, his mother was the only native Portuguese-speaking person with whom he had contact during 11 months out of each year. In Brazil, Diego started developing a contextual awareness. He realized that in Brazil he needed to speak Portuguese if he was to be understood. He started resisting English while in Brazil. That summer, Diego went to Brazil with his mother, and his father remained in the United States. When Diego's father called to talk to him, Diego spoke to his father by phone in Portuguese, and then resisted his phone calls. He thought it was one language or the other.

*Negotiating the third space.* Despite his initial resistance, a phase during which Diego saw literacy practices as right or wrong, by age 38 months Diego started to value both literacies and engage in both of them in and out of school. Evidence of this comes from Diego's lack of resistance to speaking Portuguese in public and his desire to experience both his father's and his mother's literacy practices. He started bringing elements of his father's bedtime routines to his interactions with his mother and vice versa. This is exemplified by the following literacy incidents in which Diego and each of his parents negotiate literacy:

Literacy event with Amara:

| | |
|---|---|
| Diego: | I was thinking that we could go somewhere. (INITIATES) |
| Amara: | Yeah? |
| Diego: | Yeah, let's go to the bookstore! (TAKES CHARGE) |
| Amara: | Which one? |
| Diego: | Barnes and Noble, because Borders is too far away. |
| Amara: | Are you sure? |
| Diego: | Hey, wait. We are not home. Maybe Borders is closer. Is it? (SELF-MONITORS) |
| Amara: | Yes, Borders is closer. |
| Diego: | Then, let's go there. We can get a book. (CONFIRMS) |
| Amara: | Which book? |
| Diego: | One with no words. We can tell a story from imagination. (APPLIES LEARNING) |
| Amara: | Uh-huh |
| Diego: | And I can read it with Daddy too. Yes, this is a good idea! (SELF-EVALUATES) |
| Amara: | Yeah, that's good. |
| Diego: | We're here! |
| Amara: | How do you know? |
| Diego: | [pointing to the building] Look, it says Bor-ders. |
| Amara: | Wow! You are a great reader, and you helped me get here too! Thanks! |

Literacy event with Ira, reading *Spots, Feathers, and Curly Tails* (Tafuri, 1988):

| | |
|---|---|
| Ira: | What has a curly tail? A pig has a curly tail. |
| Diego: | No. Who has a curly tail? |
| Ira: | Look, Diego, it reads What [points to word What in book] |
| Diego: | But it's who, Daddy |
| Ira: | Yes, that would have been better. You are helping the writer make the story better! |

The interactions above illustrate how, even within different literacy practices, Diego began to join lessons from both parents. With his mother, he suggested that a wordless book be purchased, as it allowed him to navigate both literacy practices. Even though the alphabetic principle graphophonics were not explicit parts of Diego's and his mother's interactions, Diego was aware, after seeing the store, what the letters B-O-R-D-E-R-S spelled. With his father, Diego brings semantic and syntactic knowledge and corrects the author's words, which for him, did not make as much sense. While Diego's father initially resisted his bid, his last turn shows his understanding of Diego's literacy practice. He validated such a practice, even if it was not part of his own childhood and idea of what counts as literacy.

While it could be claimed that there was a magical moment and things finally "clicked," it was in fact a very complex process in which third spaces emerged purposefully. From the stance of linguistic appropriation (Chouliaraki & Fairclough, 1999), it became clear by listening closely to their voices (in interviews) and looking closely at their actions (literacy practices that were becoming hybrid) the child's parents began to understand that even if conflicting, one definition of culture does not negate the other; it offers a multitude of possibilities and perspectives and may syncretically focus how existing languages, literacies, and practices create new forms (Gregory et al., 2004). In addition, as a professional educator herself, frustrated with the privileging of certain literacy practices over others, Diego's mother explained to his teachers how important it would be for the literacy practices Diego experienced at home to be included and valued in school. She went further and proposed that teachers let Diego help shape learning in his classroom according to what he knew about oral storytelling, for example. She also described specific examples of how his teachers could build upon his literacy practices, valuing and validating multiple literacies.

It took Diego nearly a year to understand that rather than choosing between Portuguese or English, he could play with language. His bedtime story time with his father and mother closely reflected the practice they each experienced as a child. Diego came to define bedtime storytime as book reading, embodied literacies (such as dancing, singing, acting and playing games), and/or oral storytelling. Bedtime literacy events were more about making sense of the world around him and spending enjoyable time with his family, rather than a book-rooted routine.

Diego gradually developed literacy skills in both languages and worlds, while improvising a third space in which American and Latino literacy practices came together, bringing pieces of one cultural/linguistic context when they fit. This is an important finding from this study, as many parents end up ceasing to speak a language due to their child's initial reaction and resistance. It takes time and effort for a child to sort out two languages and learn to navigate in three worlds. As educators, we must understand that students not necessarily choose one language or the other. Instead of telling children that they can only speak one language or practice one culture at school, teachers and parents have much to learn by creating spaces in which multiple languages may be spoken. As a result, children will likely develop a better sense of self-efficacy and self-concept (Gregory et al., 2004).

## DEVELOPING CULTURALLY APPROPRIATE PRACTICES

In order to develop culturally appropriate literacy practices, we must redefine learning in a culturally relevant and appropriate manner, as a process of social participation (Wenger, 1998) rather than the memorization of facts or repetition of sounds associated with letters on cue. In order to establish culturally appropriate practices, parents and teachers must depart from the traditionally employed banking model of education, in which knowledge is simply deposited in brains like money is in banks (Freire, 2000) and see learning as a process rather than a product. "Learning, from this perspective, occurs in co-participation and is mediated by others. It is embedded in social relationships and distributed across members of learning groups" (Gregory et al., 2004, p. 9). To develop culturally appropriate practices, the roles of teacher and learner become dynamic and blurry so that a teacher learns to teach and a child teaches to learn, engaging in cultural practices with peers and mentors. Learning primarily involves changes in participation (Larson & Marsh, 2005; Rogoff, 2003), and as such, it may have different forms across cultures without necessarily meaning that any of them are inappropriate or wrong.

In the study described here, each of the parents employed cue systems in culturally distinct ways. Even though both of them included semantics, syntax, and graphophonics in literacy activities, they did so in different orders. While Diego's mother started with semantics, then moved to syntax, and finally highlighted the graphophonics within the context, Diego's father took a different direction, starting with graphophonics, moving to sentence structure (syntax), and finally to understanding the story and context and making meaning of the text (semantics). This does not mean that one is necessarily wrong but suggests that directionalities are culturally shaped. The whole→part→whole model was employed by both, yet the time and effort employed in each phase varied considerably. Diego's father spent more time on the "parts" between the whole and Diego's mother expanded the whole, thereby delaying the "parts." Figure 10.1 illustrates the processes portrayed by Diego's parents.

Here, it is important to add a note of caution. While some of the practices displayed in this Latino American household are common to Latino

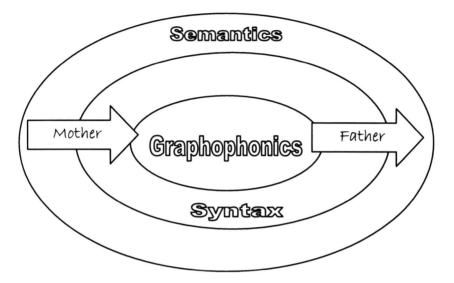

Figure 10.1.   Cultural directionality of cue systems.

and American cultures specifically, cultural practices may vary by degree and kind according to individual, location, personality, and other variables. So, while the above figure might shed light on the differences across cultures and learning models, it does not represent all Latino and American learning models and processes. The figure above is representative of this particular family. Nevertheless, it serves to challenge the idea that there is one appropriate practice for all children; individuals learn differently as they grow and develop in different sociocultural contexts. Joining Cannella (1997), we also propose the problematization and deconstruction of rigid and neatly organized learning models. In doing so, we create spaces of possibility, paying close attention to the child and his/her sociocultural background and developing experiences that will facilitate educational success in culturally complex early childhood classrooms. This fosters syncretic practices as it allows children to experiment and improvise, envisioning literacy practices as coexisting possibilities instead of mutually exclusive realms. Such a syncretic learning environment involves creating spaces for reconciling or uniting different practices, merging multiple literacy practices, and providing culturally-relevant education.

Consistent with our belief that culturally appropriate practices must be developed in order to provide an appropriate learning environment for all children, teacher-researcher Tim O'Keefe (1996) stated that kidwatching is getting to know each child as a person unique in the entire world. Diego's case study highlights a critical issue in young children's literacy development—that young children participate in multiple systems, whether linguistic, cognitive, or limited by situation. From these contexts, children learn to perform multiple identities and carry out diverse parts that are context-specific. By limiting our definition of what is appropriate in terms of literacy practices, researchers fail to acknowledge the contributions families make to their children's literacy development and, more importantly, fail to acknowledge the difficulty children may have in trying to understand possibilities in learning. Examining syncretic literacy practices offers a broader interpretation of what constitutes literacy. This study highlights the sociocultural nature of language learning (Owocki & Goodman, 2002). Even though there are general developmental patterns for literacy development, kidwatchers must know that each child is unique and learn from him, instead of trying to force specific patterns onto learning processes. One example regarding Diego is that he did not learn how to speak in sentences until he was almost 2 years old. Most of his peers were "speaking up a storm," according to his mother. However, as Diego was not only developing one but rather two languages, he had to negotiate the semantics, syntax, and graphophonics of two linguistic and cultural systems. Now, if we consider a more formal measure, at 30 months of age, Diego scored above average for his age in language skills according to the Peabody Picture Vocabulary Test-III (Dunn & Dunn, 1997) and the Rossetti Infant-Toddler Language Scale (Rossetti, 1990).

One lesson for teachers and parents is that children develop at different and unique rates, and just because one child may be slower does not mean we need to intervene. In the case of children who are navigating multiple languages and literacies, they need time to process and make sense of linguistic and cultural contexts, but ultimately their metalinguistic and metacognitive strategies will be much more advanced (Gregory et al., 2004). So, instead of immediately screening, diagnosing, and placing a child in special education, it is important to consider the level of overlap between home and school literacy systems. The more overlap, the less time the child will need to make sense of the two contexts and literacies. The less overlap, the more time the child requires (Gee, 1996). "When objects, events, and other people challenge the working model, the child adjusts it to account for new information" (Bredekamp & Copple, 1997, p. 13), many times creating a third space as a zone for language and literacy development. It is important to remember that every child possesses a wealth of literacy knowledge. According to Owocki and Goodman (2002):

Rather than building one language concept at a time, children simultaneously build models about myriad aspects of language, including its functions, formats, genres, meanings, sounds, grammars, visual features, and spelling.... When they experience moments of tension and disequilibrium, or place their focus on new literacy concepts, things may appear to fall apart.... Overall, the knowledge children develop and the way they develop that knowledge, is shaped by their sociocultural experiences. (p. 5)

## IMPLICATIONS

We believe that Diego's case offers one of many instances of negotiating a third space. At the end of each section below, we present implications for teachers who teach in culturally and linguistically complex settings, who may perceive home and school literacy practices as conflicting (Hull & Schultz, 2002), and who privilege American literacy practices over other literacy practices in their classrooms. We hope to validate the practices of teachers who see each child as a unique human being from whom they learn in order to appropriately teach, coconstructing responsive learning environments. In this final section, after exploring facets of Diego's experience learning in two languages and three worlds, we draft implications, written as hopes based on what we learned by conducting this study. They are organized in two categories: "Strengthening Home-School Connections" and "Literacy Learning in Many Languages and Worlds." While both sections contain important suggestions and components, they are by no means all-inclusive and conclusive. They are just a beginning. It is our most sincere hope that you keep adding on. We most certainly will!

### Strengthening Home-School Connections

Here, we pause to reflect on the "what ifs" of this case study. What if Diego's mother were not a professional educator? What if she did not feel comfortable articulating the different literacy practices she and Diego coconstructed in the home? How could a teacher be exposed to multiple literacy practices carried out in various homes, so they could be valued and built upon in the classroom? Here, we posit that it is extremely important that teachers create safe spaces in which children are comfortable sharing their home experiences and literacies. Furthermore, teachers can make parents inherent partners in the educational process, acknowledging that parents indeed have much to teach the teachers and that teachers value and celebrate parents' funds of knowledge in the classroom. We invite teachers to problematize traditional definitions of reading and literacy as these terms are not synonyms of book reading; instead, we believe that book reading is one thread of the cloth we call literacy practices. Finally, we suggest that teachers become ethnographers and constantly rethink and reorganize their knowledge about literacy learning as they learn with children and parents about best teaching practices. Since children do not learn multiple and complex literacy practices separately, why are they so often conceptualized and taught separately in classrooms and schools?

Implications for strengthening home-school connections include the call that educators challenge and problematize their own definitions of what counts as literacy and come to redefine literacy practices to include those forms of literacy experienced by all children and families that make up the classroom community. We hope that reading this chapter will help teachers reflect on and reassess their own literacy practices. Respecting and valuing each child's home literacy practices are a beginning in challenging our traditional definitions of functional families, families that value learning, and families that engage in varied home literacy practices. Learning with and from our students, we can all come to a more inclusive definition of literacy practices.

We believe that key elements of a culturally-appropriate definition of literacies include: (1) An inclusive approach where all family literacies are validated as venues for literacy learning; (2) A lifelong learning approach in which educators learn as ethnographers alongside children and families continuously problematizing and redefining their literacy teaching and learning; (3) Trust-building through collaborative schemes and through recognition of family's funds of knowledge; and (4) Linguistic and cultural appreciation, recognition, and reflective responsiveness, generating a coconstructed and inclusive definition of what counts as literacy practices. When parents and families feel that their traditions, rituals, and practices are being valued in schools, they are more likely to join in! We hope that you recognize and embrace a diversity of literacy practices as resources rather than as a deficit and keep adding to the list above as you learn from and with children and their families.

## Literacy Learning in Many Languages and Worlds

The implications of this study to learning in many languages and worlds are general yet important. We hope that you recognize that sociocultural experiences deeply influence literacy development (Owocki & Goodman, 2002) as was evident in the case of Diego's literacy development and the different learning models employed by his mother and father. We hope that you recognize the importance of seeing each child as an individual unique in the world and seek to learn from his/her home literacy practices, valuing them and building upon them in school. In terms of language, we hope that even if you do not speak more than one language, you value children who do, encourage them to speak in multiple languages, and have picture books available that portray the richness of cultures and languages in the classroom.

The richer the context and interactions, the richer the child's language and literacy contexts and skills become. It is important to remember, however, that the definition of "rich" is not about what is valued in traditional classrooms, but that experiences and skills are socioculturally meaningful to a particular child. Given the chance, children and families will share their riches with teachers, and teachers will come to see the wonders of each child. The first step to success in a literacy classroom is valuing and building upon home literacies. In order to do so, teachers must become learners and come to respect and appreciate multiple cultures and family systems instead of judging them. Families are not dysfunctional because they are different (Anderson & Sabatelli, 2007). Functional families come in many shapes, colors, and forms.

We thank the educators who continuously refine their definitions of literacy practices and invite all to continuously engage in learning experiences in a third space by re-envisioning classroom practices and literacy concepts based on the particular sociocultural and linguistic experiences of each individual who makes up each learning community. This is a continuous and endless job yet a valuable and rewarding one! Best of luck!

## REFERENCES

Anderson, S. A., & Sabatelli, R. M. (2007). *Family interaction: A multigenerational developmental perspective.* Boston: Allyn & Bacon.

Bredekamp, S., & Copple, C. (1997). *Developmentally appropriate practice in early childhood programs.* Washington, DC: National Association for the Education of Young Children.

Cannella, G. (1997). *Deconstructing early childhood education: Social justice and revolution.* New York: Peter Lang.

Chouliaraki, L., & Fairclough, N. (1999). *Discourse in late modernity.* Edinburgh, United Kingdom: Edinburgh University Press.

Clark, M. (1976). *Young fluent readers: What can they teach us.* London: Heinemann.

Clay, M. (2002). *An observation survey of early literacy achievement.* Auckland, New Zealand: Heinemann.

Dey, I. (1999). *Grounding grounded theory: Guidelines for qualitative inquiry.* San Diego, CA: Academic Press.

Dunn, L. M., & Dunn, L. M. (1997). *Peabody picture vocabulary test-third edition: Manual.* Circle Pines, MN: American Guidance Services.

Durkin, D. (1966). *Teaching young children to read.* Boston: Allyn & Bacon.

Farver, J. A. M., Xu, Y., Eppe, S., & Lonigan, C. J. (2006). Home environments and young Latino children's school readiness. *Early Childhood Research Quarterly, 21*(2), 196-212.

Freire, P. (2000). *Pedagogy of the oppressed.* New York: Continuum.

García Coll, C. T., Cook-Nobles, R., & Surrey, J. L. (1995). *Diversity at the core: Implications for relational theory.* Wellesley, MA: Stone Center.

Gee, J. (1996). *Social linguistics and literacies: Ideology in discourses.* London: Routledge/Falmer.

Glaser, B., & Strauss, A. (1967). *The discovery of grounded theory: Strategies for qualitative research.* New York: Aldine De Gruyter.

Gregory, E., Long, S., & Volk, D. (Eds.). (2004). *Many pathways to literacy: Young children learning with siblings, grandparents, peers, and communities.* London: RoutledgeFalmer.

Gutiérrez, K. D., Baquedano-López, P., & Tejeda, C. (1999). Rethinking diversity: Hybridity and hybrid language practices in the third space. *Mind, Culture, and Activity, 6*(4), 286-303.

Heath, S. B. (1983). *Ways with words: Language, life and work in communities and classrooms.* Cambridge, England: Cambridge University Press.

Hull, G., & Schultz, K. (Eds.). (2002). *School's out! Bridging out-of-school literacies with classroom practice.* New York: Teachers College Press.

Larson, J., & Marsh, J. (2005). *Making literacy real: Theories and practices for learning and teaching.* Thousand Oaks, CA: SAGE.

McCabe, L., & Brooks-Gunn, J. (2003). Pre- and perinatal home visitation interventions. In J. Brooks-Gunn, A. Fuligni, & L. Berlin (Eds.), *Early child development in the 21st century: Profiles of current research initiatives* (pp. 145-162). New York: Teachers College Press.

Mehan, H. (1979). *Learning lessons.* Cambridge, MA: Harvard University Press.

Moll, L. (2001). The diversity of schooling: A cultural-historical approach. In M. Reyes & J. Halcón (Eds.), *The best for our children: Critical perspectives on literacy for Latino students* (pp. 13-28). New York: Teachers College Press.

Morrow, L. (1995). Family literacy: New perspectives, new practices. In L. Morrow (Ed.), *Family literacy: Connections in schools and communities.* Newark, DE: IRA.

O'Keefe, T. (1996). Teachers as kidwatchers. In K. Short & J. Harste with C. Burke (Eds.), *Creating classrooms for authors and inquirers* (pp. 8-63). Portsmouth, NH: Heinemann.

Owocki, G., & Goodman, Y. M. (2002). *Kidwatching: Documenting children's literacy development.* Portsmouth, NH: Heinemann.

Phillips, M., Brooks-Gunn, J., Duncan, G., Klebanov, P., & Crane, J. (1998). Family background, parenting practices, and the Black-White test score gap. In C. Jencks & M. Phillips (Eds.), *The Black-White test score gap.* Washington DC: Brookings.

Raikes, H., Luze, G., Brooks-Gunn, J., Raikes, H. A., Pan, B. A., Tamis-LeMonda, C. S., et al. (2006). Mother-child bookreading in low-income families: Correlates and outcomes during the first three years of life. *Child Development, 77*(4), 924-953.

Roberts, J., Jurgens, J., & Burchinal, M. (2005). The role of home literacy practices in preschool children's language and emergent literacy skills. *Journal of Speech, Language, and Hearing Research*, *48*(2), 345-359.

Rogoff, B. (1990). *Apprenticeship in thinking: Cognitive development in social context*. Oxford, England: Oxford University Press.

Rogoff, B. (2003). *The cultural nature of human development*. New York: Oxford University Press.

Roseberry-McKibben, C. (2002). *Multicultural students with special language needs* (2nd ed.). Oceanside, CA: Academic Communication Associates.

Rossetti, L. (1990). *Infant-Toddler Language Scale*. East Moline, IL: LinguiSystems.

Routman, R. (2003). *Reading essentials: The specifics you need to teach reading well*. Portsmouth, NH: Heinemann.

Rumelhart, D. E. (1977). Toward an interactive model of reading. In S. Dornic (Ed.), *Attention and performance* (pp. 573-603). New York: Academic Press.

Sénéchal, M., & LeFevre, J. (2002). Parental involvement in the development of children's reading skill: A five-year longitudinal study. *Child Development*, *73*, 445-460.

Sparling, J. (2004). Earliest literacy: From birth to age 3. In B. Wasik (Ed.), *Handbook of family literacy* (pp. 45-56). Mahwah, NJ: Erlbaum.

Sulzby, E., & Teale, W. (1991). Emergent literacy. In R. Barr, M. Kamil, P. Mosenthal, & P. D. Pearson (Eds.), *Handbook of reading research* (pp. 727-758). New York: Longman.

Tafuri, N. (1988). *Spots, feathers, and curly tails*. New York: Greenwillow

Umek, L., Podlesek, A., & Fekonja, U. (2005). Assessing the home literacy environment: Relationships to child language comprehension and expression. *European Journal of Psychological Assessment*, *21*(4), 271-281.

Volk, D., & De Acosta, M. (2001). 'Many different ladders, many ways to climb ...': Literacy events in the bilingual classroom, homes, and community of three Puerto Rican kindergartners. *Journal of Early Childhood Literacy*, *1*(2), 193-224.

Volk, D., & Long, S. (2005). Challenging myths of the deficit perspective: Honoring children's literacy resources. *Young Children*, *60*(6), 12-19.

Vygotsky, L. S. (1978). *Mind in society: The development of higher psychological processes*. Cambridge, MA: Harvard University Press.

Wenger, E. (1998). *Communities of practice: Learning, meaning, and identity*. Cambridge, England: Cambridge University Press.

Whitehurst, G. (1992). *Family reading survey*. Stony Brook: State University of New York.

Zuniga, M. (1988). Chicano self-concept: A proactive stance. In C. Jacobs & D. Bowles (Eds.), *Ethnicity and race: Critical concepts in social work* (pp. 71-83). Silver Spring, MD: National Association of Social Workers.

# PART III

SCHOOL-HOME LITERACY CONNECTIONS AND THE
DIRECTIONS OF MINORITY LITERACY EDUCATION

CHAPTER 11

# UNDERSTANDING ENGLISH LANGUAGE LEARNERS' IDENTITIES FROM THREE PERSPECTIVES

**Sarah J. McCarthey**

Traditional views of identity have focused on identity as a unified, cohesive essence belonging to an individual whose core unfolds or develops in stages (Erikson, 1968). In contrast, social constructivist and postmodern perspectives have emphasized the constructed and dynamic nature of identity, theorizing that identity is multiple, fragmentary, and contradictory (Gee & Crawford, 1998; Sarup, 1996; Yon, 2000). Experts in multicultural education (Banks & Banks, 2004) have emphasized the variation that occurs within the cultural identity construction of members of the same ethnic/racial group due to individuals' multiple and varied membership and participation in diverse microcultures. In this chapter I focus on three theoretical perspectives that can shed light on English language learners' developing identities and contextualize them within sociocultural views of family literacy.

The perspectives of Bakhtin's (1981, 1986) dialogic theory, Wenger's (1998) theory of communities of practice, and Sfard and Pusak's (2005)

*Multicultural Families, Home Literacies, and Mainstream Schooling*
pp. 221–244

narrative theory share some characteristics that provide ways to view English language learners' identities. First, they are all deeply rooted in a sociocultural view of human learning and development; thus, identity is considered to be social in nature. Second, the theories share the view that identity is developmental and dynamic rather than a set of fixed, personality traits. Third, the theories all highlight the crucial role of language in learning and identity development. Fourth, the theories suggest that identity construction involves conflict within the socially constructed individual as well as between the individual and the society. Despite their underlying similarities, the theories differ in the ways in which "social" and "discourse" are defined in relation to identity. For example, Bahktin (1981) suggests that all of individual thinking is modeled after social interaction and differentiates "authoritative discourse" from "internally persuasive discourse"; Wenger emphasizes the nature of the community and views individual identity as the nexus of membership in multiple communities; and Sfard (2006) states, "identities are made of rather than merely expressing them (stories)." The shared emphasis on the role of social relationships and language positions these theories to create an understanding of the process of identity construction of English language learners. At the same time, each theory emphasizes different aspects of identity and allows for a closer inspection of particular home and school influences on students' identities. I use these three related perspectives (explained in greater depth in each of the cases) to highlight different aspects of students' emerging identities.

Drawing from a larger study of six Mandarin speakers and five Spanish speakers, I focus on three students to illustrate the influence of both home and school on students' emerging identities. The cases were developed from a two-year study in which a team of researchers followed students in their multiple classroom contexts (see McCarthey, García, López-Velásquez, Lin, & Guo, 2004) and interviewed the students and their parents about their language and literacy habits in English and their native languages (McCarthey & García, 2005). Each of the cases links a theoretical perspective to data collected in home and school contexts to illustrate the complexity of factors that affect students' literacy development and identity construction.

## CHUN MING FROM A BAKHTINIAN PERSPECTIVE

Bakhtin suggested that inner speech is modeled on social discourse—dialogues conducted with imagined audiences drawn from the many voices a person has encountered. He theorized that speech of the individual is shaped in continuous interaction with others' utterances and that the individual assimilates social discourse through "reciting by heart" and "retelling in one's own words" (1981, p. 341). Reciting by heart involves using another's words in the form of rules or models, "authoritative discourse," whereas retelling in one's own words is more flexible and responsive, making it possible to originate ideas. Intellectual growth in the form of "internally persuasive discourse" results from the struggle of these two forms of assimilation. Rather then being static and isolated, this idea that discourse is "half-ours and half someone-else's" (p. 345) is a creative process that can be applied to new situations. Bahktin's theories can be used to understand English language learners' development of identities by seeing their language learning as the struggle between authoritative discourse and internally persuasive discourse. The result of the conflict can be described as hybridity, producing "new cultural forms, practices, spaces, and identities created from a synthesis of diverse elements" (Manyak, 2001, p. 432). English language learners are in constant dialogue with their native language and English as they straddle two cultures and languages (Jiménez, 2000) and interweave their home, school, and peer language practices to serve a variety of purposes (Solsken, Willett, & Wilson-Keenan, 2000).

Chun Ming presents an example of a student who is developing a hybrid identity by drawing from his home and school resources. His case illustrates the ways in which an English language learner can build upon the "authoritative discourses" he has encountered learning to write in Chinese and English to produce texts that are new for him.

## Chun Ming: Developing a Hybrid Identity

Chun-Ming was a Mandarin speaker from China who came to the United States with his parents in fourth grade. Before coming to the United States, his parents had conducted research in Germany and Japan, and he lived with his grandparents in China. His father was a visiting researcher in the material science department at a major midwestern university, and his mother studied computers and accounting at a nearby community college before giving birth to another son in the United States. They lived in the university family housing, an international community, and were active in cultivating the community garden.

*Home context.* Chun-Ming spoke a dialect of Chinese, Tian-Jin, at home, but spoke Mandarin to other Mandarin-speakers. He learned some English before coming to the United States, but found it too difficult to study it in the Chinese context, "Studying English back in my own country took too much effort." Chun-Ming was very aware of the need to communicate and the role that pronunciation played in his learning of English:

> It's hard to make friends here because of your language communication problem. Sometimes because of your accent, they don't quite understand you. It's hard to make friends. You must have their pronunciation, so you can communicate.

Throughout the 2 years of the study Chun-Ming spoke in Chinese at home and his parents believed it was important for him to retain his Chinese heritage, but his mother felt somewhat conflicted:

> He is still Chinese after all. He should not forget his mother tongue. Although his Chinese proficiency cannot be as good as the children who stay in China, I hope he is still able to communicate with others in Chinese even if it is easy conversation. I don't expect him to use very difficult phrases or idioms, but I also don't want him to fail to communicate with others in Chinese once he goes back to China in the future. At least, he should know how to read the newspaper.... So, I think his English proficiency is more important. If he cannot reach the same level (of English proficiency) as American children do, he will have learning difficulties. I think his primary task is to improve English, but of course, I also pay attention to the maintenance of his Chinese.

Maintaining Chinese while learning English was a goal that was part of the larger value system for Chun-Ming's family. His mother articulated her views about maintaining Chinese culture at the same time as wanting Chun-Ming to adapt to American society:

> We don't think every aspect of American thinking is good.... This country encourages independent learning. However, such free attitudes may not be a good thing for the children since not every child is an active learner. In this case, I still hope my child can keep some Chinese traditions such as being a diligent student. But I also encourage him to develop multiple interests, for example, I let him learn violin … I also encourage him to attend field trips or extracurricular activities. Anyway, I try to make him absorb the good parts of both cultures. We want him to learn the good parts of American culture without forgetting where he comes from.

Chun-Ming's family supported his Chinese writing at home in two ways: the use of composition books sent by his grandparents from China and one-on-one tutoring with his father. His parents provided feedback to him on his writing and vocabulary use.

*School context.* During his first year in the United States (Year 1), Chun Ming spent most of his time in the English as a Second Language (ESL) classroom in which he had opportunities to write in English daily. He spent some time in the all-English classroom at the beginning and ending of the day, participating in group projects and other writing assignments.

He attended the Mandarin class for speakers from China on a daily basis for 45 minutes. The focus of this classroom was on retaining oral Chinese rather than written Chinese; however, students were required to write in Chinese to meet the district mandates of writing during the fall and spring assessments.

All of his teachers described Chun Ming as extremely bright and motivated. His fourth grade ESL teacher said, "Well, he's an excellent student. He's very, very self-directed, very, very motivated. He's a quick learner." She also noted that he had made incredible progress over the school year, "Where he is right now is quite astounding in a sense, if I compare him to other kids." His all-English fourth grade teacher noted that he was reading at the level of his English-speaking peers in her classroom. His motivation to do well carried over to his Chinese class since Mr. Guo also noted what a hard-working student he was.

For fifth grade, Chun Ming remained at the same elementary school, but was in his all-English classroom for most of the day. In this classroom, students had fewer opportunities to write, in general, and to select topics of their choice than in his previous all-English setting. He received only 45 minutes of ESL instruction, but the focus was on reading and writing. He continued to receive native language instruction daily.

*Chinese writing.* In the first year, Chun-Ming wrote two descriptive pieces required by his native language instructor. He used four-character-phrases,[1] typical of high-quality Chinese essays, to describe the beauty of the season. He also used metaphors to elaborate the image of the season. He wrote "the balloons hung on the tables or chairs are like the different colors of bubbles floating in the sky." In the piece "Autumn," Chun-Ming compared the sound of fallen leaves to that of broken glass. He wrote:

> Branches of all colors start to fall to the ground gradually. The ground is thus decorated with different colors. When you tread on them, you can hear the tittering sounds which is like the sound when you tread on the broken glass.

He further tried to bring in the metaphoric meaning of autumn as a harvesting season, by focusing on the rewards of work:

> Autumn is also a harvesting season. People plow the farm, working diligently for the harvest for years. After they reap, when they stare at what they've gained from the cost of their sweat, they smile as happy as children do.

At the end of his second year, Chun-Ming's Chinese writing reflected some language loss. For example, he used four-character phrases less frequently, he made punctuation errors, and he chose some inappropriate vocabulary (see McCarthey, Guo, & Cummins, 2005). Having fewer opportunities to write in Mandarin at home and school was beginning to take its toll. However, additional assignments given by his parents to him helped mitigate the loss. Further, Chun-Ming still wanted to develop his Chinese literacy; he explained, "In learning Chinese, the more texts you read, the more vocabulary, phrases and idioms you can learn. And these help you in organizing your writing."

*English writing*. Chun-Ming's views of English writing were very pragmatic. He did not particularly enjoy writing, but saw it as a vehicle for learning and to acquire more English, "There is no like or dislike. If you learn more, you also write more. I don't hate writing." He believed that the purpose of writing was to learn more English and that writing provided him with an opportunity to practice English, "[I] write things like compositions to practice."

There was consensus among Chun-Ming's teachers that his writing was of high quality. For example, his ESL teacher believed that his writing was very good:

> He communicates his ideas well. There is a good flow of ideas. He usually has descriptions that accompany sentences. It's not just sentences in isolation, but it's usually detail that will add more information for the writer—for the reader, rather. His vocabulary is, for the time that he has been here, at a fairly sophisticated level.

The ESL teacher occasionally provided feedback on his work through comments asking for clarification or correcting his spelling and mechanics, but this was infrequently needed. He received high grades on his writing. Most of the writing Chun-Ming did for his ESL class consisted of retellings of TV shows such as *I Love Lucy* and *The Three Stooges*, or books he had read such as *Cinderella* and *The Box Car Children*. His story summaries were filled with dialogue, interesting vocabulary, and a logical sequence. Chun-Ming seemed to be attracted to the humor and action of the "Three Stooges" saying, "That show was so much fun. The three people are catching the bad guys." His example of the "Three Stooges" (see Appendix A) is indicative of the Bakhtinian concept "half-ours and half-someone else's" in which he borrows from TV shows and popular culture to develop his identity as an English writer.

As his English improved during the second year, he wrote more about daily life and less about cartoons and TV shows. He liked to write book reports, particularly about the mystery books he read. His ESL teacher noted, "Chun-Ming makes few mistakes because I think he just memorizes rules and doesn't mess up." She went on to elaborate that his writing seemed scripted. She said:

I think he's afraid of making a mistake and afraid of branching out, and wants to use ideas that are already there, but not so much develop his own … Chun-Ming is afraid to be creative, which I think is why he relies on his journal, writing about book reports, writing about very specifically a sequential afternoon and what he did. Much more scripted writing, as opposed to more free writing.

Some of this reluctance to "be creative" or to write in scripted ways can be seen in his writing samples from Year 2. He wrote an expository piece entitled "Electricity" that describes electrons and charges (see Appendix B). The writing is somewhat formulaic as it fits the five-paragraph essay structure. The organization, sentence structure, spelling and punctuation are excellent, particularly for a second year ESL student. Over the course of two years, Chun-Ming had become a proficient English writer with his second year pieces reflecting greater clarity, coherence, and more sophisticated syntax.

*A Bakhtinian Analysis of Chun Ming.* Chun Ming was developing a hybrid identity as a bilingual/biliterate Chinese and English speaker. While he experienced some language loss in written Chinese, he wanted to maintain his Chinese identity and language. His parents' voices clearly had a strong impact on his developing identity since they valued his learning and adapting to U.S. culture at the same time as he maintained Chinese values.

Chun Ming's writing also reflects Bakhtin's theory of drawing from other's voices. His use of metaphor in his Chinese writing reflects the genre typically taught in school in China where the four-phrase phrase is valued (Huang, 2001). Likewise, his English composition on electricity, which uses the five-paragraph essay format, clearly shows the influence of English instruction. In each case, he borrows from the appropriate genre "the authoritative discourse," but transforms the work into something new for him. While the five-paragraph essay is not a "new" form for U.S. classrooms, it was new for him because it differed from what he experienced in China. His writing shows that his work is "half-ours and half-someone else's" influenced by the media, teachers, peers, and features of the genre, yet changed to express something unique. For example, he uses the forms of the five-paragraph essay, but he also adds his own voice, "That's not all about electricity. You can find out more about electricity, like static and current electricity, electro-magnets, etc. So see you next time." There also appeared to be a developmental process in which his ability to move away from scripted writing, "authoritative discourse" to "internally persuasive discourse" is developed over time. For example, his fourth grade Chinese pieces reflected the norms of Chinese writing taught in school, whereas his fifth grade Chinese writing pieces show more of an influence of the personal narrative valued in the United

States. His Chinese pieces in fifth grade reflected a hybrid construction of Chinese phrases and personal opinions. Through his writing we can see an increased sense of hybrid identity for Chun Ming that was influenced by both home and school factors.

## SUSIE FROM A COMMUNITIES OF PRACTICE PERSPECTIVE

Like Chun Ming, Susie is also influenced by home and school literacy practices. However, in her case we can see the ways in which she negotiates membership in multiple communities as she constructs her identity. These communities of practice play a significant role in her identity as an immigrant from Taiwan who focuses more on English literacy than on Chinese oral and written communication.

### Communities of Practice

Wenger (1998) suggests that we all belong to many communities of practice—some of which are more important to our identities than others. This "nexus of multimembership" (p. 158) requires us to develop competencies in different communities resulting in ongoing tensions. The process of "reconciliation ... entails finding ways of making our various forms of membership coexist" (p. 159) often across boundaries of practice. Several key aspects of Wenger's definition are important to consider: identity is (a) "lived" and thus, "more fundamentally an experience that involves participation," (b) "negotiated" assuming that it is "ongoing and pervasive", (c) "social"—"community membership gives the formation of identity a fundamentally social character," (d) "a learning process" meaning "a trajectory in time that incorporates both past and future into the meaning of the present," (e) "a nexus" that "combines multiple forms of membership" and (f) "a local-global interplay" (p. 163).

Communities of practice theories contribute to our understanding of English language learners who are members of at least two communities upon entry to the United States—their native language community and their new English-speaking community within schools. Home and school settings are "socially situated spaces where newcomers apprentice to communities of learners in order to acquire new skills and practices" (Hawkins, 2004, p. 17). While all of the students we studied were grappling with negotiating their membership in several communities, Susie's case illustrates the ways in which specific classroom contexts played a role in her identity as a Taiwanese student who was learning to write in English. Unlike Chun Ming, she had not developed competence in written Chinese before leaving Taiwan; therefore, she was not already a member of a community of Chinese writers. Her Mandarin and English teachers played a variety of roles in helping her become a member of different communities.

## Susie: Becoming an Avid English Writer

An only child, Susie was born in Taiwan, but moved to Hong Kong with her parents when she was one month old. She moved back to Taiwan when she was two or three years old, where her parents worked in a shoe factory in a large city in central Taiwan. Susie attended kindergarten and first grade in that city. When she was in second grade, her parents decided to immigrate to the United States due to their perception that the political situation in Taiwan was unstable.

In the United States, Susie's family resided in the same city where her aunt previously had immigrated. Susie's father held a part-time job at a fast food restaurant while her mother stayed home. Her family's working class status suggested that they had much in common with the working-class, less educated, Chinese immigrant families Li (2000) describes. In contrast to the model minority stereotype (McKay & Wong, 1996), her father did not think that Susie had to go to college to be a success. While her parents hoped she would attend college, her father explained that, "As long as she has normal development it is good."

Susie's parents spoke Mandarin to each other and to her at home, and she predominantly used Mandarin to communicate with them. However, similar to other immigrant children with English more advanced than their parents, she served as their English tutor. Her parents liked to practice their English with her, consulting her about English vocabulary and expressions. When she spoke too fast, they could not understand her, and she corrected their English mistakes.

Susie described English as being "better," "normal" and "familiar," and stated that she liked English better than Chinese because she "grew up in the United States." Her attitude towards Chinese was ambivalent. While she described Chinese as being "not good," "hard" and "something different," she also wished that her Chinese was better than it was to facilitate communication with her parents and to save her parents the trouble of teaching her Chinese, "I want to improve my talking in Chinese … [so] my mom doesn't have to [and] my dad won't have to waste their time to teach me Chinese anymore." Susie experienced conflict, then, between her Chinese and English language selves. While she wanted to belong to both the Chinese community of her family, she also wanted to be comfortable with English peers.

*Home contexts.* Susie did not have extensive opportunities to learn to write in Chinese in Taiwan before coming to the United States. Further, her family planned on staying in the US and wanted her to assimilate into the United. Similar to the immigrant families described by Wong Fillmore (1991), Susie's family ascribed a much lower priority to maintaining the home language and customs than they did to assimilation. Her father viewed English as a tool for assimilation:

> No matter where she is, I think English is very important. I told her that Chinese is her native language, and now that she is in America, her English definitely should be like an American's. Because you live here, you have to assimilate into this society.

Susie's parents did not write in Chinese at home, as noted by her father who said, "We do not use a lot of Chinese except speaking. We rarely write." Susie's father believed that maintaining her Mandarin speaking ability was enough, and, thus, he did not push her to develop Chinese written skills: "I do not push her Chinese. For Chinese, as long as she does the homework from the Chinese class at Karl school, that's enough. I do not force her to memorize things." He also thought that requiring her to improve her written Chinese would place an "extra burden" on her.

*School contexts.* Susie had limited Chinese literacy skills. She could not read Chinese without phonetic symbols (zhu-yin). She rarely wrote Chinese except for her Chinese homework, which included copying characters and sometimes producing summaries of the readings in the textbook. She liked to finish the routine homework of copying characters in her Chinese class so she did not need to complete the characters at home. Her Chinese teacher noted her neat handwriting, and Susie usually received rewards for completing homework in a timely fashion. However, Susie struggled to write compositions and believed that others, including her mother, saw her Chinese writing as "bad." She reported that she "can only write simple characters, such as 'small,' 'you,' and 'big,' those words." Her limited knowledge of characters greatly constrained what she could produce in a passage. Her Chinese teacher remarked that she was able to write only two or three sentences on her own, and her Chinese writing was influenced by English grammar.

During her fourth grade year, Susie participated in an all-English classroom for 125 minutes a day and an ESL classroom for 160 minutes daily. Her ESL teacher primarily was responsible for her English literacy instruction. In her fifth grade year, Susie spent most of her time in the all-English class and only 40 minutes in an advanced ESL reading/writing class. Susie's fourth grade and fifth grade all-English teachers held her in high regard. For example, Mrs. Tierney stated, "academically, she is excellent as far as reading and writing." She also mentioned that she was "very colorful in her writing—I think that goes along with her spirit; she just thinks on a whole different level." Although she scored at grade level on a standardized reading test in English toward the end of fourth grade (grade equivalent score of 4.8), her fifth grade all-English teacher felt that her reading was a bit below grade level, but believed her writing was improving all the time. She noted "she's really good with content; she's working on grammar and editing." Both all-English teachers believed that Susie was "a really hard worker" and identified her artistic ability.

Susie's ESL teacher in fourth grade held high expectations for Susie's English writing because at the beginning of fourth grade Susie had received a score of "Competent English Writer" on a writing assessment for English language learners. The teacher taught English by integrating reading, writing, listening, and speaking. To meet the diverse needs of her students, she often had them write daily summaries of what they had learned in their content-based ESL instruction and biweekly book reports, which involved retelling key components of the books they had read. She corrected their English syntax, spelling, and word choice by putting boxes on top of the writing errors, in which the students were to write the corrections, before revising the draft. Susie, who loved to communicate her thoughts through her drawing, resisted Mrs. Almasi's writing assignments. When Mrs. Almasi described Susie's attitude towards writing, she reported, "At times she's groaned and moaned because we've had a writing activity." She also believed that Susie was not putting forth the effort she could:

> At the beginning of the year, I thought that she was very, very capable, but I think she's a little bit on the lazy side. I think she would've gone a lot further had she been perhaps more willing to look at her work and evaluate it and self-correct.

The ESL teacher's perceptions of Susie appeared to affect Susie's attitude towards writing and her participation. Susie identified problems with understanding the teacher's expectations for writing in the class. For example, she reported that she had to rewrite her book report several times because the teacher did not like what she had written. Susie described it this way:

> Once I wrote the most, about five pages, and the teacher said, "No. Because you wrote many words, but you did not tell me *what the story is about.*" So she tore off all of them and asked me to write a new piece, shorter.

This event was so important to her that she referred to it again in a later interview, "Like, when we, when I read from book, and I read it, and

I did a book report, she said, 'Do it over again.' And then I give a shorter one, but that explains the story, but then she said she didn't think I read the book." Indeed, the teacher had written "I don't think you read the book" on her paper.

Susie was somewhat confused about the expectations in the fourth grade ESL class and expressed resistance when things did not go her way. When asked to discuss her writing in this class, she made comments such as, "I hate my story," "It's kind of boring," "I have nothing to say," and "I don't know what to write about." She found writing book reports frustrating and believed that her classmates would find her work uninteresting, "I think if I write a story or anything, they will think that it's boring."

In contrast, Susie bloomed as a writer in the fifth grade ESL class with Mrs. Marsh. Mrs. Marsh had students use a writing trait approach, in which students wrote about a variety of topics, shared their writing with a small group of peers, and the peers evaluated the writing according to the assigned writing trait. In addition, Mrs. Marsh gave each student a notebook, in which the student wrote and she responded to the student's work. If students wanted to keep something private, they simply wrote "don't read" and the teacher did not read the entry. Susie particularly enjoyed the responses and asked the teacher to write in the book rather than on a "post it note," a method used by the teacher to avoid writing on the students' notebooks. Mrs. Marsh reported that Susie wrote about a wide variety of topics, "it truly was like a diary. It was whatever she was feeling at the time." Mrs. Marsh also noted that Susie's writing had improved quite a bit from the beginning of the year because "she just seems to think about it more than before."

Susie's enthusiasm for English writing was evident in other school contexts as well as at home. At school, she passed notes and played word games with friends. In particular, in her fifth grade, she had a new classmate, Gail, who had been in an English-Chinese bilingual program in Taiwan. They attended the same ESL and Chinese classes and soon became very good friends. During several observations of the Chinese class, where Susie and Gail were the only students, the two girls often engaged in playful word games.

At home, she made cards for her parents, made an advertisement for her future bakery, wrote poems on her computer or on her math practice sheet when she was tired of doing math, and wrote or drew when the TV program her parents were watching did not interest her. She also made books for her parents and illustrated this book by cutting and pasting pictures from the old Chinese magazines her mother brought from Taiwan. Inspired by her fifth grade ESL teacher, she bought herself a diary to write in at home. She said, "I want to fill it all, like each page is filled with a story of my life and stuff and then I can try to lock it or something." She added, "I want to finish it, and after I finish it, maybe if I have a child, I can read it as a bedtime story." Many of these writings at home were "just for fun" or as Susie put it, "it (the idea) just came to my mind." She did not always keep these writings, but her mother tried to collect some, dated them, and sometimes wrote notes (in Chinese) on them.

A significant event in her experience as a writer was the coauthoring of a fictional story with her Taiwanese friend, Gail, that they submitted to a writing contest hosted by the school. Although contestants were not required to make their entries into the form of a book, she and Gail illustrated theirs with both hand and computer drawings. They also made a front cover and a back cover containing the story summary, reflecting the connections they saw between reading and writing (see Appendix C). Susie wrote for communicative purposes and "just for fun," sharing her spontaneous creations with her mother. Susie came to see herself as an enthusiastic writer, and her motivation clearly influenced her development as a writer in English.

*Applying communities of practice framework to Susie's case.* In applying Wenger's community of practice theory, we see that Susie had a "lived" experience that involved participation at different levels in different communities. She had little opportunity to develop writing skills prior to coming to the United States and her parents tended to focus on assimilation into the United States through learning English rather than development of Chinese literate skills. As a result, she struggled with Chinese literacy skills and did not see the purpose of writing Chinese; therefore, she was not fully engaged as a member of a community of practice of Chinese writers (Wenger, 1998). However, she was learning to participate in this community by learning to form characters at school and to write brief journal entries supported by her Chinese teacher.

Susie was continually negotiating her identity as a Chinese speaker since she was not fluent with her parents, yet she wanted to be part of that community as evidenced by her desire to not disappoint them and learn to communicate in Chinese effectively. Her identity was both social in nature and a learning process. She learned to become a member of the English writing community through the support of her fifth grade teacher and her peer, Gail. As she was provided with more freedom to choose topics of interest and explored different genres, Susie became an enthusiastic writer within several communities of practice including the ESL classroom (Wenger, 1998). Her identity as a Chinese and English speaker and an English and Chinese writer indicated that she was combining "multiple forms of membership" and reflecting "a local-global interplay" (Wenger, p. 163).

The communities of practice theory highlights Susie's membership in different communities simultaneously, and allows us to see the ways in which identity is constructed in relation to communities. In a different, but complementary manner, narrative theory emphasizes the ways in which identities are constructed within and by discourse. The story of Elena reflects the discursive nature of identity by juxtaposing narratives constructed by her and about her by teachers in different classroom and school settings as well as by her primary caregiver, her father. These stories are, at times, in conflict with one another, but reveal the complexity of a Latina who is increasingly identifying herself as "Mexican American" in a sometimes hostile environment.

## ELENA FROM A NARRATIVE THEORY OF IDENTITY

Researchers who propose a "narrative theory of identity" (Sfard & Pusak, 2005, p. 18) suggest that identities are *"discursive counterparts* (italics in original) of one's lived experiences" (p. 17). They find that "narratives authored by others are among the most important sources of our designated identities" (p. 18). Identities, then, are stories that we and others tell about ourselves (Anzaldúa, 1999). These stories about a given person might differ from one another depending on the storyteller and the audience; however, they often share family resemblances (Mishler, 1999; Sarup, 1996). Sfard and Pusak suggest that these stories can be *first-person*, in which person A tells a story about herself; *second-person* story in which A tells a story to an identified person, or *third-person* in which a story is told about A by a third person to another third person. In the analysis of Elena, I draw from these different persons to construct her story. For example, Elena provides a first-person narrative through her written work in which she provides information about her Spanish and English habits as well as information about topics that are important to her. The researcher-conducted interviews, or gathered first-person stories about her writing habits and while discussions revolving around her identity as a Mexican American provide a second-person story, and the interviews with her teachers and father present third-person stories about Elena.

### Elena: Narrating a Latina Identity

Before Elena was born, her parents immigrated to the United States from a rural part of Mexico. Elena's father had completed second grade in Mexico, and worked as a cooking assistant at a local restaurant. He moved to the local community for employment purposes, and later encouraged members of his extended family to move from a larger city to the local community. Elena had never been to Mexico although the family talked about visiting.

In fourth grade, Elena lived with her father and younger brother in a house that her father had purchased in the Unity School District. Her mother was being treated for severe depression in a hospital in another state. At the end of fourth grade, Elena's mother moved back home with the family, and her father purchased a home in the Charles School District. She was close to her extended family, which consisted of her grandparents, an uncle, two aunts, and several cousins, who lived in the area and provided support for child care and other activities.

*Home context.* Elena's father spoke Spanish, but was a very limited English speaker. Elena's mother only spoke Spanish. The adults in the extended family spoke Spanish to each other and to their children, but the children preferred speaking English to each other. Elena's father placed value on his children being bilingual, "As I tell them, later if you can speak the two languages well, then it is a benefit to you." The two main places where the children used Spanish were with their parents and adult relatives, and in the Spanish-language church that they attended.

Elena's father reported that he occasionally asked his children to write in Spanish when they wanted to do something special, "Will you take us someplace, and I tell them, 'ok, but first write [copy] something from a book in Spanish' ... I want you to write a page." He said that he was not really concerned about what they wrote, but wanted them to practice writing in Spanish. He knew that Elena had problems with writing, "She is very slow to write, whether in Spanish or English." However, he still thought that it was important for her and her brother to be biliterate: "For them, it is very important to maintain their Spanish, to be able to read and write it."

During the first year of the study, Elena did some letter writing in Spanish and a little reading in Spanish at home. She reported that her father did not correct her writing in Spanish, but only asked her if she was ready to mail her letters. Because Elena's father felt that his own literacy level was low, he said that he didn't read much in Spanish. Sometimes he bought Elena a few books in Spanish or she brought home books in Spanish or English from school. In the second year of the study, Elena's father bought the children a computer. Elena completed graphs with her cousins' names and ages, wrote essays in English, and participated in an e-mail Web site sponsored by the Spanish television network, Univisión. She said that she sometimes wrote e-mails in Spanish, pretending that she didn't know English, to see what people would say in Spanish. Elena also read books in Spanish and English to her younger cousins while on the school bus.

*School contexts.* Elena had attended preschool and grades K-2 at Brook School in the Charles School District. Elena reported that she learned to write first in English because she did not receive any literacy instruction in Spanish until second grade when Brook School initiated a part-time transitional bilingual education program. At the beginning of third grade, Elena entered the part-time transitional bilingual education program at Karl School in the Unity School District. By the end of third grade, Elena was rated as a fluent English speaker, but continued in the bilingual education program because her literacy skills in English and Spanish were quite low. In the spring of fourth grade, she scored below grade level (2.2 grade equivalent score) on a standardized reading test in English.

*Karl School.* Most of Elena's writing instruction in the first year of the study occurred in the ESL classroom. Her ESL teacher described her as "a sweet kid" who was "nurturing." She characterized Elena as "a risk taker when it comes to expressing her ideas orally, and she can come up with really magnificent ideas.... And so, she is a bright kid." Although she considered her oral Spanish to be very good, she did not think that she was literate in either language, and thought that she had problems with "phonetics" or spelling, "She stumbles on words.... She's not really strong in either one of the languages."

Elena was the only Spanish speaker in her all-English classroom. There were few opportunities for her to use both languages to think and plan writing. Writing opportunities were infrequent, but included writing a research paper on animals. She struggled to read the books to complete her project and her English writing was brief and sketchy. Elena's Spanish language class tended to emphasize correct spelling and placement of accents. Her Spanish teacher had a negative impression of Elena and her brother's abilities:

> A first grader can write better than they do in ideas, spelling, structure. ... They are not doing well in English; they aren't doing well in Spanish; they are not doing well in any class. Elena's level is kindergarten and first grade.

At the end of the school year, Elena moved to Brook School in a different district. Elena's teachers in the former district thought that the move would create more problems because they believed her home situation was unstable (e.g., the Spanish teacher thought her father was an alcoholic). Her all-English teacher commented, "She does not need a new school." However, her father explained that he made the move so that his family could live closer to his parents and other relatives to provide assistance while he was at work.

*Brook School.* In Year 2, Elena attended Brook School, which advertised that it had a transitional bilingual education program, but which actually had a part-time ESL program. Elena received 60 minutes of daily ESL instruction and 30 minutes of Title 1 instruction four days a week. The rest of the time she was in an all-English classroom. Different from her placement at Karl School, she now was placed with six other Spanish speakers in her all-English classroom, including her cousins. In addition, there were a number of other Spanish speakers at the school, with the majority of them of Mexican origin. Elena reported that she was happier at Brook School than at Karl School because "There, I missed my cousins a lot ... I like it because there I felt strange. Here, I don't feel strange."

Elena had opportunities to write in three different contexts at Brook: her all-English classroom, her Title 1 class, and her ESL class. Her Title 1 teacher supported Elena and four other ESL Latina/o fifth graders complete their monthly book reports that were required by one of the all-English teachers. She reported that initially the students wrote their book reports according to an outline, in which they just had to fill in the blanks, but by the end of the year, they were writing the book reports on their own. The teacher, Mrs. Starky, also reported that her planning time coincided with the students' lunch time, and that Elena and the other students were welcome to visit her during this time, which she called the Lunch Bunch, to chat, listen to music, or play games.

Although Mrs. Starky did not know Spanish and was not certified in ESL, she did allow the students to use both of their languages to figure out what they had read. When a child in the group did not know what "moccasins" meant, Mrs. Starky reported:

> And so I was trying to describe it and draw a little picture of it, but Elena jumped in right away and said moccasins in Spanish. And so they're always helping each other out, and I trust them to do that ... I just think that's the coolest.

Mrs. Starky thought that Elena's writing tended to be "real factual" and somewhat formulaic. She explained that the journal writing that occurred in her all-English classroom was not "a natural or free response journal" because a rubric guided students' journal writing. She also thought that Elena's writing might have been affected by the school emphasis on preparing students to do well on the state mandated writing assessment. She explained: "When I see her writing in English, I don't see her taking a creative spin.... We talk about the connections ... the text to self, text to world, and text to text. She knows all the lingo, but she's not one to go to the text-to-self very often."

Writing instruction in Elena's all-English fifth grade classroom was very explicit to prepare students for the state test that emphasized the five-paragraph essay. For example, in one assignment we observed, the teacher told students precisely how to organize their paper: "Write a paper about an invention. Tell why it is important, how life was before the invention, and the positive or negative aspects of the invention." The writing instruction that occurred in the ESL class tended to involve the completion of frames about topics they were studying or spelling tests.

*Shifts in Elena's stories about herself.* In her fourth-grade year, Elena made few references to her identity as a Latina. Her stories focused on her dream house, while most of her other pieces reflected the assignments requested in her content-based ESL instruction. She believed that she was a better writer in English than in Spanish, "I don't know much Spanish; I can't either read or write it." She also demonstrated little interest in writing.

During her fifth-grade year, Elena seemed to identify more strongly with her Latina identity. For example, on several occasions she expressed a great admiration for the Mexican-American singer Selena, "I want to be a singer! I want to be like Selena." She started reading about topics on Mexico, anticipating a trip, "Because all the adults in my family come from there. And five of the kids come from there.... Oh, I love the food! It's what I eat everyday!" She also believed that her reading and writing skills in Spanish and English were at the same level, explaining that she wrote in a particular language depending on her purposes, "Sometimes I write in Spanish, sometimes in English, because sometimes I want to pretend that I don't know English to see what they say."

Elena's motivation to write increased during fifth grade and she was engaging in a variety of writing practices at home on the family's computer. For example, she completed graphs with her cousins' names and ages and using the Internet in Spanish on an e-mail Web site sponsored by Univision. She also wrote a persuasive essay about why girls were better than boys at home.

Elena's Spanish letter is an example of the ways in which she revealed her own story in relation to her identity as a Latina. In the letter she positioned herself as connected to the Latino community, but she also hinted at the enormous challenges she faced with communicating in two languages in a hostile environment:

Querido Arturo,

En (a city) cae nieve. A se frio. Hay muchos especiales en las tiendas. Y hay artas tiendas de dollar. Hay una tienda Mexican. Hay lucas y otros dulces mexicanos. No puedes a cer amigos facis porque no to dos ablan el mis mo iduama. Para acer amigos tienes que pasar afuear y en los parkes y platicar con jente. Puedes es perar rasitas.

Elena

(Dear Arturo, it snows in (names a city). It's cold. There are many sales in the stores. And there are many dollar stores. There is a Mexican store. There are "lucas" and other mexican candy. You can't make friends easily because not everybody speak the same language. To make friends you have to go outside and in the parks and talk to people. You can expect racists. Elena.)

Her written narrative contributes to her construction of her identity as a child of immigrants growing up in the US who experiences racism. For example, she begins the piece by setting up the context of being in a cold climate, but then focuses on the Mexican store with its access to Mexican food items such as "lucas." Elena demonstrates her awareness of the linguistic and racial barriers that appear to prevent her from making friends. The sentence, "You can expect racists" as an ending to her letter is particularly telling. While she does not describe a particular incident in which she has experienced racism, the fact that she anticipates racism and is warning her friend about racism in the community reflects her own voice and her experiences as a Mexican American who is learning English but also trying to establish her identity as Mexican American.

*Elena from a narrative perspective.* The narrative approach to identity construction helps us to see Elena's development as stories told by different participants. At times, the story lines contradict one another (Mishler, 1999). For example, the Karl School teachers constructed the story of her family as a fractured family with many problems including depression and alcoholism. Yet, Elena's father told the story of drawing on family resources to provide for the children during the year of separation from their mother; he sought to provide a bilingual/biliterate environment in the best way he could by encouraging Spanish language use, helping with homework, and buying a computer.

While her ESL teacher at Karl school saw her as a nice student, two of the teachers saw Elena as a struggling student who was not fully literate in either Spanish or English, and predicted that changing schools would hinder her literacy development. In contrast, teachers at Brook School told a more positive story of Elena's growth; their stories focused on providing opportunities for her to interact with other Spanish speakers, using more structured writing activities, and allowing her to spend time in an informal environment during lunch.

Through the lens of identity-building as storytelling (Gonzalez, 2001) we can see that the stories that her father, her teachers in different school and classroom contexts, and her own stories about herself constructed who she was as a developing bilingual/biliterate person. In the case of Elena, identity can be viewed as a discursive activity in which the stories about her are not "merely expressing" her identities but are "made of" them (Sfard, in press).

## CONCLUSION

Each of the theoretical frames described above aids us in viewing English language learners from different perspectives. The Bahktinian frame applied to identity focuses on the historical view of the ways in which past encounters with multiple voices shape who we are. Chun Ming's writing reveals the voices of his parents' views of Chinese and US culture and bilingualism, his teachers' perspectives on the use of genres, the influence of the media, and his previous experiences with Chinese and English texts. The "communities of practice" perspective focuses on the influence of context and the role of the community in engaging learners. It allows us to see how Susie was in the process of moving in and out of different communities, developing a "nexus of multimembership" (p. 158). She wanted to become a part of the community of Chinese speakers, but she seemed even more motivated to become part of the community of engaged, active English writers. Finally, the identity as narrative lens helps us understand how different audiences and perspectives shape who we are. Elena's father, teachers at different schools with whom she engaged in different contexts, and she herself all had their viewpoints about who she was. While their stories overlapped at times, they also conflicted with one another. The narrative view allows us to understand how identity is constructed and provides a bridge between identity and learning. Each perspective provides the potential for explaining how English language learners become who they are as they negotiate the terrain of learning a new language in a new country.

In this chapter I have presented each case in relation to one theory. However, all of these theories could be used to frame the ways in which all of the students in the study negotiated their home and school contexts because the theories share many characteristics. For example, the theories all derive from social constructivist foundations, consider identity as multiple and constructed, and highlight the role of language in learning. Therefore, in tandem the theories offer richly textured analyses that can offer insights into how to assist English language learners in becoming bilingual, biliterate, and bicultural. Together, the theories and cases contribute to our knowledge about how students from diverse backgrounds are influenced by home and school contexts in constructing their multiple and dynamic identities.

# APPENDIX A:
## CHUN MING'S THREE STOOGES

April 8. Mon.

The three stooges

At Cooking

This is a short story. It's very funny
And this story is about the three stooges, Moe
Larry and Shemp.

The stooges ran to a restaurant. A customer came. He ordered chicken soup. Shemp
got a chicken and put hot water through it
in the bowl. Then he took the water out. This
was called "Chicken Soup." As he threw
the soup to the customer, the soup was
thrown to Moe and sprayed out all over him.
Moe said, "Ouch!" Then he hit Shemp's
face and said, "What's the matter
with you? Hurry up, a customer wants
eggs!" Shemp began to cook the eggs. The
fire was so big. Shemp threw the eggs onto Moe's
face. And all customers ate nothing. They were
going to shut down the restaurant because
the kitchen workers couldn't cook anything for them.
So they got some police officers and the officer
arrested the stooges.

Very Good!

## APPENDIX B: CHUN MING'S ELECTRICITY

Electricity
Have you ever felt a shock when you
touch your friend?

Have you ever seen a balloon sticking
to your cloth after rubbing it on your
hair?

Light, sound and electricity are all
forms of energy. Everything is made of
atoms. An atom contains electrons and
protons. Electrons have a negative charge
and protons have a positive charge. If
an object gains or loses electrons, it has
an electric charge. An object that has
gained electrons has a negative electric
charge. An object that has lost
electrons has a positive electric charge.

When you rub a balloon on your
hair, it became positively charged because
it's losing electrons. Electrons were rubbed
off. Opposite charges attract each other,
so the balloon will stick to your cloth.

Objects sometimes repel other. This is
because they have the same charge. If
you put two magnets together, and they
repel each other, that means they have
the same charge. Unlike charges attract
each other, like charges repel each
other. This attraction and pulsion is called
electric force.

That's not all about electricity. You
can find out more about electricity, like
static and current electricity, electro-
magnets, etc. So, see you next time.

## APPENDIX C: SUSIE'S COVER PAGE FOR STORY CONTEST

WOLFY WAS A BABY WOLF THAT
THOUGHT HIS PARENTS LIKED HIS
SISTER BETTER. HE THOUGHT THAT
LEAVING HOME AND SURVIVING ON
HIS OWN WAS THE ONLY CHOICE.
WOULD HE SURVIVE? WOULD HE
CHANGE HIS MIND AND STAY?
READ THIS BOOK AND FIND OUT.

## NOTE

1.  Although Chinese phrases may contain more or less than four characters, four-character phrases are frequently used and play essential roles in developing Chinese vocabulary. Some phrases originate from history, others from classical literature, and others from oral communication. The teaching of four-character phrases is considered an important part of the language arts curriculum in Chinese-speaking countries (Huang, 2001).

## REFERENCES

Anzaldúa, G. (1999, October). *Nos/otros: "Us" vs. "them" (Des) conciementos y comprisos*. Presentation at the Conference of Territories and Boundaries: Geographies of Latinidad, University of Illinois at Urbana-Champaign.

Bakhtin, M. M. (1981). *The dialogic imagination*. Austin: University of Texas Press.

Bakhtin, M. M. (1986). *Speech genres and other late essays*. Austin: University of Texas Press.

Banks, J. A., & Banks, C. A. (Eds.) (2004). *Handbook of research in multicultural education* (2nd edition). San Francisco: Jossey Bass.

Erikson, E. (1968). *Identity: Youth and crisis*. New York: W.W. Norton.

Gee, J., & Crawford, V. (1998). Two kinds of teenagers: Language, identity, and social class. In D. Alvermann, K. Hinchman, D. Moore, S. Phelps, & D. Waff (Eds.), *Reconceptualizing the literacies in adolescents' lives* (pp. 225-245). Mahwah, NJ: Erlbaum.

Gonzalez, N. (2001). *I am my language: Discourses of women and children in the borderlands*. Tucson: University of Arizona Press.

Hawkins, M. R. (2004). Researching English language and literacy development in schools. *Educational Researcher, 33*(3), 14-25.

Huang, F. J. (2001, June). The art of Chinese. *Guo Wen Tian Di*, 86-90.

Jiménez, R. T. (2000). Literacy and the identity development of Latina/o students. *American Educational Research Journal, 37*, 971-1000.

Li, G. (2002). *"East is east, west is west"? Home literacy, culture, and schooling*. New York: Peter Lang.

Manyak, P. C. (2001). Participation, hybridity, and carnival: A situated analysis of a dynamic literacy practice in a primary-grade English immersion class. *Journal of Literacy Research, 33*, 423-465.

McCarthey, S. J., García, G. E., López-Velásquez, A., Lin, S., & Guo, Y. (2004). Understanding writing contexts for English Language Learners. *Research in the Teaching on English, 38*, 351-394.

McCarthey, S. J., Guo, Y. H., & Cummins, S. (2005). Understanding changes in Mandarin elementary students' L1 and L2 writing. *Journal of Second Language Writing, 14*(2), 71-104.

McCarthey, S. J., & Garcia, G. E. (2005). English language learners' writing practices and attitudes. *Written Communication, 22*(1), 36-75.

McKay, S. & Wong, S. L. (1996). Multiple discourses, multiple identities: Investment and agency in second language learning among Chinese adolescent immigrant students. *Harvard Educational Review, 66*(3), 577-608.

Mishler, E. G. (1999). *Storylines: Craft artists' narratives of identity.* Cambridge, MA: Harvard University Press.

Sarup, M. (1996). *Identity, culture, and the postmodern world.* Athens: University of Georgia Press.

Sfard, A. (2005). Telling identities by the company they keep: A response to the critique by Mary Juzwik. *Educational Researcher, 35*(9), 22-27.

Sfard, A. (2006). Telling identities by the company they keep: A response to the critique by Mary Juzwik. *Educational Researcher, 35*(9), 22-27.

Sfard, A., & Prusak, A. (2005). Telling identities: In search of an analytic tool for investigating learning as a culturally-shaped activity. *Educational Researcher, 34*(4), 14-22.

Solsken, J., Willett, J., & Wilson-Keenan, J. (2000). Cultivating hybrid texts in multicultural classrooms: Promise and challenge. *Research in the Teaching of English, 35*(2), 179-212.

Wenger, E. (1998). *Communities of practice: Learning, meaning, and identity.* Cambridge, England: Cambridge University Press.

Wong Fillmore, L. (1991). When learning a second language means losing the first. *Early Childhood Research Quarterly, 6*, 323-346.

Yon, D. (2000). *Elusive culture: Schooling, race, and identity in global times.* Albany: State University of New York Press.

CHAPTER 12

# OLD TENSIONS, NEW VISIONS

## Implications of Home Literacies for Teacher Education Programs, K-12 Schools, and Family Literacy Programs

### Jennifer D. Turner and Patricia Edwards

Why do some children become engaged literacy learners and others do not? This is one of the most enduring questions for literacy researchers and educators. For decades, literacy scholars have considered the role that school-related factors, such as teachers, materials, and instructional approaches, play in the literacy development of elementary students (e.g. B. Taylor & Pearson, 2002; Turner, 2005; Wharton-McDonald, Pressley, & Hampston, 1998). Although several of these studies mention home-related factors, such as parent involvement in school (e.g., attending parent teacher conferences and other school events) and home-school communication, such factors are not usually given prominence within this research.

More recently, out-of-school factors have gained increasing attention from educators, parents, and policymakers (Arzubiaga, Rueda, & Monzo, n.d.). A critical "out of school" factor—literacy practices within homes

*Multicultural Families, Home Literacies, and Mainstream Schooling*
pp. 245–268
Copyright © 2009 by Information Age Publishing
245

and families—has been the subject of intense discussion over the past ten years (Gadsden, Ray, Jacobs, & Gwak, 2006). Much of this discussion has been guided by the premise that home literacies play a significant role in literacy development and schooling: the family serves as children's earliest learning environment, and parents are the first and most important teachers in their lives (Edwards, Pleasants, & Franklin, 1999; Haney & Hill, 2004). However, this discussion of home literacies has also raised concerns about the low literacy achievement of "at-risk" children, and the challenges associated with involving poor and/or culturally-diverse parents in their children's educational lives have been raised, and has lead to heated debates about what constitutes good parenting, appropriate parent involvement, and acceptable literacy practices in homes and families (Arzubiaga et al., n.d.; Edwards, 2004; Gadsden et al., 2006). As a result, "parent involvement and parent-child literacy engagement, over time, has become a national priority, on the one hand, and the problems associated with both have been framed as unique to low-income and low-income minority families on the other hand" (Gadsden et al., 2006, p. 157).

Clearly, the concept of home literacies is both controversial and complex. While some literacy scholars and educators think that *all* home literacies greatly contribute to children's literacy acquisition in mainstream schools, others view home literacy as a "risk factor" for culturally and linguistically diverse children because their family practices may not reflect those valued in schools. As literacy scholars and educators, we, the authors of this chapter, believe that this controversial view of home literacies has serious consequences for the field. One such consequence is the disconnection between theory, practice, and research related to home and family literacies (Edwards, 2003). According to Purcell-Gates (2000), "research in the area of family literacy is lagging behind policy and practice. Public perception about its role in children's learning, public and private funding, and program implementations are all outpacing empirically based knowledge" (p. 866). We are not suggesting that controversy is not a useful tool in literacy research and education, for we recognize that healthy debate supports the spirit of inquiry. Our concern, however, is that the controversies and tensions surrounding the issue of home literacies are so polarizing that they seem to mitigate the advancement of the field. Some literacy scholars take up particular positions in the debate on home literacies without listening to the perspectives of others. Other scholars attempt to avoid these tensions by remaining "neutral" and conducting studies which "simply report new understandings" (Edwards, 2003, p. 100).

In an effort to move beyond the acrimony within the field, we examine the powerful role that home literacies play in three educational contexts: teacher education programs, K-12 schools, and family literacy programs. In each context, we examine the "old" tensions, conflicts, and controversies that have dominated the discourse on home literacies, illustrating how these contentious debates often hinder the work of literacy researchers and educators rather than advance the progress of the field. Recognizing that a comprehensive review of home and family literacies research is beyond the scope of this chapter, we offer a synthesis of relevant studies that provide particular "snapshots" of the field. We conclude the chapter by highlighting a "new" vision of home literacies and its implications for implementing research and practice that makes a difference in university, public school, and adult education classrooms.

## HOME LITERACIES AND TEACHER EDUCATION PROGRAMS

Within the past decade, literacy scholars (e.g., Barr, Watts-Taffe, and Yokota, 2000; Hoffman & Pearson, 2000) have called for literacy teacher education programs to rethink how they address issues of diversity. Diversity has recently become a "hot topic" in teacher education for two reasons. First, demographic projections suggest that students in American schools will be increasingly diverse, yet the teaching force remains white, monolingual, and middle-class (Ladson-Billings, 1999). Second, as Au and Raphael (2000) argue, the new millennium has centered on images of literacy that are more multifaceted and complex (e.g., new literacies), and these "changing definitions of literacy and the literacy curriculum have important implications for educating students of diverse backgrounds" (p. 149).

Despite the increased attention that literacy teacher education programs have given to diversity, preservice teachers are still not adequately prepared to identify, affirm, and build upon their students' home literacies. Why? One reason is that teacher preparation programs have not yet resolved a difficult tension: Given the curriculum, and the limited timeframe of the program, when and where should preservice teachers be taught about the importance of students' home literacies? Since the National Council for Accreditation of Teacher Education standards shifted toward multiculturalism in 1979, nearly all literacy teacher education programs have identified diversity as an important curricular theme (Hollins & Guzman, 2005). Yet the reality is that teacher education programs have typically relegated issues to diversity to one specific course (Ladson-Billings, 1999). Literacy teacher education programs may have an especially difficult time "making room" in the curriculum for diversity courses because they are more concerned with including more rigorous content-specific literacy courses which develop novice teachers' pedagogical content knowledge, subject matter knowledge, and repertoire of instructional strategies (Wellman & Wold, 2006).

Consequently, there are very few studies which describe how literacy teacher education programs have addressed issues related to home literacies, or diversity in general, in a systematic and effective way. A notable exception is a study of programmatic change conducted by Keehn and her colleagues (2003) at the University of Texas at San Antonio. Analyses of faculty interviews, survey data, and other program-related artifacts (e.g., meeting notes) revealed substantive changes in the quality of the program, including creating new structures to support program goals (e.g., adding more field-based literacy courses, creating a common syllabus), redesigning the delivery system (e.g., using a "block" design for methods coursework), and designing a system to support adjunct faculty. As part of these changes, Keehn and her colleagues note that (a) the common course syllabi "specifically identify ... and activities to focus attention on issues of diversity" (p. 235); (b) they hired a field placement coordinator to facilitate placement in schools with diverse student populations; and (c) course instructors were making a more concerted effort to systematically add issues of diversity into their coursework (e.g., requiring that students complete a community literacy investigation). Unfortunately, the information that we can learn about making diversity-related changes in literacy teacher education programs is quite limited; this study offered very little detail about the specific types of diversity issues (e.g., race, ethnicity, language, home literacies) that were addressed by these changes, nor did it provide much information about the effectiveness of these diversity-related changes (e.g., how did these change affect preservice teachers' conceptions about and strategies for teaching diverse students).

Currently, much of the progress in the integration of home literacies (and other diversity-related issues) into literacy teacher education has been made by individual course instructors. Most of these studies are situated within literacy methods courses, and highlight pedagogical practices that teacher educators use to support preservice teachers' capacity to identify, build upon, and affirm students' home literacies (e.g., Boling, 2003; Clark & Medina, 2000; Florio-Ruane, 2001; Kidd, Sanchez, & Thorp, 2004; Schmidt, 1998; Turner, 2006). Narrative-based pedagogies, including reading family stories (Clark & Medina, 2000; Florio-Ruane, 2001), writing their own family stories (Schmidt, 1998), and writing family stories of their students (Kidd, Sanchez, Thorp, 2004), are frequently mentioned as important teacher educator practices. Other strategies include using case-based methods (e.g., videos of effective classroom teachers in diverse settings) to help preservice teachers consider how students draw upon their own home literacies within the classroom (Boling, 2004), and developing writing activities (e.g. "the vision project") as spaces where teacher education students can articulate their own conceptions of culturally responsive literacy pedagogy and explore how they could draw upon students' home literacy experiences and knowledge within their classroom literacy instruction (Turner, 2006).

Literacy teacher educators have also conducted numerous small-scale studies on targeted field experiences in multicultural schools and classrooms. For example, Jones and Blendinger (1994) organized field experiences that provided opportunities for preservice teachers to develop and enact multiple ways to communicate with minority families, including (a) implementing activities that supported home-school communication; (b) organizing an at-home reading project; (c) conducting parent-teacher conferences, and (d) actively learning about the wide range of activities used by teachers and schools to involve parents. Along similar lines, Lazar and Weisberg (1996) designed a tutoring program for struggling readers that provided a conversational "space" for White preservice teachers and parents to talk with one another. Importantly, these conversations represented a "cultural exchange" in which the parents described their children's home literacies, and the preservice teachers used this information to design culturally relevant and meaningful literacy lessons. Studies by Xu (2000), and Wolf, Ballentine, and Hill (2000) demonstrate how fieldwork, in conjunction with literacy methods coursework, can offer a productive context for preservice teachers to better understand how to connect with students' and families' cultural and linguistic practices. Although most of these studies report positive effects for preservice literacy teachers, these claims are limited due to the short-term nature of the investigation (Hollins & Guzman, 2005). Overall, however, it should be noted that integrating home literacies into literacy coursework and fieldwork seems to be a productive first step because this helps preservice teachers learn how to build positive relationships with students and families from diverse backgrounds.

As we reviewed this body of work, we discovered a second source of tension for teacher education programs: there is no one "best way" to educate preservice teachers about children's home literacy practices. In light of the public's heightened awareness of the importance of reading, and the pressures of accountability and standards-based reform, literacy teacher education programs are striving to move towards research-based practices that are proven to enhance the quality of the preparatory experience (Young & Draper, 2006). This is a time of "incredible impatience within the policy world" (Pearson, 2001, p. 5), yet literacy teacher education programs are being asked to make important curricular decisions based upon a research base that is quite limited (Young & Draper, 2006).

Again, literacy teacher educators have taken the initiative to generate new information by examining their own classroom practices. Several studies focus on enhancing preservice literacy teachers' awareness of their own cultural identities and home literacies. Allen and Hermann-Wilmarth

(2004) for example, designed their literacy teacher education course as a "cultural construction zone" where preservice teachers could openly discuss and (de)construct their own cultural identities. Through autobiographical writing, and other extended activities, preservice teachers began to closely examine the home literacy practices which shaped their literacy learning (e.g., parents read to them at bedtime) and their perceptions of diversity and schooling (e.g., parents held negative views of minority people). Similarly, Schmidt's (1998) ABC model uses autobiographical writing, biographical "life stories" gathered through interviewing, and cross-cultural analyses of these texts, to enhance preservice teachers' cross-cultural understanding and communication with minority families. These studies demonstrate how narrative texts help preservice teachers to know themselves and understand others (Schmidt, 1999) through critical self-reflection.

Other teacher education practices help preservice teachers to develop greater respect for and deeper understandings of the multiple and varied cultural practices, linguistic knowledge, and family experiences that students bring into the classroom. Florio-Ruane (2001) and Clark and Medina (2000) created spaces for their preservice teachers to read and respond to a wide variety of ethnic autobiographies, and learned about literacy, culture, and identity in their own lives and communities as well as in the lives of people whose backgrounds differed widely from their own. Several teacher educators expand preservice teachers' understandings of multiple home literacies by encouraging them to use inquiry-based methods to learn about their students, and the literacies embedded within their families. For example, in their literacy methods course Kidd et al. (2004) encouraged the preservice teachers to select a focus family whose cultural background was different than their own, and to spend time with those families at their homes and in their communities. Based on this information, the preservice teachers composed "family stories" which described their cultural and linguistic backgrounds (e.g., stories about immigration experiences, popular cultural proverbs) and illustrated their home literacy practices (e.g., child-rearing practices, traditions and rituals).

## HOME LITERACIES AND K-12 SCHOOLS

For years, improving parent involvement has been a critical goal for teachers, administrators, and schools (Edwards, 2004). Yet despite the resounding calls for extending the family's role in children's learning, the reality in most schools remains "high rhetoric and low practice" (Edwards, et al., 1999).

There are several reasons why schools have struggled to develop successful family-school partnerships. One of the most critical problems is that there are thorny problems within the field of parent involvement research. In their review, Baker and Soden (1998) identified several of the problems most difficult to untangle:

> While most practitioners and researchers support the policy direction of increased parent involvement, few agree about what constitutes effective involvement. Confusion persists regarding the activities, goals, and desired outcomes of various parent involvement programs and policies. A major source of this confusion is the lack of scientific rigor in the research informing practice and policy. Because of this, less is known about parent involvement than commonly is assumed. Nonetheless, early studies suggesting the importance of parent involvement are treated as definitive, regardless of the equivocal nature of the data, and they are used to support the position that all types of parent involvement are important. Moreover, many programs and policies promoting parent involvement are not explicitly based on the evidence that does exist. Reliance on such compromised data may lead to unrealistic expectations of what parent involvement programs and practices actually are able to accomplish. (p. 3)

Clearly, there are several factors at work together which contribute to the problem of understanding parent involvement in schools. Perhaps the most prevalent problem is the shifting definition of parent involvement. The meaning and definition of family-school partnerships, family involvement, and parent involvement varies widely (Moles, 1987). According to Ascher (1988), "parent involvement may easily mean quite different things to different people" (p. 10), including:

> advocacy: parents sitting on councils and committees, participating in the decisions and operation of schools. It can mean parents serving as classroom aides, accompanying a class outing or assisting teachers in a variety of other ways, either as volunteers or for wages. It can also conjure up images of teachers sending home notes to parents, or of parents working on bake sales and other projects that bring schools much needed support. Increasingly, parent involvement means parents initiating learning activities at home to improve their children's performance in school: reading to them, helping with homework, playing educational games, discussing current events, and so on. Sometimes, too, parent involvement is used more broadly to include all the ways in which home life socializes children for school. (p. 10)

Given these multiple definitions of parent involvement, teachers have not figured out exactly what they want parents to do. Parent involvement is "hit or miss" in most schools because it is not synchronized around the curriculum, and there is no master schedule for parent involvement across teachers or across grade levels. Without careful planning and organization at the school level, individual classroom teachers are held responsible for working with parents and obtaining their support in the educational process. Making matters worse, while the definitions of parent involvement that Ascher identified may appear to be inclusive, some scholars have noted that these practices work to exclude parents from culturally and linguistically diverse backgrounds who may not have the cultural capital valued by schools (Edwards, Danridge, McMillon, & Pleasants, 2001). As a result, traditional definitions of home-school partnerships are quite narrow, with the school talking *to* families rather than working *with* them (Edwards et al., 1999).

To broaden definitions of home-school connections and family involvement, Morrison (1998) describes four approaches to parent involvement. As the most common and traditional way to approach parent involvement, *the Task Approach* seeks to involve parents in order to get assistance completing specific tasks that support the school or classroom program (e.g., working as tutors, classroom aides, chaperones on trips, clerical helpers). In the *Process Approach,* families are encouraged to participate in certain activities that are important to the educational process, such as curriculum planning, textbook review and selection, membership on task forces and committees, teacher review and selection, and helping to set behavior standards. The *Developmental Approach,* which is exemplified in cooperative preschools, community schools, and Head Start programs, seeks to help parents and families develop skills that benefit themselves, children, schools, professionals, and families and, at the same time, enhance family growth and development. A *Comprehensive Approach* to parent and family involvement includes elements of all of the preceding approaches, especially the developmental approach. It goes beyond the other three approaches, however, in that it makes the family the *center* or *focus* of activities. This method does not seek involvement from parent or family members for the sake of involvement or the benefit of a particular agency. Rather it works with, in, and through the family system to empower, assist, and strengthen the family. Thus, a comprehensive approach also provides involvement through family development and support programs, including parenting workshops, home visitations, substance abuse education and treatment programs, discussion and support groups, job training and referral programs, and basis skills training programs. As a result, all family members are helped, including children.

A comprehensive approach to parent involvement presumes that schools and teachers acknowledge and appreciate the home literacy practices enacted by students and their families. And while many teachers have good intentions, and would like to be "open" to differences in home literacies, this is not often the case. Krevotics and Nussel (1994) explain

> Many teachers find themselves ill-prepared to comprehend the multiple cultures that students bring to the classroom, let alone bring dignity and respect for those cultures. They are taught subject matter, but not what to do when the subject matter does not pertain to the life experiences of the students. Teacher education programs rarely prepare teachers to make education meaningful to diverse groups of students [and their parents]. (p. xi)

Unfortunately, some teachers have an extremely difficult time making connections with families that practice different home literacies. In Edwards' (1993) work with minority parents and white teachers in a rural Louisiana community (Donaldsonville Elementary School), teachers were quite open about their frustrations. One particularly vocal teacher was Mrs. Elliott (all names that appear in this chapter are pseudonyms), a first-grade teacher at Donaldsonville Elementary School. In several interviews, Mrs. Elliot expressed her concerns about the difficulty in attempting to collaborate with minority parents, especially those who have limited reading skills and are unfamiliar with school-based literacy:

> Tonya's mother is a nightmare. I can't get her to come in too see me, even though I have sent at least five notes home. She is extremely uncooperative and defensive. I encouraged her to read to her child and I even tried to tell her during our parent-teacher conference about what she could do at home to help Tonya gain more confidence in her reading and writing ability. But she didn't say "I understand and I will try to do something about it." Instead she said nothing. It was as if she didn't hear anything I was saying to her. Nothing has worked, and I don't know what else to do. I am feeling helpless and angry, because I feel that I am not getting any support from Tonya's mother. I don't understand parents who think that it is the teacher's responsibility to teach their children, and they don't have to do anything, but send them to school.

Comments like these have been made by well-intentioned teachers who have exhausted all of their strategies for connecting and working with parents. Mrs. Elliot clearly understands that the traditional forms of home-school communication are not working, yet she does not know what to do. Literacy scholars like Edwards and her colleagues (1999) have developed ideas that help practicing teachers to understand and communicate more effectively with parents from diverse racial, ethnic, socioeconomic, and linguistic backgrounds. They provide a framework for collecting early home literacy information through parent stories. After all, as a child's first and most important teacher, a parent can offer memories of specific formative interactions, observations on early learning efforts, and thoughts on how their own backgrounds have impacted a child's attitude toward school. In sharing their anecdotes and observations, parents give teachers the keys to unlock a vault of social, emotional, and educational variables. These parent stories give classroom teachers access to knowledge that was not obvious, but very beneficial if they utilize the information gained from these stories. Parent stories have the potential of helping teachers to incorporate students' home literacy experiences in the classroom and empower parents to participate in their child's education in personally meaningful ways.

In listening to parents from minority and/or poor backgrounds, there is a tension that has perplexed many literacy scholars and educators. We know that parents from diverse backgrounds want teachers to affirm their cultural knowledge, language, and home literacy practices (Neito, 1996). We also know that many parents from diverse backgrounds want to support their children's education and they want their children to develop proficiency in the power code (Delpit, 1995; Gadsden et al., 2006; Li, 2006). Yet some of these families do not enact and engage in home literacy practices that reflect the knowledge, skills, and conventions associated with the culture of power (Delpit, 1995). So the question then becomes: How do we help parents who have nonmainstream home literacy practices to acquire mainstream home literacy practices? And if we teach families these mainstream home literacy practices, does that mean that we view them as deficient or disadvantaged?

These questions highlight the controversy around the concept of *adaptation*. Wiley (1996) explains that adaptation involves the expectation that children and adults, who are held to have substandard knowledge and skills, to acculturate or learn to match or measure up to the norms of those who control the schools, institutions, and workplace (p. 147). Scholars who support adaptation have claimed that many poor, minority, and immigrant parents want to give their children linguistic, social, and cultural capital to deal in the marketplace of schools (Gallimore, Weisner, Kaufman, & Bernheimer, 1989; Super & Harkness, 1986). They have also suggested "when schools fail to provide parents with factual, empowering information and strategies for supporting their child's learning, the parents are even more likely to feel ambivalence as educators [of their own children]" (Clark, 1988, p. 95).

Supporters of the *adaptation perspective* recognize that parents' home literacy practices can support children's literacy development in school. Activities such as telling stories and singing songs encourage the acquisition of literacy skills (Glazer, 1989; Moss & Fawcett, 1995; National Education Goals Panel 1997; Sonnenschein, Brody, & Munsterman 1996). Reading to children is perhaps the most well-known activity for developing children's literacy skills and their lifelong love of reading (Anderson,

Hiebert, Scott, & Wilkinson, 1985; Doake, 1986; Gallimore & Goldenberg, 1989; Huey, 1908; Teale, 1981). However, there is an extensive body of research describing the difficulty lower SES mothers have with sharing books with their young children (Farron, 1982; Heath 1982a, 1982b, 1986; Heath, Branscombe, & Thomas, 1985; Heath & Thomas, 1984; McCormick & Mason, 1986; Ninio, 1980; Snow & Ninio, 1986). Some researchers have argued, therefore, that "simply to inform parents about the importance of reading to their children is not sufficient. We must move beyond telling lower SES parents to showing them how to participate in parent-child book reading interactions with their children" (Edwards, 1989, p. 250). As a result, several key *adaptation* studies involve showing parents how to read to their children or assisting them with school-like literacy events (Darling &Hayes, 1989; Edwards, 1993; Handel, 1992; Rodriguez-Brown, Li, & Albom 1999; Winter & Rouse, 1990).

But controversies about meanings of "educating" parents to enact mainstream home literacy practices (i.e., parent book reading) have emerged from the adaptation perspective. Several researchers have warned of the danger of "blaming the victim" in a deficit-model of learning development and they pointed out the embeddedness of literacy in home life (Anderson & Stokes, 1984; Erickson, 1989; Hearron, 1992; D. Taylor & Dorsey-Gaines, 1985). Others have claimed that teaching these types of mainstream home literacy practices promote "victim blaming" (Cairney, 1997; Garcia, 1994; Nieto, 1993; Shockley, 1994, Street, 1995), and implies that the homes of poor, minority, and immigrant children are "lacking in literacy" (Anderson & Stokes, 1984; Auerbach, 1989; Chall & Snow, 1982; Delgado-Gaitan, 1987; Erickson, 1989; Goldenberg, 1984). A final criticism of the adaptive perspective is that teaching parents to engage in home literacy practices that are valued in schools (e.g., parent-child book reading, assisting with homework) has "perpetuated the 'we know, you don't know' dichotomy" (Shockley, 1994, p. 500). To a large extent, these controversies around the adaptation perspective have contributed to the difficulties that schools have in creating successful partnerships with parents (Edwards, 2003, 2004).

## HOME LITERACIES AND FAMILY LITERACY PROGRAMS

One might assume that there is a strong relationship between home literacies and family literacy programs; after all, the concept of home literacies seems to be at the very heart of such programs. However, that is not the case. Kendrick, Anderson, Smythe, and McKay (2003) explain, "historically, family literacy programs and family literacy research have had an uneasy relationship" (p. 245). This relationship is troubled, in part, because there is no consensus about the definition of home/family literacy. In her extensive review, Purcell-Gates (2000) identified three definitions that are commonly used to describe home literacy practices. The first definition views family literacy as "descriptive of the ways in which literacy does and does not mediate the lives of families" (Purcell-Gates, 2000, p. 859). This definition seems to be primarily used by home literacy researchers, who conduct ethnographies to richly illustrate and interpret the literacy practices that parents and children enact within their homes (e.g., Anderson & Stokes, 1984; Heath, 1983; Li, 2002; Purcell-Gates, 1995; D. Taylor, 1985; D. Taylor & Dorsey-Gaines, 1985; Zentella, 2005).

The second definition centers on the image of family literacy as an instructional program serving parents and children. Purcell-Gates (2000) explains: "during the span of time in which [ethnographic family literacy research] was conducted, the term *family literacy* was appropriated by those whose purpose was to teach parents to incorporate mainstream literacy practices into their lives as a way of improving the academic performance of their children" (p. 859). This is perhaps the most commonly-used definition in the current marketplace, because it describes the goals and objectives of federally-funded and locally-supported parent education programs across the country (Riley, Robinson, & Conaty, 1993). Emerging from the second term, the third definition of family literacy refers to a research program that documents the outcomes of the instructional programs (Purcell-Gates, 2000).

Of the three definitions for family literacy, the second is the most controversial. Purcell-Gates (2000) explains:

> Should the term and construct of *family literacy* be interpreted as primarily descriptive or pedagogical? And if pedagogical, what should the nature of that pedagogy be? There is real difference and disagreement among researchers and educators as to the answers to these questions. (pp. 858-859)

As family literacy shifted from a descriptive, research-based term to a pedagogical concept, literacy scholars contend that the ideological divisions among literacy educators and scholars became apparent (Kendrick et al., 2003; Purcell-Gates, 2000). These ideological divisions stem from an ethical dilemma concerning the purpose of family literacy programs: If family literacy programs truly honor and affirm multiple home literacy practices, should non-mainstream parents be "taught" to enact family practices that are valued by the mainstream? In other words, are family literacy programs interested in "educating" families from diverse cultural and linguistic backgrounds because they view them and their home literacy practices from a deficit perspective?

Scholars like Auerbach (1989), D. Taylor (1997) and Kendrick and her colleagues (2003) vehemently argue that

> while many family literacy programs purport to be inclusive and to value a range of literacy practices, most operate from a deficit perspective aimed at teaching parents from non-mainstream groups to engage in literacy practices found in middle-class homes that are valued and built on in school" (Kendrick et al., 2003, p. 255).

Family literacy researchers have taken steps in opposition of what they perceive as a deficit view of home literacy practices. In the late 1990s, Denny Taylor (1997) and a group of family literacy researchers and providers came together to issue a set of international principles which they believed represented poor and/or minority families as capable units whose needs result from economic, social, and political oppression. Through these principles, they asserted that "family programs must begin with a mutual respect and collaborative stance with families and view literacy as a vehicle for changing the oppressive forces in their lives" (Purcell-Gates, 2000, p. 859). More recently, scholars have also attempted to address this issue in their research. For example, in their comparative study of the images of family literacy portrayed by Canadian elementary school children and by family literacy programs, Kendrick and her colleagues (2003) found very striking results. The children, who were enrolled in Grades 1 or 2, drew pictures of a wide variety of home literacy practices (e.g., reading in a tent, doing homework, playing computer, writing stories) with various people (e.g., mothers, fathers, cousins and other extended family members, siblings, friends). In contrast, the family literacy programs used traditional images and representations of home literacy practices (e.g. mother and children reading together, families appearing to be of European descent) most frequently on their Web sites. Based on these findings, Kendrick and her colleagues suggest that family literacy organizations do not select images reflecting the lived experiences of their clients because they "are influenced by what Auerbach (1989) considered the prevailing view of family literacy, which tends to be a deficit model of 'fixing families'" (p. 256).

However, some scholars assert that there are family literacy programs that do affirm the home literacy practices of the parents whom they serve, and that they empower these parents by helping them to access and acquire the power code (Delpit, 1995). Padak and Rasinski (2003), for example, identify several important benefits for parents involved in family literacy programs, including (a) greater opportunities to learn literacy than in typical adult education programs; (b) increased reading achievement and writing ability; (c) greater knowledge about parenting options and child development; and (d) enhanced social awareness and self-advocacy. These benefits have been confirmed by other researchers. In Primavera's (2000) study of 100 adult participants in family literacy workshops, parents reported an increase in confidence, self-esteem, parental efficacy, literacy competence, and interest in educating themselves and their children. Fossen and Sticht (1991) found that ninety-percent of the mothers participating in their Intergenerational Literacy Action Research Project, which involved basic-skills instruction and job training in community-based programs, had become more aware of the influence that they had on their children's educational achievements, and could articulate strategies that they used to work with their children, as a result of participating in the program.

Literacy researchers have also found that parents who participate in family literacy programs have greater capacity to support their children's literacy learning in school (Cook-Cottone, 2004; Edwards, 1995; Edwards & Danridge, 2001; Gadsden et al., 2006; Morrow & Young, 1997). Cook-Cottone (2004) posits that many effective family literacy programs have adopted sociocultural approaches to working with families and children. In these social constructivist-based programs, families are "mentored in the use of literacy tools and provided the necessary scaffolding for effective transmission of literacy knowledge from parent to child. In other words, the family literacy program functions as a Vygotskian mentor to the family ... who in turn become mentors to the child" (p. 209). Cook-Cottone suggests that family literacy programs which utilize sociocultural approaches to educating parents capitalize on the power of the cultural, linguistic, and social practices that families enact with their children by utilizing home literacy as a bridge for apprenticing parents (and their children) into the mainstream literacy practices (e.g. reading to children, helping with homework, visiting libraries) valued in school. Similarly, studies conducted by Edwards and her colleagues (Edwards, 1995; Edwards & Danridge, 2001; Edwards et al., 2001) and by Gadsden et al. (2006), clearly demonstrate that parents, especially those from minority and/or poor backgrounds, place high value on literacy and education, and they often participate in family literacy workshops and programs because they *want* to learn specific strategies and techniques that they can use at home to support their children's literacy learning. Consequently, these studies suggest that non-mainstream parents who participate in family literacy programs might view their acquisition of school-based literacy practices as a tool of empowerment rather than as an indication that they are disadvantaged or deficient.

## NEW VISIONS OF RESEARCH AND PRACTICE IN HOME LITERACIES: IMPLICATIONS FOR TEACHER EDUCATION PROGRAMS, K-12 SCHOOLS, AND FAMILY LITERACY PROGRAMS

In this chapter, we have highlighted the multiple sources of controversy, conflict, and confusion within the area of home literacies. We argue that these tensions have polarized literacy researchers and educators, and as a result, advancements in home literacies' research have significantly lagged behind policy and practice (Purcell-Gates, 2000). By discussing how acrimonious debates about home literacies play out in teacher education programs, K-12 schools, and family literacy programs, we not only sought to raise literacy scholars and instructors' awareness of these critical issues, but also to offer new directions to professionals committed to families and children.

We conclude this chapter, on a positive and hopeful note. We understand that recognizing and valuing the family and home literacy practices of students—whether they are in university classrooms, K-12 schools, or adult literacy programs—is critical to their success. As literacy scholars and educators, we believe that it is our responsibility to affirm the cultural and linguistic "identity kits" that our students bring with them into the classroom. Yet we also strongly believe that as educators who have acquired mainstream literacy practices, it is our professional responsibility to help others acquire those practices that are valued in our schools and society.

How can literacy researchers and educators working in university classrooms, K-12 schools, and family literacy programs accomplish both of these tasks? We offer a set of recommendations that could frame "new visions" of scholarship, practice, and policy related to home literacies. We use the term "new visions" deliberately, to acknowledge that there is not one single "vision" that can resolve all of the tensions and debates around home literacy practices. Consequently, we view our recommendations as "guiding principles" that literacy scholars, literacy teacher educators, K-12 teachers, and family literacy instructors can use to develop research agendas and educational programs that help families to support the literacy development of their children.

### Commit to Conducting Research That Makes a Difference

Literacy scholars and researchers have long recognized the importance of home literacies research. Yet some of these studies have not had much impact on classroom literacy instruction. It is important that the scholarly work generated from this line of inquiry reaches university, K-12, and adult literacy classrooms across the country. As Edwards (2003) stated,

"We must refrain from doing research where we, as a research community, are the only ones who learn from this research. We must commit ourselves to conducting research that has implications for practitioners, and we must do the work of disseminating that research" (p. 100). We do not deny that literacy researchers may feel tremendous pressure to come in, work with their participants, and exit the field as quickly as possible because publishing is a requirement of tenure. However, we must also remember that the time and energy that families, children, teachers, and family literacy instructors are invaluable, and we owe it to them to share our research in ways that provide answers to the complex educational issues and problems in their lives.

## Expand the Image of "Researcher"

Literacy researchers and educational scholars at the university level have typically conducted research on the literacy practices of families (e.g., Heath, 1983; Li, 2002; Purcell-Gates, 1995; Taylor, 1995). However, we believe that expanding the image of researcher to include K-12 practitioners, culturally-diverse students and families, teacher education students, community leaders, and family literacy instructors, would advance the field in two important ways. First, literacy researchers who work collaboratively with practitioners and parents/children would learn much more meaningful information about the local definitions of parent involvement and home literacy practices that are enacted within particular communities. This type of insider knowledge is critical because there are multiple definitions of parent involvement and these definitions change across contexts (Ascher, 1988; Edwards, 2004). Second, there is a gap between the research on home literacies and the practice and policy of such research (Purcell-Gates, 2000). However, literacy scholars may be able to bridge that gap by (a) working with practitioners to create programs and classrooms that successfully build upon families' literacy practices, (b) by working with community leaders to establish programs and workshops that give parents the training and skills that they need to improve their employment opportunities; and (c) by working with parents to understand the benefits of participating in these programs for themselves and their children.

## Listen Harder and Longer to Parent Voices

In light of the voluminous work conducted on families and their home literacy practices during the last few decades, one might assume that we know "everything we need to know" about parents and children. However, this is not the case. Much more descriptive work needs to be done that highlights the importance of family lives and multiple literacies in a range of home and communities representing cultural diversity, linguistic diversity, and economic diversity (Au & Raphael, 2000). In addition, literacy scholars like Pat Edwards (Edwards et al., 1999) and Vivian Gadsden (Gadsden et al., 2006) remind us that we need to listen to parents in substantive and significant ways because they have important insights about their children and their literacy learning at home. Teachers want parents to be deeply involved in their children's literacy education, yet few know how to communicate effectively with diverse parents. Although some research has been conducted on successful frameworks for fostering positive relationships between parents and teachers (e.g., Edwards & Danridge, 2001; Edwards et al., 1999), we need more research that addresses the topic of home-school connections if we want to help preserve and inservice teachers develop the dispositions, knowledge, and skills for connecting with parents from different backgrounds.

## Expand Notions of "Parents" and "Parenting"

Edwards (2004) contends that many schools have difficulties enhancing parent involvement and building upon the home literacies of their students because they believe that there is a "one-size-fits-all" approach to parent involvement. Some schools have tried to implement what they had read about or seen other schools doing to involve parents; not realizing that individual schools must examine the type of parent involvement initiatives they create based on the needs of parents in their school. Consequently, when schools used the "same terminology," as that of another school, and it does not work the way the other school's family-school partnership worked, they come away confused and discouraged. What literacy researchers, especially those working in the field of home literacies, must understand is that parent involvement is situated within particular communities, and it can be different from school to school and community to community.

Thus, as literacy researchers, we must be sensitive to and respectful of the local definitions of parent involvement within particular schools and communities. These local definitions may include *business partnerships, home-school partnerships,* and *home-school-community partnerships.* These types of partnerships can be categorized as "local" because they consider how local community members (e.g., community organizations, business owners/employees, community leaders) can join with parents, teachers, and administrators to become more actively involved in family or parent involvement initiatives. This "team model" of schooling, which is the foundation for "Accelerated Schools" in California and those developed by Comer (1980), positions parent involvement as a powerful element, and strives to empower all parents rather than just a few parent volunteers (Seeley, 1989). In these partnerships, parent involvement is not a separate project, rather it is an integral part of the school's comprehensive plan to mobilize all available resources (e.g., parents, neighbors, community leaders) in an effort to help children achieve. As literacy researchers and educators, we can learn a great deal from these partnerships because they show us that "parents" can come in different forms. For many students, other people—grandmothers, aunts and uncles, siblings, Big Brother/Big Sister organizations, community leaders and youth workers (e.g. Future Farmers of America), and court-appointed guardians (i.e., foster parents)—act as parents, and they should be welcomed and involved within the classroom as much as possible (Edwards, 2004; Heath & McLaughlin, 1991).

## Use Home Literacies as a Bridge to Mainstream Literacy Practices

As literacy researchers and educators, we know that children have to know the culture of power in order to do well in school (Delpit, 1995). Auerbach (1989) agrees that "authority is vested in those belonging to the mainstream culture, the literacy practices of the mainstream become the norm and have higher status in school contexts" (p. 173). We also recognize that many parents from culturally and linguistically diverse backgrounds want to support their children's literacy development in school, yet they do not have the necessary tools. Consequently, we believe that teachers, family literacy instructors, and other educators can successfully help non-mainstream parents to acquire the home literacy practices (e.g., parent-child book reading) and the norms, conventions, and discourses that are highly valued in school. Like Cook-Cottone (2004), we believe that parents' home literacy practices can be used as a bridge to mainstream literacy practices. When family literacy instructors and other literacy educators view parents as knowledgeable experts, they are more likely to draw upon the culture power of the family. Consequently, we should not assume that all literacy educators who teach mainstream home literacy practices consider these families to be deficient or disadvantaged. Research suggests that family literacy programs can reach and teach parents about the power code in culturally appropriate and respectful ways (Cook-Cottone, 2004). Equally important, many families from diverse backgrounds might see the opportunity to access and acquire the power code as a source of empowerment and inspiration (Edwards, 2004; Padak & Raskinki, 2003).

In closing, we believe that the future of home literacies research can and will be bright. Despite the current controversies and conflicts, we envision a time when literacy researchers will work together and join other literacy educators in building new teacher education classrooms, K-12 classrooms, and family literacy programs that are transformative and empowering. Let us move forward and make these visions a reality for all children and their families.

## REFERENCES

Allen, J. B., & Hermman-Wilmarth, J. (2004). Cultural construction zones. *Journal of Teacher Education, 55*, 214-226.

Anderson, A. B., & Stokes, S. J. (1984). Social and institutional influences on the development and practice of literacy. In H. Goelman, A. Oberg, & F. Smith (Eds.), *Awakening to literacy* (pp. 24-37). Exeter, NH: Heinemann.

Anderson, R. C., Hiebert, E., Scott, J. A., & Wilkinson, I. A. G. (1985). *Becoming a nation of readers: The report of the commission of reading.* Washington, DC: The National Institute of Education.

Arzubiaga, A., Rueda, R., & Monzo, L. (n.d.). *Family matters related to the reading engagement of Latina/o children.* Retrieved August 11, 2006 from http://www.ciera.org/library/reports/inquiry-1/1-015/1-015h.html

Ascher, C. (1988). Improving the school-home connection for poor and minority urban students. *The Urban Review, 20*(2), 109-123.

Au, K. H. (2000). Literacy education in the process of community development. In T. Shanahan & F. Rodriquez (Eds.), *Forty-ninth yearbook of the National Reading Conference* (pp. 61-77). Chicago: National Reading Conference.

Au, K. H., & Raphael, T. (2000). Equity and literacy in the next millennium. *Reading Research Quarterly, 35*, 170-188.

Auerbach, E. (1989). Toward a socio-cultural approach to family literacy. *Harvard Educational Review, 59*, 165-181.

Barr, R., Watts-Taffe, S., & Yokota, J. (2000). Preparing teachers to teach literacy: Rethinking preservice literacy education. *Journal of Literacy Research, 32*, 463-470.

Boling, E. (2004). Preparing novices for teaching literacy in diverse classrooms: Using written, video, and hypermedia cases to prepare literacy teachers. In C. M. Fairbanks, J. Worthy, B. Maloch, J. V. Hoffman, & D. L. Schallert (Eds.), *53rd yearbook of the National Reading Conference* (pp. 130-158). Oak Creek, WI: National Reading Conference.

Cairney, T. H. (1997). Acknowledging diversity in home literacy practices: Moving towards partnership with parents. *Early Child Development and Care, 127/128*, 61-73.

Clark, R. M. (1988). Parents as providers of linguistic and social capital. *Educational Horizons, 66*(2), 93-95.

Clark, C., & Medina, C. (2000). How reading and writing literacy narratives affect preservice teachers' understandings of literacy, pedagogy, and multiculturalism. *Journal of Teacher Education, 51*, 63-76.

Comer, J. P. (1980). *School and power.* New York: The Free Press.

Cook-Cottone, C. (2004). Constructivism in family literacy practices: Parents as mentors. *Reading Improvement, 41*, 208-216.

Darling, S., & Hayes, A. (1988-89). *Family literacy project final project report.* Louisville, KY: National Center for Family Literacy.

Delpit, L. (1995). *Other people's children: Cultural conflict in the classroom.* New York: The New Press.

Doake, D. B. (1986). Learning to read: It starts in the home. In D. R. Tovey & J. E. Kerber (Eds.), *Roles in literacy learning: A new perspective* (pp. 2-9). Newark, DE: International Reading Association.

Edwards, P. A. (2003). The impact of family on literacy development: Convergence, controversy, and instructional implications. In C.M. Fairbanks, J. Worthy, B. Maloch, J. V. Hoffman, & D. L. Schallert (Eds.), *52nd yearbook of the National Reading Conference* (pp. 92-103). Oak Creek, WI: National Reading Conference.

Edwards, P. A. (2004). *Children's literacy development: Making it happen through home, school, and community connections.* New York: Allyn & Bacon.

Edwards, P. A. (1995). Empowering low-income mothers and fathers to share books with young children. *The Reading Teacher, 48*, 558-564.

Edwards, P. A. (1993). *Parents as partners in reading: A family literacy training program* (2nd Ed.). Chicago: Childrens Press.

Edwards, P. A. (1989). Supporting lower SES mothers' attempts to provide scaffolding for bookreading. In J. Allen & J. Mason (Eds.), *Risk makers, risk takers, risk breakers: Reducing the risks for young literacy learners* (pp. 222-250). Portsmouth, NH: Heinemann.

Edwards, P. A., & Danridge, J. C. (2001). Developing collaborations with parents: Some examples. In V. J. Risko & K. Bromley (Eds.), *Collaboration for diverse learners: Viewpoints and practices* (pp. 251-272). Newark, DE: International Reading Association.

Edwards, P. A., Danridge, J. C., McMillon, G. T. & Pleasants, H. M. (2001). Taking ownership of literacy: Who has the power? In P. R. Schmidt & P. B. Mosenthal (Eds.), *Reconceptualizing literacy in the new age of pluralism and multiculturalism* (pp. 111-136). Greenwich, CT: Information Age.

Edwards, P. A., Pleasants, H. M., & Franklin, S. H. (1999). *A path to follow: Learning to listen to parents.* Portsmouth, NH: Heinemann.

Florio-Ruane, S. (2001). *Teacher education and the cultural imagination: Autobiography, conversation, and narrative.* Mahwah, NJ: Erlbaum.

Fossen, S. V. & Sticht, T. G. (1991). *Teach the mother and reach the child: Results of the Intergenerational Literacy Action Research Project of Wider Opportunities for Women.* Washington, DC: Wider Opportunities for Women.

Gadsden, V. L., Ray, A., Jacobs, C., & Gwak, S. (2006). Parents' expectations and children's early literacy: Reimagining parent engagement through parent inquiry. In R. T. Jimenez & V. O. Pang (Eds.), *Race, ethnicity, and education: Language and literacy in schools* (pp. 157-176). Westport, CT: Praeger.

Gallimore, R., Weisner, R., Kaufman, S. & Bernheimer, L. P. (1989). The social construction of ecocultural niches: Family accommodation of developmentally delayed children. *American Journal of Mental Retardation, 94*(3), 216-230.

Garcia, E. (1994). *Understanding and meeting the challenge of student cultural diversity.* Boston: Houghton Mifflin.

Goldenberg, C. C. (1984, October). *Low-income parents' contributions to the reading achievement of their first-grade children.* Paper presented at the meeting of the Evaluation Network/Evaluation Research Society, San Francisco.

Glazer, S. (1989). Oral language and literacy. In D. S. Strickland & L. M. Morrow (Eds.), *Emerging literacy: Young children learn to read and write* (pp. 16-26). Newark, DE: International Reading Association.

Handel, R. E. (1992). The partnership for family reading: Benefits for families and schools. *The Reading Teacher, 46*(2), 117-126.

Haney, M., & Hill, J. (2004). Relationships between parent-child teaching and emergent literacy in preschool children. *Early Child Development and Care, 174,* 215-228.

Heath, S. B. (1982a). Questioning at home and at school: A comparative study. In G. Spindler (Ed.), *Doing ethnography of schooling: Education anthropology in action* (pp. 102-129). New York: Hold, Rinehart and Winston.

Heath, S. B. (1982b). What no bedtime story means: Narrative skills at home and school. *Language in Society, 11*(2), 49-76.

Heath, S. B. (1983). *Ways with words: Language, life, and work in communities and classrooms.* New York: Cambridge University Press.

Heath, S. B., Branscombe, A., & Thomas, C. (1985). The book as narrative prop in language acquisition. In B. Schieiffelin & P. Gilmore (Eds.), *The acquisition of literacy: Ethnographic perspective.* Norwood, NJ: Ablex.

Heath, S. B., & McLaughlin, M. W. (1991). Community organizations as family. *Phi Delta Kappan, 72*(8), 576-580.

Heath, S. B., & Thomas, C. (1984). The achievement of preschool literacy for mother and child. In H. Goelman, A. Oberg, & F. Smith (Eds.), *Awakening to literacy* (pp. 51-72). Portsmouth, NH: Heinemann.

Huey, E. B. (1908). *The psychology and pedagogy of reading.* New York: MacMillan.

Hoffman, J., & Pearson, P. D. (2000). Reading teacher education in the next millennium: What your grandmother's teacher did know that your granddaughter's teacher should. *Reading Research Quarterly, 35,* 28-44.

Hollins, E., & Guzman, M. (2005). Research on preparing teachers for diverse populations. In M. Cochran-Smith & K. Zeichner (Eds.), *Studying teacher education* (pp. 477-548). Mahwah, NJ: Erlbaum.

Jones, L. T., & Blendinger, J. (1994). New beginnings: Preparing future teachers to work with diverse families. *Action in Teacher Education, 16,* 79-86.

Keehn, S., Martinez, M., Harmon, J., Hedrick, W., Steinmetz, L., & Perez, B. (2003). Teacher preparation in reading: A case study of change in one university-based undergraduate program. In C. M. Fairbanks, J. Worthy, B. Maloch, J. Hoffman, & D. Schallert (Eds.), *52nd yearbook of the National Reading Conference* (pp. 230-244). Oak Creek, WI: National Reading Conference.

Kendrick, M., Anderson, J., Smythe, S., & McKay, R. (2003). What images of family literacy reveal about family literacy practices and family literacy programs.

In C. M. Fairbanks, J. Worthy, B. Maloch, J. Hoffman, & D. Schallert (Eds.), *52nd yearbook of the National Reading Conference* (pp. 245-258). Oak Creek, WI: National Reading Conference.

Kidd, J. K., Sanchez, S. Y., & Thorp, E. K. (2004). Listening to the stories families tell: Promoting culturally responsive language and literacy experiences. In C. M. Fairbanks, J. Worthy, B. Maloch, J. Hoffman, & D. Schallert (Eds.), *53rd yearbook of the National Reading Conference* (pp. 246-265). Oak Creek, WI: National Reading Conference.

Ladson-Billings, G. (1999). Preparing teachers for diversity: Historical perspectives, current trends, and future directions. In L. Darling-Hammond & G. Sykes (Eds.), *Teaching as the learning profession: Handbook of policy and practice* (pp. 86-124). San Francisco: Jossey-Bass.

Lazar, A., & Weisberg, R. (1996). Inviting parents' perspectives: Building home-school partnerships to support children who struggle with literacy. *The Reading Teacher, 50*, 228-237.

Li, G. (2002). *East is east, west is west? Home literacy, culture, and schooling.* New York: Peter Lang.

McCormick, C., & Mason, J. (1986). Intervention procedures for increasing preschool children's interest in and knowledge about reading. In W. H. Teale & E. Sulzby (Ed.), *Emergent literacy: Writing and reading* (pp. 90-115). Norwood, NJ: Ablex.

Moles, O. (1987). Who wants parent involvement? Interests, skills, and opportunities among parents and educators, *Education and Urban Society, 19*, 137-145.

Morrison, G. S. (1998). *Early childhood education today* (7th ed.). Upper Saddle River, NJ: Prentice-Hall.

Morrow, L., & Young, J. (1997). A family literacy program connecting school and home: Effects on attitude, motivation, and literacy achievement. *Journal of Educational Psychology, 89*, 736-742.

Moss, B., & Fawcett, G. (1995). Bring the curriculum of the world of the home to the school. *Reading & Writing Quarterly: Overcoming Learning Difficulties, 11*, 247-256.

National Education Goals Panel. (1997). *Special early literacy report, 1997.* Washington, DC: U.S. Government Printing Office.

Nieto, S. (1992). *Affirming diversity: The sociopolitical context of multicultural education.* New York: Longman.

Ninio, A. (1980). Ostensive definition in vocabulary teaching. *Journal of Child Language, 7*, 565-573.

Padak, N., & Rasinski, T. (2003). *Family literacy programs: Who benefits?* Kent State University, OH: Ohio Literacy Resource Center. (ED 480 716).

Pearson, P. D. (2001). Learning to teach reading: The status of the knowledge base. In C. M. Roller (Ed.), *Learning to teach: Setting the research agenda* (pp. 4-19). Newark, DE: International Reading Association.

Primavera, J. (2000). Enhancing family competence through literacy activities. *Journal of Prevention and Intervention in the Community, 20*, 85-101.

Purcell-Gates, V. (1995). *Other people's words: The cycle of low literacy.* Cambridge, MA: Harvard University Press.

Purcell-Gates, V. (2000). Family literacy. In M. L. Kamil, P. B. Mosenthal, P. D. Pearson, & R. Barr (Eds.), *Handbook of reading research* (Vol. 3, pp. 853-870). Mahwah, NJ: Erlbaum.

Riley, R. W., Robinson, S. P., & Conaty, J. C. (1993). *Parents' literacy and their children's success in school: Recent research, promising practices, and research implications.* Retrieved August 11, 2006 from http://www.ed.gov/pubs/OR/ResearchRpts/parlit.html

Rodriguez-Brown, F. V., Li, F, R., & Albom, J. B. (1999). Hispanic parents' awareness and use of literacy-rich environments at home and in the community. *Education and Urban Society, 32*(1), 41-58.

Schmidt, P. (1998). The ABCs of cultural understanding and communication. *Equity & Excellence in Education, 31*, 28-38.

Seeley, D. S. (1989). A new paradigm for parent involvement. *Educational Leadership, 47*(2), 46-48.

Shockley, B. (1994). Extending the literate community: Home-to-school- and school-to-home. *The Reading Teacher, 47*, 500-502.

Snow, C. E., & Ninio, A. (1986). The contribution of reading books with children to their linguistic and cognitive development. In W. H. Teale & E. Sulzby (Ed.), *Emergent literacy: Writing and reading* (pp. 116-138). Norwood, NJ: Ablex

Sonnenschein, S., Brody, G., & Munsterman, K. (1996). The influence of family beliefs and practices on children's early reading development. In L. Baker, P. Afferbach, & D. Reinking (Eds.), *Developing engaged readers in school and home communities* (pp. 3-20). Mahwah, NJ: Erlbaum.

Super, C., & Harkness, S. (1986). The developmental niche: A conceptualization at the interface of child and culture. *International Journal of Behaviour Development, 9*, 1-25.

Taylor, B., & Pearson, P. D. (Eds.). (2002). *Teaching reading: Effective schools, accomplished teachers.* Mahwah, NJ: Erlbaum.

Taylor, D. (1985). *Family literacy: Children learning to read and write.* Exeter, NH: Heinemann.

Taylor, D. (Ed.). (1997). *Many families, many literacies: An international declaration of principles.* Portsmouth, NH: Heinemann.

Taylor, D., & Dorsey-Gaines, C. (1985). *Growing up literate: Learning from inner city families.* Portsmouth, NH: Heinemann.

Teale, W. H. (1981). Parents reading to their children: What we know and need to know. *Language Arts, 58*, 902-911.

Turner, J. D. (2005). Orchestrating success for African American readers: The case of an effective third-grade teacher. *Reading Research and Instruction, 44*, 27-48.

Turner, J. D. (2006). "I want to meet my students where they are!": Preservice teachers' visions of culturally responsive reading instruction. *National Reading Conference Yearbook, 55*, 309-323.

Xu, S. (2000). Preservice teachers integrate understandings of diversity into literacy instruction: An adaptation of the ABCs model. *Journal of Teacher Education, 51*, 135-142.

Wellman, D. K., & Wold, L. S. (2006). Teacher preparation programs link literacy teaching with the demands of teaching in schools. In S. D. Lenski, D. L. Grisham, & L. S. Wold (Eds.), *Literacy teacher preparation: Ten truths teacher edu-*

*cators need to know* (pp. 54-63). Newark, DE: International Reading Association.

Wharton-McDonald, R., Pressley, M., & Hampston, J. M. (1998). Literacy instruction in nine first-grade classrooms: Teacher characteristics and student achievement. *Elementary School Journal, 99*, 101-128.

Wiley, T. G. (1996). *Literacy and language diversity in the United States.* Center for Applied Linguistics and Delta Systems.

Winter, M., & Rouse, J. (1990). Fostering intergenerational literacy: The Missouri parents as teachers program. *The Reading Teacher, 43*, 382-386.

Wolf, S. A., Ballentine, D., & Hill, L. A. (2000). "Only connect!": Cross-cultural connections in the reading lives of preservice teachers and children. *Journal of Literacy Research, 32*, 533-569.

Young, J. R., & Draper, R. J. (2006). Literacy teacher preparation is based on research. In S. D. Lenski, D. L. Grisham, & L. S. Wold (Eds.), *Literacy teacher preparation: Ten truths teacher educators need to know* (pp. 2-13). Newark, DE: International Reading Association.

Zentella, A. C. (2005). *Building on strength: Language and Literacy in Latino Families and Communities.* New York: Teachers College Press.

# PART IV

## HOME LITERACIES AND MAINSTREAM SCHOOLING: A CONCLUSION

CHAPTER 13

# SAY IT TODAY THEN SAY IT DIFFERENTLY TOMORROW

## Connecting Home and School Literacies

**Diane Lapp**

As I read the papers in this well prepared volume I was reminded that one's literacy, no matter in which home it begins, is multidimensional, interactive, and generative. It was also intriguing to be reminded of the significant effects that home and school literacy practices have on the learning of multiple languages and how when at odds these powerful influences can unfortunately cause emotional, social, and educational collisions for the child. This understanding forefronts the unified, primary theme of this collection which is that schools must evaluate their current practices to determine if they provide a positive interplay between home and school language experiences and communities.

As each author highlighted differences among families and cultural groups it also became clear that the early language exposures of one's home must be viewed by educators as providing the entry point for one's later and continuing school experiences. The papers in this widely documented collection serve to remind us that across each school day as chil-

*Multicultural Families, Home Literacies, and Mainstream Schooling*
pp. 271–276
Copyright © 2008 by Information Age Publishing
All rights of reproduction in any form reserved.

dren participate in learning events with their classmates they draw from the experiences shared in their homes. This expanded view of the utility of language supports conversations and investigations regarding the relationship between one's language and one's access to desired situational and personal mobility and opportunity (Edwards, 2007; Hymes, 1972; Smitherman, 1995).

To more fully understand the relationships among language, its use at home, and its utility in the school community these researchers have shared their work among families situated in their homes and community settings. They acknowledge that each child's early experiences must be understood, validated, cherished and celebrated by teachers if they are to thrive as learners. Their shared perception that every child regardless of culture or affluence has a repertoire of home language experiences that can be drawn from, by an insightful teacher, as a means to impact academic and school successes repeats throughout this text. This insight becomes the second unifying theme that ties these chapters together.

As they shared the stories of children from many cultures, their families, and their school experiences I was reminded of the work of Cazden, John, and Hymes (1972) that cautioned educators that instruction must support and grow from the power of the home language. Hymes (1981) also noted that "it may sometimes seem that there are only two kinds of English in the United States, good English and bad English" (p. v) and that "the United States is a country rich in many things, but poor in knowledge of itself with regard to language" (p. v). Collectively these researchers encouraged educators to be cognizant of the racist implications of rejection of any language variety that is not Academic English.

The stories shared decades later by the authors of *Multicultural Families, Home Literacies, and Mainstream Schooling* support this thinking while offering a unfortunate school profile about those who do not speak what is believed to be the good English (Bernstein, 1970). This profile promulgates a deficit image of the speaker as well as the speaker's language which, when played out in schools casts them in a downward spiral of failure. Many of the children we have come to know through this volume would be lumped within this profile if it were not for the insightful instruction of many of their teachers.

Throughout this work we see these authors offering multiple ways of incorporating a sociolinguistic sensitivity into instructional practice. Each of these examples illustrates the unified focus of providing students with in-school literacy experiences that emerge as an extension of their home literacy practices without disparaging their families and communities. The authors make us privy to instructional moves that will suggest to students that there are different variations of English; that, for example are often situationally efficient. Such instruction conveys a model of different but not deficit (Gorski, 2006); a model that eradicates classism rather than one that attempts to repair economically poor children (Payne, 2005); a model that affords students choices of the structures they select to use to communicate their ideas to an intended audiences.

Collectively engaging, this body of work, *Multicultural Families, Home Literacies, and Mainstream Schooling* edited by Guofang Li, sensitizes readers to dimensions of classrooms that may be unready for children who have been historically disenfranchised or academically unsuccessful. Perhaps more importantly, the work of these researchers opens to the *possibilities* for all children, drawing implications for change through classroom practices. Through these researchers' eyes and unified voice, readers will come to know children from various cultures and languages--children whose home literacy practices have provided fertile (but perhaps unrecognized or under-used) foundations for their school literacy experiences. Further, these researchers offer both specific and nuanced insights that speak to teacher educators who are committed to preparing teachers who will be exhilarated rather than dismayed by children whose early worlds differ from their own. Their work highlights three major areas of focus for the preparation of future teachers who (1) know and appreciate the home literacies of their students, (2) coconstruct with their students a classroom culture of inclusion, and (3) support their students in understanding that learning is a continuous process for people of all ages.

*First,* comes the recognition that we must prepare teachers who know how to make positive, pragmatic use of the insights they acquire about each child's family, cultural membership, family stories, language use, and home literacy practices. To ensure this not be superficial, future teachers must be guided into contexts and situations that offer them opportunities to acquire authentic experiences and knowledge that will, in turn, support their designing of instructional plans that validate and link home, community, and academic literacies. We cannot afford *not* to prepare teacher candidates for the high-stakes environments described by the researchers of this text. Failure to fully know and respect each home context is failure to prepare future teachers to succeed in effectively impacting the lives of their future students.

Designing experiences that ensure this level of knowing is where teacher educators will be put to the test; those of us who prepare teachers will need to go beyond merely providing candidates with the experience of a "cultural plunge" which involves visits to areas with which they are unfamiliar. While "visits" may serve as valuable first steps that expose future teachers to many factors of diversity among families living in high poverty communities, they must have opportunities to be more than voyeurs; they must be present in the homes and communities of their students if they are to get inside their hearts and heads to understand the social and culture dimensions of literacy development and dissonance. With this understanding, they must then have carefully guided and scaffolded support to learn to transfer their new understandings into classroom practice. This can only happen if teacher educators *also* come to fully understand the worlds of the children for whom they prepare future teachers. As these researchers have shown in their work, this depth of understanding can decrease the discord between children's home experiences and expectations and those encountered in classrooms.

Teacher educators must continually ask how a teacher who has never been taught to acknowledge and appreciate students' differences can be expected to utilize this information to design instruction and to continuously assess and refine practice against a growing understanding about how their students' home literacies support their school learning? Answering this question requires an evaluative self-dialogue on the part of teacher educators about what they must also learn in order to design teacher preparation programs where together with teacher candidates they discuss how insights learned about children's experiences *out of school* can positively support *within* school learning.

To begin, each teacher educator must also engage in a personal introspection to decide if he/she is prepared to work beside future teachers in settings described by these researchers. Acknowledging that one's insights come from personal perspectives opens to the need for a reflective stance on teaching. The studies shared as family stories by the contributors to this text highlight the need for reflection as a beginning point for future teachers and their mentors rather than solely an outcome for candidates in teacher preparation programs.

Second, teacher educators must prepare future teachers who know how to coconstruct with their students a classroom culture that acknowledges that the differences in children's home cultures do not represent deficits. This can be learned by contrastively analyzing home and school literacy experiences and practices. To do so is imperative in order to make learning in school more effective for every student. Teachers can only understand this by hearing the voices of their students even when those voices must be intuited. These researchers make a plea for the preparation of insightful teachers who see how their students' individual voices reflect different ways of acquiring and practicing new learning. They further urge us to realize that students must be supported in using these individualities to coconstruct learning with their teachers and classmates. This vision exists within environments where teachers value the language and experiences children bring to school and use these to promote continued learning. What teachers believe, value and do will be reflected in their teaching and conveyed to their students.

*Third,* the researchers suggest that future teachers must support each child's developing insight that contextual and situational learning dissonance exists for everyone at one time or another. This knowledge will allow them to be challenged by the struggles of learning rather than experiencing a feeling of failure. Pursuing knowledge is learned as students see their teachers' demonstrations of the act of learning and receive support and encouragement to develop their many literacies in new arenas. Students need to realize that as anyone, even their teachers, attempts to build a new base of knowledge they question, struggle, acquire new language and concepts, pose new questions, consult document and human experts, and marvel at the accumulation of their new insights and challenges. Students become aware through the eyes of their teachers that this is the joy, albeit challenge of learning experienced by everyone. This can easily be seen as many teacher educators and classroom teachers attempt to become technologically proficient. Many can easily share their vulnerabilities with students who generally outpace them in understanding and creating "multiliteracies."

The researchers of this volume offer us the important urgency and stepping-stones needed to prepare teachers who are able to share instruction with students without violating their home languages and cultures. We can infer their pleas for the authentic preparation of teachers who will have the insights and know how to transfer what they have learned from spending time in the communities and the families of children into effective classroom practice. We can further surmise that this implied connection would enable children to become full participants at school while not alienating themselves from their home cultures and languages. Children will be supported in realizing that their literacies, like their identities, are individual, multiple, and yet overlapping and provide important stepping stones for future learning.

Taken together, these researchers' papers task us with sharing their message with our colleagues, administrators, and legislators with the hopes that their insights become part of the preparation of future teachers. The authors of the chapters in *Multicultural Families, Home Literacies, and Mainstream Schooling* tackle difficult concepts and questions with authority and grace because of their practical experience as teachers, teacher educators and researchers. Their papers share a unified focus that offers insights about the cultural and social implications of family practices that teacher educators and future teachers can use to create teaching and learning experiences that cause every child to know and value their power and potential as learners.

To this end this research shows us how to provide students with opportunities to use their indigenous home languages (Smitherman & van Dijk, 1988) to explore other structured language varieties (Labov, 1972) and their situational usage patterns. The final theme these authors have shared is to support every student as they acquire the language facility to reason and structure arguments in both their native vernacular and academic English. Their having this continuum of linguistic knowledge will ensure that their literacy "is not a single entity that occurs in different contexts, but a social practice that varies according to the particular use to which it is put in each context" (Ball & Farr, 2003, p. 435). After reading this volume it will become the aim of every educator to create instructional interventions that serve as a bridge rather than a barrier between the home literacy and school literacy practices of students so that they will be able sustain and create successful language relationships within whatever domains become the social and professional realities of their futures.

## REFERENCES

Ball, A., & Farr, M. (2003). Language variations, culture and teaching the English language arts. In J. Flood, D. Lapp, J. Squire, & J. Jensen (2003), *Handbook of research on teaching the English language arts* (2nd ed., pp. 435-445). Mahwah, NJ: Erlbaum.

Bernstein, B. (1970). Social class, language, and socialization. In P. P. Giglioli (Ed.), *Language and social context: Selected readings* (pp. 157-178). London: Penguin.

Cazden, C., John, V. P., & & Hymes, D. (1972) *Functions of language in the classroom.* New York: Teachers College Press.

Edwards, P. A. (2007). *The education of African American students: Voicing the debates, controversies and solutions.* Presidential address to the National Reading Conference, Austin, TX.

Gorski, P. (2006). Savage unrealities. *Rethinking Schools, 21*(2). http://www.rethinkingschools.org/archive/21_02/sava212.shtml

Hymes, D. (1981). Foreword. In. C. Ferguson & S. B. Heath (Eds.), *Language in the USA* (pp. v-ix). New York: Cambridge University Press.

Labov, W. (1972). *Language in the inner city: Studies in Black English vernacular.* Philadelphia: University of Pennsylvania Press.

Payne, R. K. (2005). *A framework for understanding poverty* (4th ed). Highlands, TX: aha! Process.

Smitherman, G. (1995). Students' right to their own language. A retrospective. *English Journal, 84*(1), 21-27.

Smitherman, G., & van Dijk, T. A. (Eds.). (1988). *Discourse and discrimination.* Detroit, MI: Wayne State University.

# ABOUT THE CONTRIBUTORS

## ABOUT THE EDITOR

**Guofang Li** is an associate professor of second language and literacy education in the Department of Teacher Education, Michigan State University. Her research interests focused on three interrelated areas of concerns: (a) Asian immigrant children's home literacy practices; (b) cultural conflicts and educational dissensions between Asian immigrant parents and mainstream schools/teachers regarding literacy learning and instruction; and (c) Asian children's social processes of learning, especially the impact of the "model minority" myth, social class, and cultural identity on language and literacy development. Li's major publications include three sole-authored books, *Culturally Contested Literacies: America's "Rainbow Underclass" and Urban Schools* (Routledge, 2008). *Culturally Contested Pedagogy: Battles of Literacy and Schooling between Mainstream Teachers and Asian Immigrant Parents* (SUNY Press, 2006, winner of 2006 Ed Fry Book Award, National Reading Conference), *"East is East, West is West"? Home Literacy, Culture, and Schooling* (Peter Lang, 2002), and two coedited volumes *"Strangers" of the Academy: Asian Women Scholars in Higher Education* (Stylus, 2006), and *Model Minority Myths Revisited: An Interdisciplinary Approach to Demystifying Asian American Education Experiences* (IAP, 2008).

## ABOUT THE CONTRIBUTORS

**Patricia A. Edwards** is a professor of teacher education at Michigan State University and past president of the National Reading Conference (2006-2007). She is the author of *A Path to Follow: Learning to Listen to Parents* (Heinemann, 1999) and *Children's Literacy Development: Making it Happen Through School, Family, and Community Involvement* (Allyn & Bacon, 2004).

She is widely published and a recognized national authority on family literacy and role of parents in the learning-to-read-and-write process.

**Billie Enz** is the associate dean of the School of Educational Innovation and Teacher Preparation at Arizona State University's Polytechnic Campus. Dr. Enz is a member of the early childhood faculty and teaches language and literacy courses. She has authored numerous articles and textbooks in this area. Dr. Enz has also authored several books on new teacher development and mentor training. She is a member of the Commission of Early Childhood Literacy for the International Reading Association, and immediate past president of the Literacy Development in Young Children special interest group. Her most recent grants involve family literacies in different cultures.

**Trevor Cairney** is master of new college and adjunct professor of education at the University of New South Wales in Sydney, Australia. He has been researching and writing about literacy for over 30 years and has written seven books and over 200 book chapters and journal articles. His research and publications have been concerned with text comprehension and composition, the sociocultural foundations of literacy and the relationship between home, school, and community.

**Maria R. Coady** is an assistant professor of ESOL/bilingual education in the School of Teaching and Learning at the University of Florida. Dr. Coady teaches courses related to second language acquisition and the sociocultural context of education for English language learners. Her research includes bilingualism and biliteracy development for language minority (mainly Spanish-speaking) students in U.S. public schools. She also conducts research and directs literacy projects with migrant farmworker families in north central Florida.

**Catherine Compton-Lilly** is an assistant professor in curriculum and instruction at the University of Wisconsin–Madison. She taught in the public schools of New York State for 18 years. She is the author of *Reading Families: The Literate Lives of Urban Children* (Teachers College Press, 2003) and *Confronting Racism, Poverty and Power,* (Heinemann, 2004). Her most recent book, *Rereading Families* (Teachers College Press, 2007), follows the families from her first book into Grades 4 and 5. This book documents the second phase of a 10-year longitudinal study. Dr. Compton-Lilly is the author of several articles and book reviews and is the editor-in-chief of *Networks,* a teacher research on-line journal. Her research interests focus on literacy learning in urban communities and crafting instruction that builds on the strengths and abilities of children.

**Jaime Dice** is a doctoral candidate in the Department of Child and Family Development at the University of Georgia. Her research interests include cognitive factors influencing individual differences in the development of attention in early childhood as well as early childhood education.

**Dawn Foley** is a senior lecturer and program coordinator of the Early Childhood Program in the School of Education at Arizona State University at the Polytechnic Campus. She is also a doctoral student in the Early Childhood program at the Tempe Campus. As the lead literacy instructor at ASU Poly, her favorite courses to teach are puppetry and children's literature. Dawn's interests include early language and literacy development, play and creative dramatics as a conduit to facilitate learning in these areas.

**Diane Lapp** is a professor of reading and language arts in teacher education at the San Diego State University. She is especially interested in issues related to first and second language/literacy acquisition and development. She has coauthored with Dr. James Flood several college textbooks and many curriculum materials for school aged children which have been published by Macmillan/McGraw Hill. In addition she is also the coauthor of two major research handbooks, *The Handbook of Research on the Communicative and Visual Arts* and *The Handbook of Research on Teaching the English Language Arts*. She has served as the editor of three International Reading Association texts and has been a member of the editorial board of the *Reading Teacher, Reading Research and Instruction, Reading Research Quarterly*, and *Journal of Reading Behavior*.

**Patricia (Paddy) Lynch** received her PhD in elementary education from the University of South Carolina, and currently teaches fifth grade science and social studies in the year-round school that has been her professional home for the last 15 years. Her interests include exploring the ways in which inquiry-based science and the arts support literacy learning, and her work has been featured in *Primary Voices, Early Childhood Education*, and *Art Education*.

**Sarah McCarthey** is professor of curriculum and instruction at the University of Illinois. Her research focuses on the ways in which students construct their identities as readers and writers within home and classroom contexts. She has published articles in *Reading Research Quarterly* (2001), *Research in the Teaching of English* (2004), *Written Communication* (2005), and *Journal of Second Language Writing* (2005). She is currently looking at the impact of NCLB on teachers' writing instruction in several states and working with teachers to understand the ways in which they integrate writing into their science instruction. She taught elementary school for eight years and has worked collaboratively with teachers since she began her graduate work at Stanford University and Michigan State University. She is currently coeditor of *Research in the Teaching of English*.

**Hye-Young Park** is working toward a PhD at the University of Illinois at Urbana-Champaign. Her research interests are language transfer, multiple identity, and experimental writing issues as they relate to bilingualism and multiculturalism. She is the president of The Language and Literacy Graduate Student Organization in the Department of Curriculum and Instruction at the University of Illinois at Urbana-Champaign. She is also a secretary in the International Association of Educators.

**Leslie Reese** is a professor in the Department of Teacher Education at California State University, Long Beach, where she is the coordinator of the Dual Language Development MA Program. Her research interests include home-school connections, literacy development among Latino children, immigration, and classroom action research. She is currently co-principal investigator of a longitudinal study of language and literacy development among children in urban public school settings in Mexico.

**Mariana Souto-Manning** is an assistant professor of child and family development at the University of Georgia. From a critical perspective, her research examines the sociocultural and historical foundations of early schooling, language development, literacy practices, cultures, and discourses. She studies how young children, families, and early childhood teachers from diverse backgrounds shape and are shaped by discursive practices, employing a methodology that combines discourse analysis with ethnographic investigation.

**Jennifer Danridge Turner** is an assistant professor in reading education at the University of Maryland, College Park. She received her PhD in educational psychology with a specialization in Literacy from Michigan State University in 2003. Dr. Turner's current research focuses on effective literacy teachers and teaching for African American elementary students. She has authored or coauthored articles in leading literacy journals, including *The Reading Teacher*, *Reading Research and Instruction*, *Literacy Teaching and Learning*, and the *Journal of Adolescent and Adult Literacy*. Dr. Turner has served as a member of the Urban Diversity Initiatives Commission for the International Reading Association, and is the new cochair of the Ethnicity, Race, and Multilingual Committee for the National Reading Conference.